OECD-FAO Agricultural Outlook 2017-2026

Please cite this publication as:
OECD/FAO (2017), *OECD-FAO Agricultural Outlook 2017-2026*, OECD Publishing, Paris.
http://dx.doi.org/10.1787/agr_outlook-2017-en

ISBN 978-92-64-27547-8 (print)
ISBN 978-92-64-27550-8 (PDF)
ISBN 978-92-64-27548-5 (epub)

Series: OECD-FAO Agricultural Outlook
ISSN 1563-0447 (print)
ISSN 1999-1142 (online)

FAO
ISBN 978-92-5-109808-0

Photo credits: Cover © Original cover concept designed by Juan Luis Salazar. Adaptations by OECD.

Corrigenda to OECD publications may be found on line at: *www.oecd.org/about/publishing/corrigenda.htm*.

Foreword

The food and agriculture sector is faced with a critical global challenge: to ensure access to safe, healthy, and nutritious food for a growing world population, while at the same time using natural resources more sustainably and making an effective contribution to climate change adaptation and mitigation. Through this annual collaboration and other studies, the Organisation for Economic Co-operation and Development (OECD) and the Food and Agriculture Organization of the United Nations (FAO) are working together to provide information, analysis and advice, to help governments achieve these essential objectives.

This is the 13th joint edition of the OECD-FAO Agricultural Outlook. *It provides ten-year projections to 2026 for the major agricultural commodities, as well as for biofuels and fish. The pooling of market and policy information from experts in a wide range of participating countries provides a benchmark necessary for assessing the opportunities and threats to the sector. This year's* Agricultural Outlook *includes a special focus on Southeast Asia, a region where agriculture and fisheries have developed rapidly and undernourishment has been significantly decreased, but also a region that is on the front line of the effects of climate change and where there are rising pressures on natural resources.*

The Agricultural Outlook *comes in the context of a wider set of international efforts to address food security and agricultural issues. Two global initiatives stand out:*

- *The UN Sustainable Development Goals (SDGs) set ambitious targets to be achieved by 2030. Among these, the first goal is to end poverty in all its forms everywhere, while the second goal pledges to end hunger, achieve food security and improved nutrition, and promote sustainable agriculture. The two goals are related as more than three-quarters of the world's poor depend on agriculture not only for their food, but also for their livelihoods.*
- *Under the United Nations Framework Convention on Climate Change's 2015 Paris Agreement, 195 countries have committed to take action to contain the increase in global average temperatures to well below 2°C above pre-industrial levels. Climate change poses a threat to sustainable food production, but agriculture, which accounts for more than a fifth of all greenhouse gas emissions, can be an active part of the solution*

The Agricultural Outlook *supports these global initiatives by providing a benchmark against which to assess the implications of alternative policies that seek to increase the availability of food sustainably while mitigating greenhouse-gas emissions. Such policies include both supply-side measures, such as measures for increasing sustainable productivity growth in agriculture, and demand-side measures for encouraging the reduction of waste and overconsumption.*

The OECD and FAO are working across the board to support the global effort to eradicate poverty and tackle climate change. In 2016, Agriculture Ministers convened at both the OECD and FAO in order to chart directions for future policies that can meet these commitments. At the OECD meeting, Ministers stressed that policies must promote the resilience, as well as the productivity and sustainability of the agriculture and food sector and rural communities. They also recognised that achieving those shared goals will require sustained international co-operation. At the FAO meeting, which also involved Trade Ministers, they underlined the importance of agricultural commodities for growth in developing and less developed countries and cautioned about the risks posed by climate change. They also stressed the importance of market transparency and policy predictability, as well as the role that trade can play in adapting to climate change.

Because the areas of projected food demand growth differ from the areas where supply can be increased sustainably, international trade will take on particular importance in the attainment of the SDGs, as well as in adapting to and mitigating climate change. The 11th WTO Ministerial Conference, to be held in Buenos Aires in December of this year, will undoubtedly be guided by the need to ensure the agricultural sector makes these global contributions effectively, while also addressing specific food-security concerns in developing countries.

Food security and agricultural issues have received specific attention in international fora such as the G20 and the G7. A significant initiative was the G20's Agricultural Market Information System (AMIS), which is housed at the FAO and to which the OECD and other international organisations contribute. With food prices now closer to long-term trend levels, it is important that the structural issues that remain are not neglected. Moreover, food markets are inherently volatile, and today's relative stability is no reason for complacency.

More than ever, we must all work together to improve the sustainability of food systems and ensure global food security and healthy nutrition. We hope that our collaborative effort on the annual production of this report will continue to provide governments and all other stakeholders with a key element of the information they need to reach the goals set in the 2030 Agenda for Sustainable Development and the Paris Agreement

Angel Gurría,
Secretary-General
Organisation for Economic
Co-operation and Development

José Graziano da Silva,
Director-General
Food and Agriculture Organization
of the United Nations

Acknowledgements

The *Agricultural Outlook, 2017-2026*, is a collaborative effort of the Organisation for Economic Co-operation and Development (OECD) and the Food and Agriculture Organization (FAO) of the United Nations. It brings together the commodity, policy and country expertise of both organisations and input from collaborating member countries to provide an annual assessment of prospects for the coming decade of national, regional and global agricultural commodity markets. The baseline projection is not a forecast about the future, but rather a plausible scenario based on specific assumptions regarding macroeconomic conditions, agriculture and trade policy settings, weather conditions, longer term productivity trends and international market developments.

The *Agricultural Outlook* is jointly prepared by the OECD and FAO Secretariats.

At the OECD, the baseline projections and *Outlook* report were prepared by members of the Trade and Agriculture Directorate: Marcel Adenäuer, Jonathan Brooks (Head of Division), Koen Deconinck, Annelies Deuss, Armelle Elasri (publication co-ordinator), Gen Furuhashi, Hubertus Gay (Outlook co-ordinator), Céline Giner, Gaëlle Gouarin, Claude Nenert, Graham Pilgrim and Grégoire Tallard of the Agro-Food Trade and Markets Division, and for fish and seafood by James Innes and Antonia Leroy of the Natural Resources Policy Division. The OECD Secretariat is grateful for the contributions provided by visiting experts Ashwina Aubeeluck (Agriculture and Agri-Food Canada), and Si Zhizhi (Chinese Academy of Agricultural Sciences). The organisation of meetings and publication preparation were provided by Helen Maguire and Michèle Patterson. Technical assistance in the preparation of the *Outlook* database was provided by Eric Espinasse and Frano Ilicic. Many other colleagues in the OECD Secretariat and member country delegations provided useful comments on earlier drafts of the report.

At the Food and Agriculture Organization of the United Nations, the projections were prepared by economists and commodity officers from the Trade and Markets Division (EST) under the leadership of Boubaker Ben-Belhassen (EST Division Director) and Josef Schmidhuber (EST Division Deputy Director) with the overall guidance of Kostas Stamoulis (Assistant Director-General, Economic and Social Development Department). The core projections team consisted of ElMamoun Amrouk, Sergio René Araujo Enciso, Pedro Arias, Eduard Bukin, Emily Carroll, Merritt Cluff, Hannah Fried, Yasmine Iqbal, Holger Matthey (Team Leader) and Jorge Soguero Escuer. Commodity expertise was provided by Abdolreza Abbassian, Paulo Augusto Lourenço Dias Nunes, Michael Griffin, Shirley Mustafa, Adam Prakash, Peter Thoenes, G. A. Upali Wickramasinghe and Di Yang. Input on special topics and boxes was provided by Katinka de Balogh, Matthew Burnett, Wantanee Kalpravidh, Ekaterina Krivonos, Pascal Liu, Juan Lubroth and Francesco N. Tubiello. We thank visiting expert Tracy Davids from the Bureau for Food and Agricultural Policy at the University of Pretoria. Stefania Vannuccini from the FAO Fisheries and Aquaculture Department contributed, with technical support from Pierre Charlebois. Advice on fishmeal and fish oil issues was provided by Enrico Bachis from the Marine Ingredients Organisation (IFFO). Research assistance and database preparation were provided by Claudio Cerquiglini, Julie Claro, Emanuele Marocco and Marco Milo. Jiyeon Chang provided valuable input into the drafting of the overview chapter. This edition also benefited from comments made by other colleagues from FAO and member country institutions and was closely reviewed by Günter Hemrich, Michelle Kendrick, Anna Lartey, Regina Laub, José Rosero Moncayo, Marco Sánchez Cantillo, Rob Vos and Natalia Winder Rossi. FAO's James Edge, Yongdong Fu, Pedro Javaloyes, Jessica Mathewson, Raffaella Rucci and Juan Luis Salazar provided invaluable assistance with publication and communication issues.

Chapter 2 of the *Outlook*, "Southeast Asia: Prospects and challenges", was prepared by the Secretariats at FAO and OECD led by Jared Greenville of the Development Division of the Trade and Agriculture Directorate and Merritt Cluff. Contribution in OECD besides before mentioned members of the Trade and Agricultural Directorate was provided in form of the box on "The potential role of agriculture in the future development of Myanmar" by Martha Baxter of the OECD Development Centre. Input from FAO on special topics and boxes was provided by Sumiter Broca, Fang Cheng, Cristina Coslet, David Dawe, Aziz Elbehri and Shirley Mustafa.

Finally, information and feedback provided by the International Cotton Advisory Committee, International Dairy Federation, International Grains Council, International Sugar Organization, Marine Ingredients Organisation (IFFO) and World Association of Beet and Cane Growers is gratefully acknowledged.

The complete *Agricultural Outlook*, including more detailed commodity chapters, the full statistical annex and fully documented Outlook database, including historical data and projections, can be accessed through the OECD-FAO joint internet site: *www.agri-outlook.org*. The published *Agricultural Outlook 2017-2026* report provides: an overview of global agriculture and prospects; an in-depth analysis of the outlook for Southeast Asian agriculture and a consideration of some of the challenges facing the sector; and short snapshots for each commodity with associated statistical tables. The more detailed commodity chapters and an extended statistical annex are contained in the OECD's iLibrary version of the report.

Table of contents

Acronyms and abbreviations 11

Executive Summary 15

Chapter 1. **Overview of the *Agricultural Outlook 2017-2026*** 17
- The setting: Record production levels and abundant stocks led to continued price decreases in 2016 18
- Summary of macroeconomic conditions and policy assumptions 18
- Consumption 21
- Production 34
- Trade 41
- Prices 48
- Risks and uncertainties 53
- Notes 57
- References 57

Chapter 2. **Southeast Asia: Prospects and challenges** 59
- Introduction 60
- Developments in agriculture and fisheries in Southeast Asia 61
- Medium-term outlook 82
- Notes 96
- References 96

Chapter 3. **Commodity snapshots** 101
- Cereals 102
- Oilseeds and oilseed products 104
- Sugar 107
- Meat 110
- Dairy and dairy products 113
- Fish and seafood 116
- Biofuels 119
- Cotton 122
- Annex: **Commodity snapshot tables** 125

More detailed commodity chapters as well as the Glossary, Methodology and Statistical Annex are available on line at *http://dx.doi.org/10.1787/agr_outlook-2017-en*

Tables

2.1. Contextual indicators for selected countries in Southeast Asia, 2015 61
2.2. Self-sufficiency targets of ASEAN members 78
3.A1.1. World cereal projections 126
3.A1.2. World oilseed projections 128
3.A1.3. World sugar projections 130
3.A1.4. World meat projections 131
3.A1.5. World dairy projections: Butter and cheese 132
3.A1.6. World dairy projections: Powders and casein 133
3.A1.7. World fish and seafood projections 134
3.A1.8. World biofuel projections 136
3.A1.9. World cotton projections 137

Figures

1.1. Current market conditions for key commodities 19
1.2. Annual growth in consumption for key commodity groups, 2007-16 and 2017-26 22
1.3. Regional shares in commodity consumption growth, 2016-26 23
1.4. Fish: Regional shares in demand growth and per capita food consumption 24
1.5. Pigmeat: Regional shares in demand growth and per capita food consumption . 25
1.6. Beef and veal: Regional shares in demand growth and per capita food consumption 26
1.7. Poultry: Regional shares in demand growth and per capita food consumption .. 27
1.8. Fresh dairy products: Regional shares in demand growth and per capita food consumption 27
1.9. Per capita food consumption of meat and fish in 2026 28
1.10. Per capita food use of cereals in 2026 29
1.11. Per capita calorie availability by food category 30
1.12. Per capita protein availability by food category 30
1.13. Feed: Regional shares in demand growth and total use 31
1.14. Growth in biofuel production, 2000-26 32
1.15. Growth in demand for maize (left) and vegetable oil (right), by use 34
1.16. Increase in maize production due to area expansion and yield growth, 2016-26 . 35
1.17. Trends of global land use of agriculture 36
1.18. Average annual crop land change for selected countries 37
1.19. Maize yields in the United States and globally 37
1.20. Milk production in selected countries 38
1.21. Meat production, by type and country 40
1.22. Fish production 40
1.23. Growth in trade volumes by commodity 41
1.24. Evolution of trade volume for merchandise trade and agricultural trade 42
1.25. Impact on agro-food trade of policies, reforms and drifts 44
1.26. Share of production traded 44
1.27. Share of production traded for selected commodities 45
1.28. Imports as share of domestic cereals demand in selected Middle Eastern and African countries 46
1.29. Export shares of the top 5 exporters in 2026, by commodity 46
1.30. Import shares of top 5 importers in 2026, by commodity 48
1.31. Medium-term evolution of commodity prices in real terms 49

1.32. Long-term price of maize in real terms ... 49
1.33. Average annual real price change for agricultural commodities, 2017-26 ... 50
1.34. Evolution of individual commodity prices in real terms ... 51
1.35. GDP growth rates in OECD and selected developing countries ... 55
2.1. The Southeast Asian region ... 60
2.2. Agricultural and fisheries sectors share of employment and GDP ... 62
2.3. Distribution of farm size in Southeast Asia ... 63
2.4. Production growth in Southeast Asia ... 63
2.5. Agricultural production in Southeast Asia ... 64
2.6. Southeast Asia agricultural production shares by country, 2013 ... 65
2.7. Marine and inland fishery production in Southeast Asia ... 66
2.8. Contribution to fishery production by country ... 66
2.9. Composition of agricultural output growth in Southeast Asia, by period (%) ... 68
2.10. There is scope to improve a number of areas of the enabling environment ... 70
2.11. Main agro-food export and import products ... 74
2.12. Net exports of rice ... 74
2.13. ASEAN and world GVC participation ... 76
2.14. Past and projected GDP per capita growth in Southeast Asia ... 82
2.15. Changes in consumption in Southeast Asia ... 83
2.16. Net agriculture and fish production across Southeast Asia ... 85
2.17. Southeast Asian versus world agriculture and fish production ... 85
2.18. Changes in major production activities in Southeast Asia ... 86
2.19. Global copra production by region ... 87
2.20. Changes in major production activities in Southeast Asia ... 88
2.21. Area and yield changes for major production activities in Southeast Asia ... 89
2.22. Changes in the trade balance of major commodities in Southeast Asia ... 92
2.23. Contributions to changes in the trade balance of major commodities in Southeast Asia ... 92
2.24. Sources of changes in calorie and protein intake in Southeast Asia ... 93
3.1. World cereal prices ... 103
3.2. Exports of oilseeds and oilseed products by region ... 105
3.3. World nominal and real sugar prices ... 108
3.4. World meat prices ... 112
3.5. Per capita consumption of processed and fresh dairy products ... 114
3.6. Regional contributions to world fish and seafood production ... 117
3.7. Evolution of ethanol blending in gasoline fuels and of biodiesel blending in diesel fuels ... 120
3.8. Cotton consumption by region ... 123

Follow OECD Publications on:

http://twitter.com/OECD_Pubs

http://www.facebook.com/OECDPublications

http://www.linkedin.com/groups/OECD-Publications-4645871

http://www.youtube.com/oecdilibrary

OECD Alerts http://www.oecd.org/oecddirect/

This book has...

StatLinks
A service that delivers Excel® files from the printed page!

Look for the *StatLinks* at the bottom of the tables or graphs in this book. To download the matching Excel® spreadsheet, just type the link into your Internet browser, starting with the *http://dx.doi.org* prefix, or click on the link from the e-book edition.

Follow FAO on:

Food and Agriculture Organization of the United Nations

www.twitter.com/FAOstatistics
www.twitter.com/FAOnews

www.facebook.com/UNFAO

www.linkedin.com/company/fao

www.youtube.com/user/FAOoftheUN

Acronyms and abbreviations

ACP	African Caribbean and Pacific countries
AEC	ASEAN Economic Community
AGEI	Agricultural Growth Enabling Index
AMIS	Agricultural Market Information System
ARC	Agricultural Risk Coverage (US Farm Bill Instrument)
ASEAN	Association of South East Asian Nations
ASF	African Swine Fever
Bln	Billion
Bln L	Billion litres
BRIC	Emerging economies of Brazil, Russian Federation, India and China
BRICS	Emerging economies of Brazil, Russian Federation, India, China and South Africa
Bln t	Billion tonnes
CAP	Common Agricultural Policy (European Union)
CCAFS	Climate Change, Agriculture and Food Security
CCC	Commodity Credit Corporation
CFP	Common Fisheries Policy (European Union)
CETA	Comprehensive Economic and Trade Agreement
ChAFTA	China-Australia Free Trade Agreement
CIF	Cost, insurance and freight
CIS	Commonwealth of Independent States
CPI	Consumer Price Index
CPIF	Consumer Price Index for Food
CRP	Conservation Reserve Program (United States)
CSP	Conservation Stewardship Program (United States)
CTA	Technical Centre for Agricultural and Rural Cooperation
cts/lb	Cents per pound
CUFTA	Canada-Ukraine Free Trade Agreement
CVD	Countervailing duty
c.w.e.	Carcass weight equivalent
DDGs	Dried Distiller's Grains
dw	Dressed weight
EBA	Everything-But-Arms Initiative (European Union)
EISA	Energy Independence and Security Act of 2007 (United States)
El Niño	Climatic condition associated with the temperature of major sea currents
EMEs	Emerging Market Economies
EPA	US Environmental Protection Agency
EPAs	Economic Partnership Agreements
ERS	Economic Research Service of the US Department for Agriculture
est	Estimate
EU	European Union

EU15	Fifteen member states that joined the European Union before 2004
EU28	Twenty eight member states of the European Union
FAO	Food and Agriculture Organization of the United Nations
FDP	Fresh dairy products
FDI	Foreign direct investment
FFV	Flex fuel Vehicles
FOB	Free on board (export price)
FMD	Foot and Mouth Disease
FTA	Free Trade Agreement
G-20	Group of 20 important developed and developing economies (see Glossary)
GDP	Gross domestic product
GDPD	Gross domestic product deflator
GHG	Greenhouse gas
GIEWS	Global Information and Early Warning System on Food and Agriculture
GM	Genetically modified
GVCs	Global value chains
ha	Hectares
HFCS	High fructose corn syrup
hl	Hectolitre
IEA	International Energy Agency
IFA	International Fertilizer industry association
IFAD	International Fund for Agricultural Development
IFPRI	International Food Policy Research Institute
IGC	International Grains Council
ILUC	Indirect Land Use Change
IMF	International Monetary Fund
IPCC	Intergovernmental Panel on Climate Change
IUU	Illegal, unreported and unregulated (fishing)
kg	Kilogrammes
kha	Thousand hectares
kt	Thousand tonnes
La Niña	Climatic condition associated with the temperature of major sea currents
LAC	Latin America and the Caribbean
Lao PDR	Lao People's Democratic Republic
lb	Pound
LDCs	Least Developed Countries
lw	Live weight
MBM	Meat and bone meal
MDGs	Millennium Development Goals
MENA	Middle East and North Africa
MERCOSUR	Mercado Común del Sur / Common Market of South America
MFA	Multi-fibre Arrangement
Mha	Million hectares
mln	Million
Mn L	Million litres
MPS	Market Price Support
Mt	Million tonnes

NAFTA	North American Free Trade Agreement
OECD	Organisation for Economic Cooperation and Development
OIE	World Organisation for Animal Health
OLS	Ordinary Least Squares
OPEC	Organization of Petroleum Exporting Countries
p.a.	Per annum
PCE	Private consumption expenditure
PEDv	Porcine Epidemic Diarrhoea virus
PLC	Price Loss Coverage (US Farm Bill instrument)
PoU	Prevalence of Undernourishment
PPI	Producer Price Index
PPP	Purchasing power parity
PSE	Producer Support Estimate
R&D	Research and development
RED	Renewable Energy Directive in the European Union
RFS / RFS2	Renewable Fuels Standard in the United States, which is part of the Energy Policy Act
RIN	Renewable Identification Numbers prices
rse	Raw sugar equivalent
RTA	Regional Trade Agreements
r.t.c.	Ready to cook
r.w.e.	Retail weight equivalent
SDG	Sustainable Development Goals
SFP	Single Farm Payment (European Union)
SMP	Skim milk powder
SPS	Single payment scheme (European Union)
t	Tonnes
t/ha	Tonnes/hectare
TFP	Total Factor Productivity
TPP	Trans Pacific Partnership
tq	Tel quel basis
TRQ	Tariff rate quota
UN	The United Nations
UNDP	United Nations Development Programme
UNEP	United Nations Environment Programme
UNFCCC	United Nations Framework Convention on Climate Change
URAA	Uruguay Round Agreement on Agriculture
US	United States
USDA	United States Department of Agriculture
VIFEP	Vietnam Institute of Fisheries and Economic Planning
WFP	World Food Programme
WHO	World Health Organization
WITS	World Integrated Trade Solution
WMP	Wole milk powder
wse	White sugar equivalent
WTO	World Trade Organization
WWF	World Wide Fund for Nature

Currencies

ARS	Argentinean peso	KRW	Korean won
AUD	Australian dollars	MXN	Mexican peso
BDT	Bangladeshi taka	MYR	Malaysian ringgit
BRL	Brazilian real	NZD	New Zealand dollar
CAD	Canadian dollar	PKR	Pakistani rupee
CLP	Chilean peso	RUB	Russian ruble
CNY	Chinese yuan renminbi	SAR	Saudi riyal
DZD	Algerian dinar	THB	Thai baht
EGP	Egyptian pound	TRL	Turkish lira
EUR	Euro (Europe)	UAH	Ukrainian grivna
IDR	Indonesian rupiah	USD	US dollar
INR	Indian rupees	UYU	Uruguayan peso
JPY	Japanese yen	ZAR	South African rand

Executive Summary

The *Agricultural Outlook 2017-26* is a collaborative effort of the OECD and FAO prepared with input from the experts of their member governments and from specialist commodity organisations. It provides a consensus assessment of the medium term (ten year) prospects for agricultural and fish commodity markets at national, regional and global levels. This year's edition contains a special focus on the agriculture and fish sectors of Southeast Asia.

The context for this year's *Outlook* is record production and abundant stocks of most commodities in 2016, keeping prices well below the peaks experienced in the last decade. Average prices of cereals, meats and dairy products continued to decline, while prices of oilseeds, vegetable oils, and sugar saw a slight rebound in 2016.

Over the outlook period, demand growth is projected to slow considerably. The primary sources of growth in the last decade were first the People's Republic of China, where rising meat and fish demand caused the consumption of feed to grow by almost 6% per year, and second the global biofuel sector, where the use of feedstock inputs grew by almost 8% per year. The replenishment of cereal stocks by 230 Mt over the last decade also augmented demand. These recent drivers are not anticipated to support markets in the same way over the medium term, and no other sources to replace them are foreseen.

Growth in food demand for virtually all commodities in the *Outlook* is anticipated to be less than in the previous decade. Globally, per capita food demand for cereals is anticipated to be largely flat, with growth only expected in least developed countries. Meat consumption prospects are seen as limited on the basis of recent trends in many countries, where dietary preferences, low incomes and supply-side constraints curb consumption growth. Additional calories and protein are expected to come mainly from vegetable oil, sugar and dairy products. Overall, "convergence" towards western diets appears limited.

By 2026, calorie availability is projected to reach 2 450 kcal per day on average in least developed countries and exceed 3 000 kcal per day in other developing countries. Still, food insecurity will remain a critical global concern, and the co-existence of malnutrition in all its forms poses new challenges in many countries.

The demand growth for ethanol and biodiesel has weakened due to lower fossil fuel prices and fewer incentives from government policies. Even though energy prices are projected to increase, the derived demand for biofuel feedstocks, especially maize and sugarcane for ethanol and vegetable oil for biodiesel, will grow slowly, except in key developing countries where demand increases are driven by more pro-active domestic policies.

Future growth in crop production will be attained mostly by increasing yields. Yield growth is projected to decrease slightly, but output could be raised by closing large yield gaps that continue to persist, especially in Sub-Saharan Africa. The global cereal area will only increase marginally, while a further expansion of soybean area is projected to satisfy the demand for animal feed and vegetable oil.

Growth in meat and dairy production will be achieved from both larger herds and higher output per animal, with large differences in the intensity of production continuing to persist. Growth in poultry production accounts for almost half of total meat production expansion over the decade. Milk production growth is expected to accelerate compared to the previous decade, most notably in India and Pakistan.

Aquaculture dominates growth in the fish sector, as capture fish production is determined by the current level of stocks and governed by policies to limit over-fishing. China will maintain a share above 60% of global fish production. Farmed fish production is the fastest growing protein source among the commodities in the *Outlook*.

The growth in agriculture and fish trade is projected to slow to about half the previous decade's growth rate. However, trade will represent a broadly constant share of the sector's output over the coming decade. Generally, agricultural trade has proven to be more resilient to macroeconomic fluctuations than trade in other goods. Given relatively high protection in the farm sector, agricultural trade growth could be boosted by further market liberalisation.

Food imports are becoming increasingly important for food security, particularly in Sub-Saharan Africa, North Africa, and the Middle East. While for some countries this may reflect greater demand but insufficient natural resources for growing food domestically, in other cases it may indicate agricultural development problems which need attention.

Net exports are projected to increase from the Americas, Eastern Europe and Central Asia, while net imports are expected to increase across other Asian and African countries. Exports remain concentrated in a few supplying countries contrasting with widely dispersed imports. This may imply a greater susceptibility of world markets to supply shocks, stemming from natural and policy factors, rather than demand shocks.

Under the *Outlook's* expected fundamental supply and demand conditions, real prices of most agricultural and fish commodities are anticipated to follow a slightly declining trend, keeping them below previous peaks over the next ten years. Prices of agricultural commodities are subject to considerable volatility and may show large deviations from their long-term trends for an extended period of time.

Southeast Asia

The special chapter of the *Outlook* focusses on the countries of Southeast Asia, where economic growth has been strong and the agriculture and fish sectors have developed rapidly. Broad based growth has enabled the region to significantly reduce undernourishment in recent years.

However, the growth of agriculture and fisheries in the region has led to rising pressure on natural resources, affecting the export-oriented fish and palm oil sectors in particular. The *Outlook* projects palm oil production growth to slow considerably as the main producer countries focus on sustainable development.

Improved resource management and increased R&D will be needed to achieve sustainable productivity growth. Policies in support of rice production could also be reoriented to facilitate the diversification of agriculture. Given the region's sensitivity to climate change, investments to facilitate adaption are required.

Chapter 1

Overview of the Agricultural Outlook 2017-2026

This chapter provides an overview of the latest set of quantitative medium-term projections for global and national agricultural markets. The projections cover production, consumption, stocks, trade and prices for 25 agricultural products for the period 2017 to 2026. The chapter starts with a description of the state of agricultural markets in 2016. In the next sections, consumption and production trends are examined, with a focus on regional developments. The chapter also reviews trade patterns showing the relative concentration of exports and dispersion of imports across countries for different commodities. The chapter concludes with global agricultural price projections and a discussion of uncertainty which might affect price projections. Growing demand for agricultural commodities is projected to be matched by efficiency gains in production which will keep real agricultural prices relatively flat.

The statistical data for Israel are supplied by and under the responsibility of the relevant Israeli authorities.The use of such data by the OECD is without prejudice to the status of the Golan Heights, East Jerusalem and Israeli settlements in the West Bank under the terms of international law. The position of the United Nations on the question of Jerusalem is contained in General Assembly Resolution 181(II) of 29 November 1947, and subsequent resolutions of the General Assembly and the Security Council concerning this question.

The setting: Record production levels and abundant stocks led to continued price decreases in 2016

For most cereals, meat types, dairy products and fish, the 2016 production level was either the highest on record, or a close second. These exceptional production levels, along with stagnant demand and high levels of existing stocks, led to further declines in prices for most commodities (Figure 1.1). Oilseeds, biodiesel, cotton and fish saw a modest price recovery compared to 2015, and the sugar price continued its upward path.

Conditions in agricultural markets are heavily influenced by macro-economic variables such as global GDP growth (which supports demand for agricultural commodities) and the price of crude oil (which determines the price of several inputs into agriculture, and influences the demand for cereals, sugar crops, and vegetable oils through the market for biofuels). In 2016, global GDP growth remained low at 2.9%, the slowest growth rate since 2009. Crude oil prices, which had been low since mid-2014, increased at the end of 2016 following an agreement of both OPEC and non-OPEC producers to reduce output in 2017. However, throughout most of the year, oil prices were low by historical standards. In combination with sluggish GDP growth, this contributed to the price decreases observed in agricultural markets in 2016.

Summary of macroeconomic conditions and policy assumptions

This *Agricultural Outlook* presents a baseline scenario that is considered plausible given a range of assumptions on the macro-economic, policy and demographic environment. Box 1.4, at the end of the Overview chapter, describes in detail the main macroeconomic and policy assumptions that are adopted in the baseline projections. Compared to 2016, GDP growth is expected to pick up slightly in developed economies over the next ten years, but to slow in emerging markets and developing countries. Developing countries will continue to drive global population growth; however global population growth is projected to slow to 1% per year over the next decade. Inflation is projected to remain low in OECD countries and the People's Republic of China (hereafter "China"). In Brazil and the Russian Federation, inflation will come down from recent high levels, aided by currency stabilisation. Nominal oil prices are expected to increase at an average rate of 4.8% per year over the outlook period, from USD 43.8 per barrel in 2016 to USD 89.5 per barrel by 2026.

The baseline projections in the *Agricultural Outlook* assume current policy settings continue into the future. In particular, the decision of the United Kingdom to leave the European Union, officially communicated by the British government on 29 March 2017, is not included in the projections as the terms of departure have not yet been determined. In the current *Outlook*, projections for the United Kingdom are therefore retained within the European Union aggregate.

Figure 1.1. **Current market conditions for key commodities**

Current market conditions	Production Index Average 2006-2016 = 100	Price Index Average 2006-2016 = 100

Cereals

World production reached a historical high in 2016, especially for wheat and maize following bumper crops in key exporters. The resulting surplus, along with maize destocking policies in China, led to continued declines in prices.

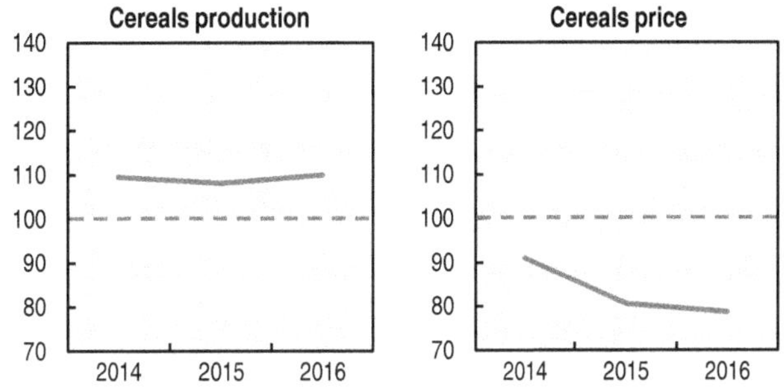

Oilseeds

Soybean production increased strongly in 2016 due to record crops in the United States and Brazil. World aggregate production of other oilseeds (rapeseed, sunflower seed and groundnuts) increased for the first time in three years. Following the 2015 decline, vegetable oil production recovered in 2016. Although oilseed prices increased in 2016, they remain below the average prices of the past decade.

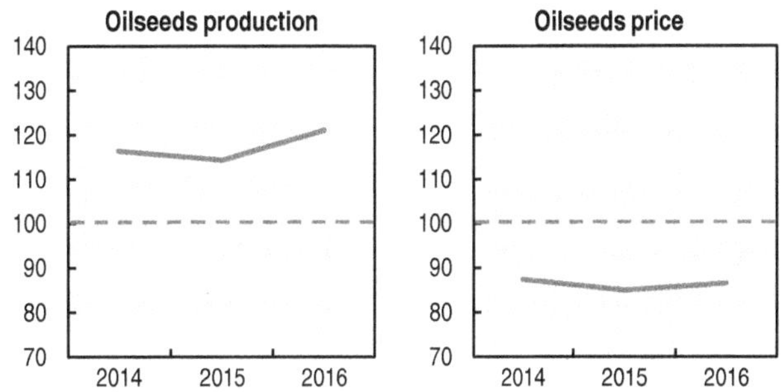

Sugar

Production in the 2016/17 season is expected to be insufficient to cover demand. Production setbacks occurred in key exporters Brazil and Thailand, and in India, the second largest producer. Sugar prices remain relatively high. Prices for high fructose corn syrup, the main alternative to sugar, also increased in 2016.

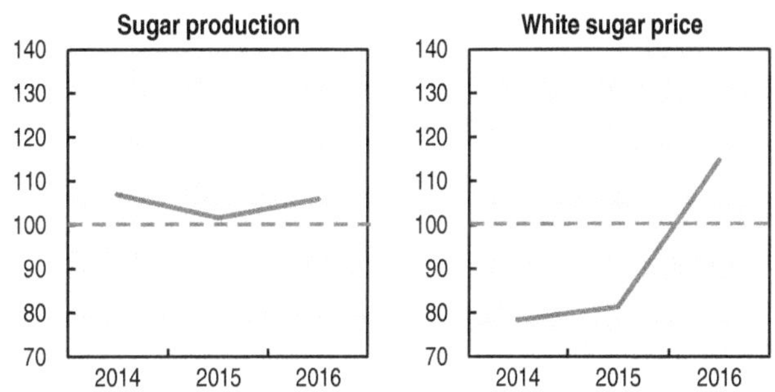

Meat

Overall production increased by only 1% in 2016, the second lowest rate in the last decade. Production of poultry and bovine meat expanded while pigmeat and sheep meat production declined. Despite a recovery near the end of the year, prices in 2016 were on average below the 2015 level. Relatively low feed costs and growing livestock inventories contribute to decreasing prices.

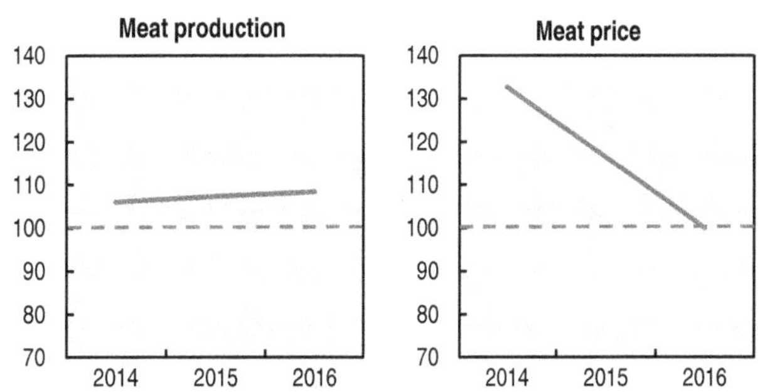

Note: All graphs expressed as an index where the 2006-16 average is set to 100. Production refers to global production volumes. Prices are nominal. More information on market conditions and evolutions by commodity can be found in the Commodity Snapshots in Chapter 3, the commodity snapshot tables in the Annex, and the online commodity chapters.

Source: OECD/FAO (2017), "OECD-FAO Agricultural Outlook", OECD Agriculture statistics (database), *http://dx.doi.org/10.1787/agr-data-en.*

StatLink *http://dx.doi.org/10.1787/888933520914*

Figure 1.1. **Current market conditions for key commodities** *(Cont.)*

Current market conditions	Production Index Average 2006-2016 = 100	Price Index Average 2006-2016 = 100

Dairy

While world milk production increased slightly in 2016, production by important exporters (Australia, New Zealand and Argentina) slumped. As a result, prices started to recover in the second half of 2016, especially for butter and whole milk powder (WMP). However, due to low prices in the beginning of 2016, the average price for the year was lower than in 2015.

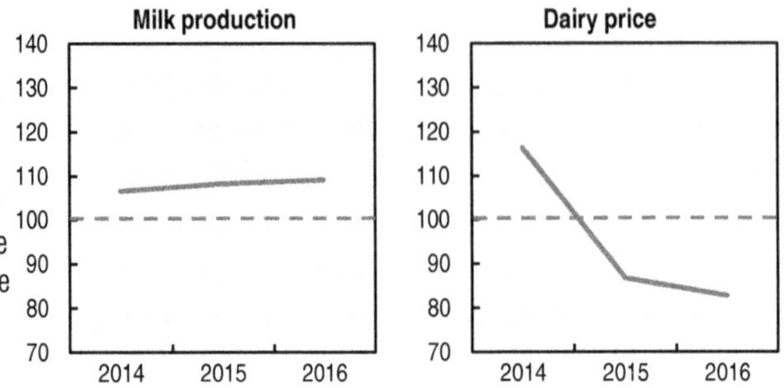

Fish

Production expanded by a modest rate of 1% in 2016. Growth came from aquaculture as capture fisheries experienced lower catches mainly due to the impact of El Niño in selected Latin American countries. The average fish trade price increased in 2016, supported by sustained demand, in particular for a number of highly traded seafood commodities.

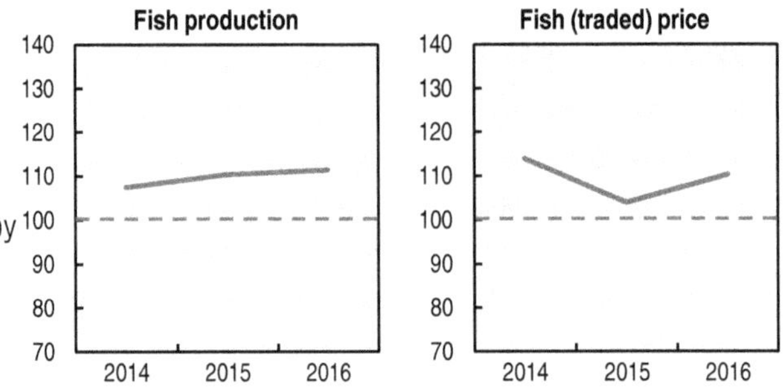

Biofuels

Demand for biofuels was sustained by obligatory blending and by higher demand for fuel due to low energy prices. Non-mandated demand was limited except in Brazil, where policies in major states favour hydrous ethanol. Policy decisions stimulated biofuels production in 2016 through mandate increases and favourable taxes or subsidies in several countries. Prices of biodiesel and ethanol stabilised in 2016.

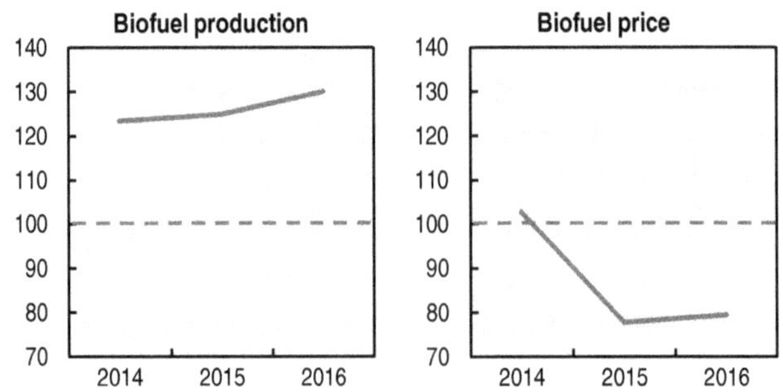

Cotton

Production recovered by 7% in 2016, following a strong drop in 2015. Production increased in almost all major cotton producing countries due to improved yields. Processing stagnated, while world stocks are high at eight months of consumption. As a result, prices remained under pressure in 2016.

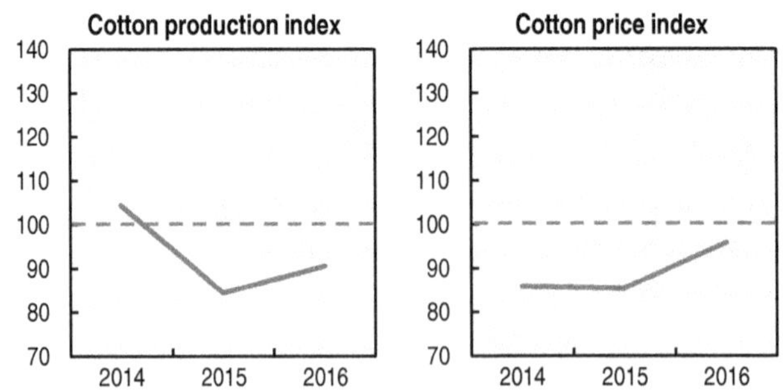

Note: All graphs expressed as an index where the 2006-16 average is set to 100. Production refers to global production volumes. Prices are nominal. More information on market conditions and evolutions by commodity can be found in the Commodity Snapshots in Chapter 3, the commodity snapshot tables in the Annex, and the online commodity chapters.

Source: OECD/FAO (2017), "OECD-FAO Agricultural Outlook", OECD Agriculture statistics (database), *http://dx.doi.org/10.1787/agr-data-en.*

StatLink *http://dx.doi.org/10.1787/888933520914*

Consumption

Global demand growth will slow compared to the previous decade

The last decade has seen unprecedented growth in the demand for agricultural products. Between 2004-06 and 2014-16, the total consumption of cereals (wheat, maize, rice, and other coarse grains) increased from 2.0 bln t to 2.5 bln t, adding almost 500 Mt of additional demand. To put this in perspective, total domestic utilisation of cereals (including for non-food uses) in the United States was around 350 Mt in 2016. Similarly, the total consumption of poultry increased from 81 Mt in 2004-06 to 113 Mt in 2014-16, an increase of 32 Mt. The 2014-16 domestic utilization of poultry in the United States was 17 Mt. Demand for fish for human consumption also increased remarkably, growing from 111 Mt in 2004-06 to 149 Mt in 2014-16, an increase of 38 Mt; fish consumption in the United States in 2014-16 was 7 Mt. Over the last ten years, agricultural markets thus experienced a demand increase of historical proportions.

This increase was driven by two main factors: the rise of China and the growth in biofuel production. In China, income growth pushed up food demand. In particular, higher demand for meat and intensification of livestock production boosted demand for animal feed. In the developed world, food demand stagnated, but biofuel support policies strengthened the global demand for maize, sugarcane and vegetable oils.

While these factors will continue to influence global demand for agricultural products, their relevance will diminish relatively over the coming decade. Demand growth in China is slowing down, as income growth moderates and the propensity for households to spend additional income on food declines. The evolution of biofuels markets is heavily driven by policies and crude oil prices, and hence harder to forecast based on demographic and economic trends. Current policies and expected moderate crude oil prices appear likely to lead to a lower growth in biofuel production from agricultural crops compared to the last decade.

As a result, this *Outlook* projects that across most commodities, the growth in total demand (including non-food uses) will slow considerably compared to the previous decade (Figure 1.2). For most commodity groups, including cereals, meat, fish and vegetable oil, growth rates will be cut by around half. This slowdown will be particularly pronounced for the demand for vegetable oil, which was the fastest-growing commodity over the past decade, driven in part by biofuel policies. For sugar, however, the growth rate will decrease only moderately as the increase in per capita consumption is expected to contribute as much as the increase in population over the next decade.

A major exception to this trend is fresh dairy products. Projected growth rates for fresh dairy for the coming decade are higher than those experienced over the past ten years, driven by increasing per capita demand in developing countries, most notably India. For other dairy products such as cheese, butter, skimmed milk powder and whole milk powder (not shown in Figure 1.2), consumption growth slows compared to the previous decade, but remains at levels above those of cereals, meat or fish. Dairy, together with vegetable oil and sugar, will have the highest growth rates.

In contrast with the previous decade, the overall growth in agricultural demand over the outlook period will be mainly driven by population growth. The solid areas in Figure 1.2 indicate the share of the growth rate attributable to population growth, while the shaded areas indicate the contribution of growth in per capita consumption (including non-food consumption). For instance, the growth of cereal consumption for all uses will be around

Figure 1.2. **Annual growth in consumption for key commodity groups, 2007-16 and 2017-26**

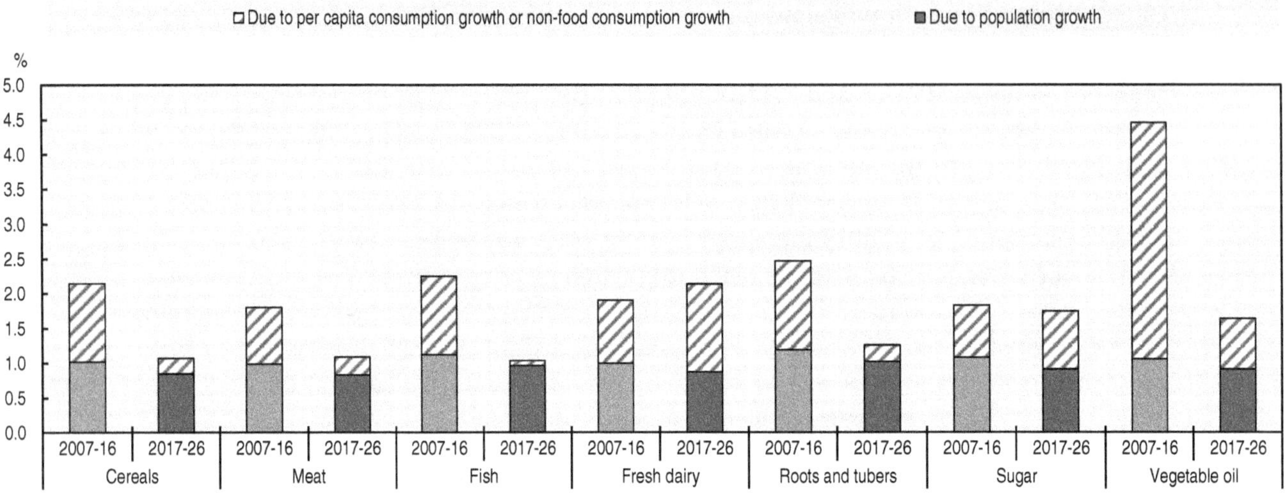

Note: The population growth component is calculated assuming per capita demand remains constant at the level of the year preceding the decade. Growth rates refer to total demand (for food, feed and other uses).

Source: OECD/FAO (2017), "OECD-FAO Agricultural Outlook", OECD Agriculture statistics (database), *http://dx.doi.org/10.1787/agr-data-en*.

StatLink *http://dx.doi.org/10.1787/888933520933*

1.1% per year over the next decade. If per capita consumption (including non-food) had remained at current levels, population growth by itself would induce a growth of 0.9% per year over the baseline period. The remaining share of 0.2% p.a. can be attributed to factors such as income growth and consumption preferences that impact both food and non-food consumption of cereals. Across commodity groups consumption growth over the previous decade was due to a roughly even split between population growth and increase in per capita consumption (including non-food). Over the next decade, however, per capita consumption growth will only play an important determining role for sugar, dairy, and vegetable oils. Higher per capita growth explains the higher overall growth rates for these commodities. The growth in fresh dairy consumption is exceptional, with the result that fresh dairy shows the highest consumption growth rate among the key commodities of the *Outlook*. However, trade of fresh dairy products will remain limited and, as a result, growth in consumption will have a limited impact on world dairy markets.

Projections indicate relatively low growth in total meat consumption, as per capita consumption is expected to level off in many middle-income countries with a high preference for meat, especially China. In the Least Developed Countries, meat demand will continue to be constrained by limited income growth in poor rural and urban households.

China, India and Sub-Saharan Africa drive global growth

The world's population will increase from 7.3 to 8.2 billion over the course of the outlook period. Almost all of this population growth will occur in developing countries. In Sub-Saharan Africa, the population will increase from 974 million to 1.3 billion, an increase of 289 million; the population of India will grow from 1.3 billion to 1.5 billion, an increase of almost 150 million. Together, Sub-Saharan Africa and India will account for 56% of total population growth over the next decade, while India overtakes China as the world's most populous country.

Given their strong population growth, India and Sub-Saharan Africa will also drive a large share of global demand. In addition, China will continue to contribute to demand for several key commodities (Figure 1.3). For cereals, total consumption (including for non-food uses) is expected to increase by 338 Mt over the outlook period. Of this, 38% will come from China, India and Sub-Saharan Africa. This share is lower for wheat and maize (where developed countries play a larger role), but higher for rice (where India alone accounts for 27% of the increase in consumption) and other coarse grains (where Sub-Saharan Africa accounts for 41% of the global consumption increase).

Figure 1.3. **Regional shares in commodity consumption growth, 2016-26**

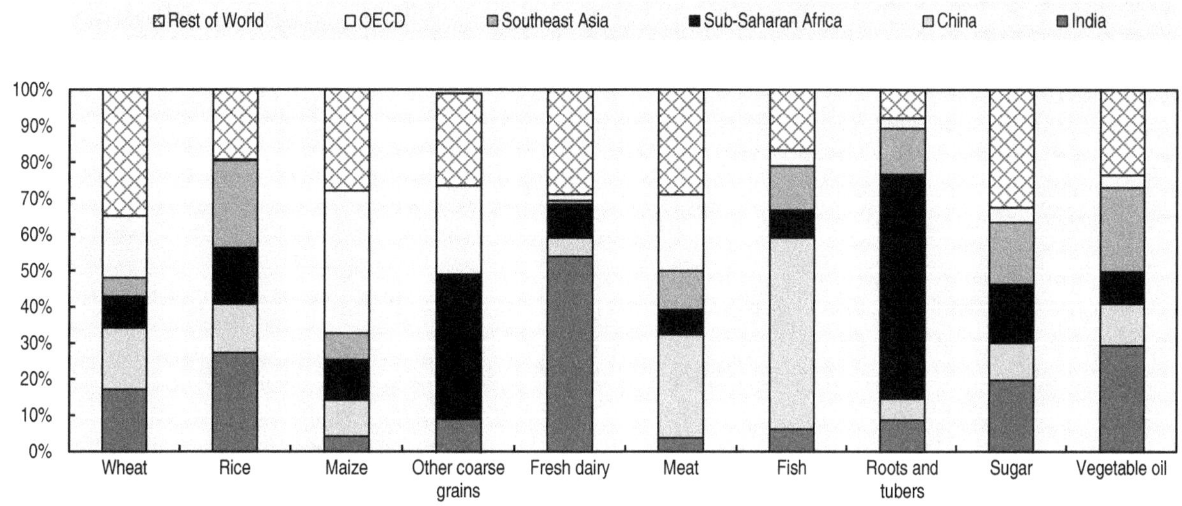

Note: Demand growth compares 2026 to baseline (2014-16) average. Southeast Asia includes Indonesia, the Philippines, Malaysia, Thailand, Viet Nam, Lao PDR, Myanmar and Cambodia.

Source: OECD/FAO (2017), "OECD-FAO Agricultural Outlook", OECD Agriculture statistics (database), *http://dx.doi.org/10.1787/agr-data-en.*

StatLink *http://dx.doi.org/10.1787/888933520952*

China accounts for large shares of the additional consumption of meat (29%) and especially fish (53%), two commodities where the demand growth from India and Sub-Saharan Africa is lower. For instance, India accounts for only 4% of the additional meat consumption. India is a bigger driver of additional demand for fresh dairy products (54%) and vegetable oil (29%), while Sub-Saharan Africa accounts for 62% of the increase in roots and tubers.

Figure 1.3 also indicates the role played by Southeast Asia (Indonesia, Philippines, Malaysia, Thailand, Viet Nam, Lao PDR, Myanmar and Cambodia) in demand growth in the coming decade. These countries will contribute to an important degree to the additional demand for rice (24%) and vegetable oil (23%), as well as sugar (17%), fish (12%) and roots and tubers (13%). By contrast, their role is lower for other commodities, fresh dairy in particular. These issues are discussed further in Chapter 2.

Lower consumption growth in China is reducing global consumption growth

As the preceding discussion makes clear, China will continue to play an important role in consumption growth for many commodities. However, compared with the previous decade, consumption growth will be considerably lower in China in the coming decade, a trend which leads to lower growth at the global level.

In the last decade, China was responsible for 21 Mt of additional fish consumption out of a global growth in consumption of 31 Mt (Figure 1.4). This growth was driven by an increase in per capita food consumption of fish from 30 kg/capita in 2007 to 42 kg/capita in 2016, a level two-thirds higher than the OECD average of 25 kg/capita. Over the next decade, Chinese per capita food consumption of fish is projected to increase further to 50 kg/capita. However, this represents a smaller increase than what was witnessed in the previous decade. At a global level, the effect is a strong reduction in the annual growth of consumption. As global per capita food consumption remains stable over the next decade, total growth in consumption of fish is practically equal to global population growth, as shown in Figure 1.2.

Figure 1.4. **Fish: Regional shares in demand growth and per capita food consumption**

(a) Regional shares in global consumption growth(left), (b) Per capita consumption by region (right)

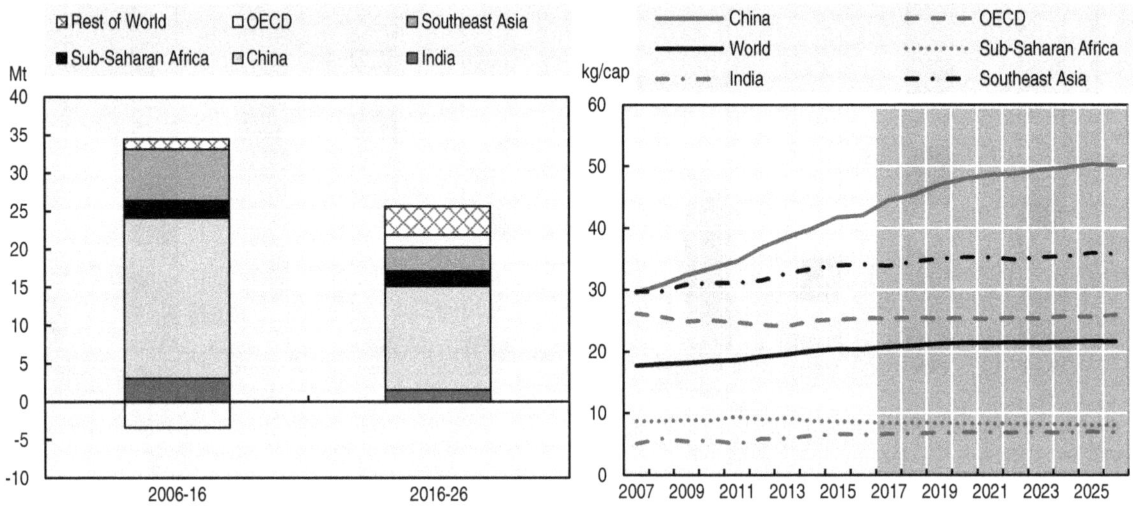

Note: Consumption growth compares 2004-06 average to 2014-16 average, and 2014-16 average to 2026. Southeast Asia includes Indonesia, the Philippines, Malaysia, Thailand, Viet Nam, Lao PDR, Myanmar and Cambodia.

Source: OECD/FAO (2017), "OECD-FAO Agricultural Outlook", OECD Agriculture statistics (database), *http://dx.doi.org/10.1787/agr-data-en*.

StatLink *http://dx.doi.org/10.1787/888933520971*

Likewise, annual consumption of pigmeat increased by 18 Mt in the last decade, of which 11 Mt (or 59%) was consumption growth in China (Figure 1.5). For the coming decade, the projected consumption growth for pigmeat is considerably lower at 11 Mt. This lower global consumption growth is almost exclusively explained by developments in China. After strong growth over the past decade, per capita consumption in China has reached 40 kg/capita in 2016, one-third above the OECD average. Over the outlook period, consumption growth is projected to be around one-third of the level observed in the last decade, resulting in a strong reduction in the growth of pigmeat consumption.

Most pigmeat consumed in China is produced domestically, but evolutions in the demand for meat have indirect effects on other markets through the derived demand for feed. In this way, evolutions in China also contribute to a lower growth in global demand for maize and soybeans over the next decade, as discussed below.

Global growth patterns shift as growth in demand in China decreases

Chinese growth in demand has been characterised by a strong increase in consumption of animal-based protein (fish, pigmeat) and associated feed demand.

Figure 1.5. **Pigmeat: Regional shares in demand growth and per capita food consumption**

(a) Regional shares in global consumption growth (left), (b) Per capita consumption by region (right)

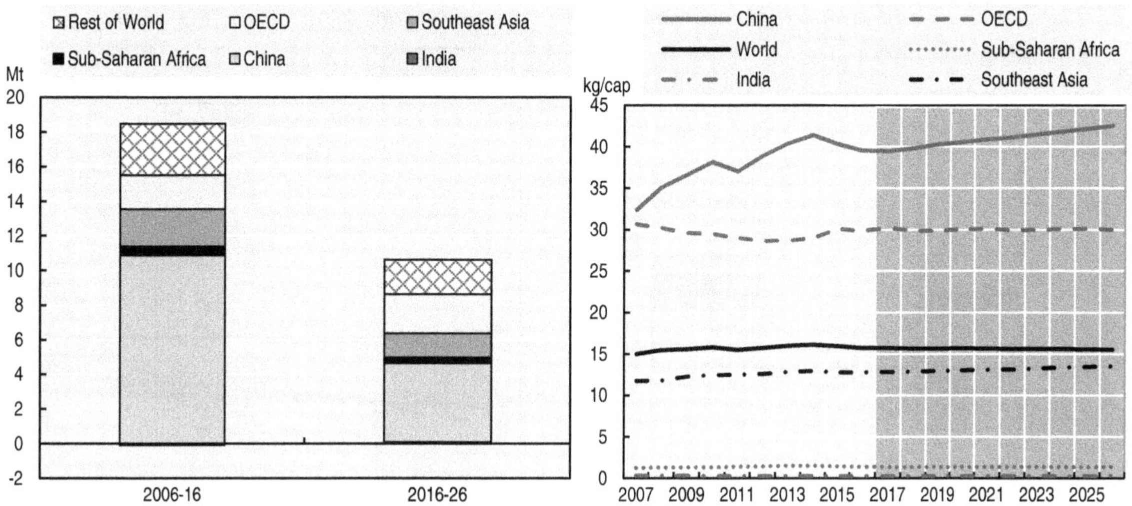

Note: Demand growth compares 2004-06 average to 2014-16 average, and 2014-16 average to 2026. Southeast Asia includes Indonesia, the Philippines, Malaysia, Thailand, Viet Nam, Lao PDR, Myanmar and Cambodia. Per capita consumption expressed in retail weight.
Source: OECD/FAO (2017), "OECD-FAO Agricultural Outlook", OECD Agriculture statistics (database), *http://dx.doi.org/10.1787/agr-data-en.*

StatLink *http://dx.doi.org/10.1787/888933520990*

Consumption preferences in areas where strong population and income growth is expected in the projection period will differ from those of China, suggesting that future consumption growth will unfold in different directions.

Growth of pigmeat consumption will be limited as high demand for pork over the last decade was largely driven by Chinese consumption preferences, which are unlike those elsewhere in the world where strong population and income growth are expected.

For fish, as Figure 1.4 indicates, it seems unlikely that consumption increases in other countries can replicate the large growth seen in the past decade. This growth was driven by a strong increase in per capita consumption (of 12 kg/capita) in the world's most populous country, China. By contrast, per capita consumption of fish in India is currently below 10 kg/capita, a level which is expected to remain stable over the outlook period. Given similar food preferences, Southeast Asian countries could potentially increase their per capita fish consumption to the levels observed in China over the long run. However, although the total population of this region is large, it is only about half that of China's. Finally, Sub-Saharan Africa currently has a low per capita consumption of fish and this is projected to decrease further over the outlook period due to limited supply capacity. Hence, over the medium term it seems unlikely that other countries will drive global demand for fish to the same degree as China has done in recent years.

In markets where China's role is traditionally less pronounced, there is also no clear trend for other regions to drive growth in the future. For instance, the growth in demand for beef and veal meat was 6 Mt over the last decade and is projected to grow to 9 Mt in the next decade (Figure 1.6). Average per capita consumption in developing countries will remain at only about one-third of that of developed countries by 2026, but the bulk of beef and veal demand growth will continue to be driven by population growth in developing countries. Demand for bovine meat in the United States, which had decreased in recent years, is expected to recover. However, given already-high consumption levels, developed

Figure 1.6. **Beef and veal: Regional shares in demand growth and per capita food consumption**

(a) Regional shares in global consumption growth (left), (b) Per capita consumption by region (right)

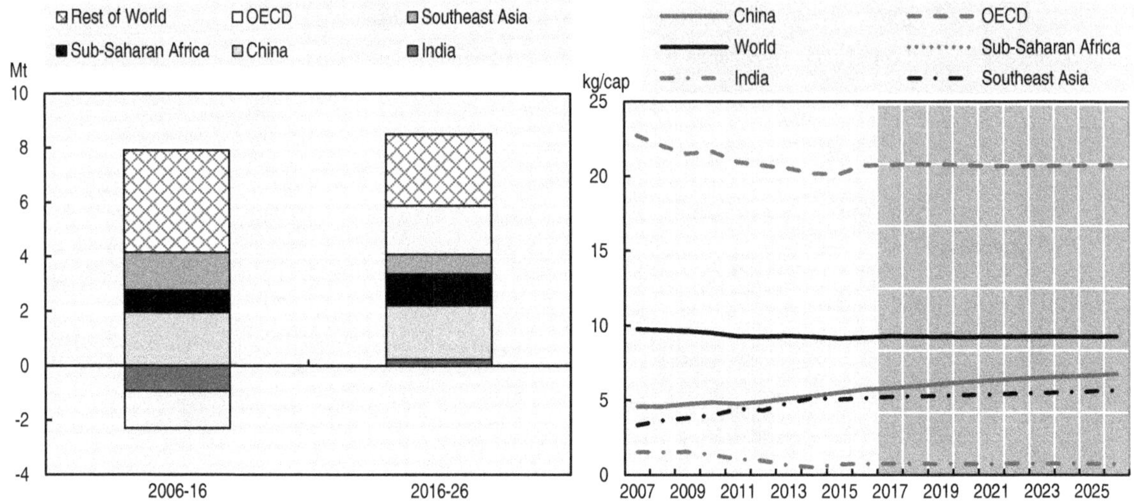

Note: Demand growth compares 2004-06 average to 2014-16 average, and 2014-16 average to 2026. Southeast Asia includes Indonesia, the Philippines, Malaysia, Thailand, Viet Nam, Lao PDR, Myanmar and Cambodia. Per capita consumption expressed in retail weight.
Source: OECD/FAO (2017), "OECD-FAO Agricultural Outlook", OECD Agriculture statistics (database), *http://dx.doi.org/10.1787/agr-data-en*.

StatLink *http://dx.doi.org/10.1787/888933521009*

countries are not expected to increase per capita meat consumption levels much further. Nor are developing regions showing signs of increasing their per capita beef and veal consumption levels by much. In Sub-Saharan Africa, per capita beef and veal consumption is projected to remain low over the projection period, but total consumption expands strongly due to the rapidly increasing population. At a global level, per capita consumption is expected to remain stable, and beef and veal demand is therefore expected to grow at a similar rate to population growth.

The strong growth in poultry consumption last decade by 32 Mt was driven to a large extent by OECD countries (7 Mt) together with Brazil (3 Mt) and the Russian Federation (2 Mt). As demand growth in these countries will be more modest in the future, total consumption growth for poultry is expected to be 18 Mt in the next decade, only half of the increase over the past ten years. Based on its continued per capita consumption increase, China will remain a strong engine of growth in the global poultry market over the *Outlook* period. Per capita consumption in India is expected to grow by 30%, but originating from a low base, hence its overall share in global demand growth will remain low. In Sub-Saharan Africa, per capita consumption will remain stagnant, and overall consumption growth will be in proportion to population growth (Figure 1.7).

The demand for sheep (not shown here) is expected to increase by 3.2 Mt over the next decade, an acceleration compared with the previous decade, when demand grew only 2 Mt. The acceleration in demand is mostly due to China, where per capita consumption is projected to increase from 3.5 to 4.2 kg per capita, and Sub-Saharan Africa, where per capita consumption remains flat at around 2.2 kg per capita but where strong population growth drives higher demand. These per capita consumption levels are above the global average, which remains flat at around 2 kg per capita. At a global level, however, consumption and production of sheep meat is modest in comparison with other meat types.

Figure 1.7. **Poultry: Regional shares in demand growth and per capita food consumption**

(a) Regional shares in global consumption growth (left), (b) Per capita consumption by region (right)

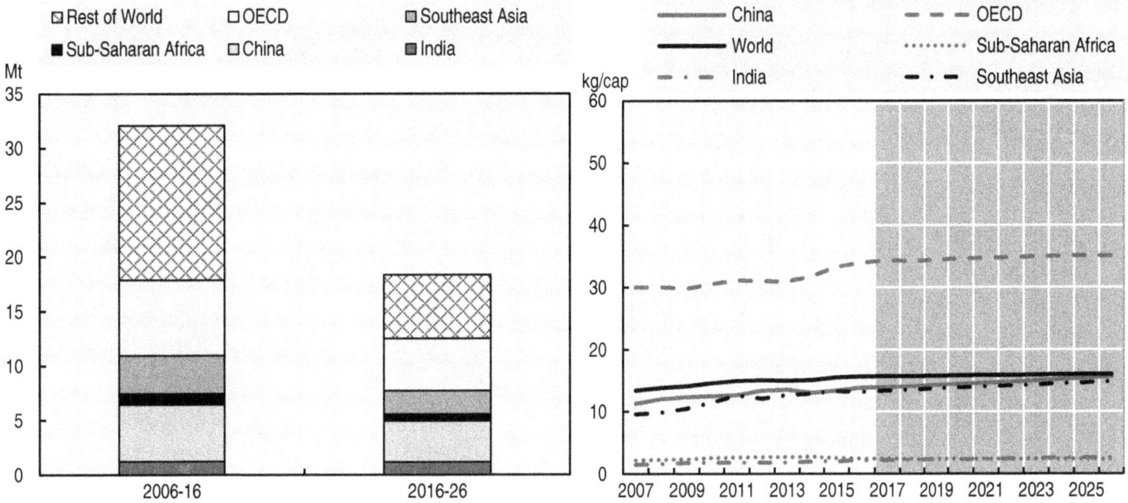

Note: Demand growth compares 2004-06 average to 2014-16 average, and 2014-16 average to 2026. Southeast Asia includes Indonesia, the Philippines, Malaysia, Thailand, Viet Nam, Lao PDR, Myanmar and Cambodia. Per capita consumption expressed in retail weight.
Source: OECD/FAO (2017), "OECD-FAO Agricultural Outlook", OECD Agriculture statistics (database), *http://dx.doi.org/10.1787/agr-data-en.*

StatLink http://dx.doi.org/10.1787/888933521028

The growth in consumption of dairy products will be led by an increase in the consumption of fresh dairy products. As shown in Figure 1.8, total consumption of fresh dairy products is expected to be 104 Mt higher at the end of the outlook period; more than half of this increase is due to continued demand growth in India. Per capita consumption of fresh dairy products in India has shown a strong increase in the past decade, as shown in the second panel of Figure 1.8. This trend is expected to continue and contrasts with

Figure 1.8. **Fresh dairy products: Regional shares in demand growth and per capita food consumption**

(a) Regional shares in global consumption growth (left), (b) Per capita consumption by region (right)

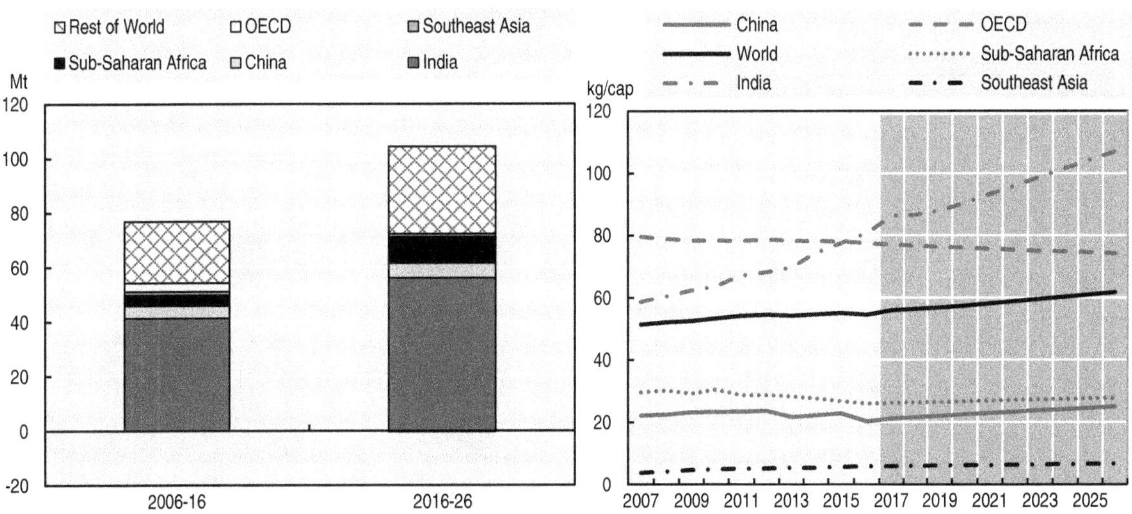

Note: Demand growth compares 2004-06 average to 2014-16 average, and 2014-16 average to 2026. Southeast Asia includes Indonesia, the Philippines, Malaysia, Thailand, Viet Nam, Lao PDR, Myanmar and Cambodia.
Source: OECD/FAO (2017), "OECD-FAO Agricultural Outlook", OECD Agriculture statistics (database), *http://dx.doi.org/10.1787/agr-data-en.*

StatLink http://dx.doi.org/10.1787/888933521047

decreasing consumption in the developed world. Per capita consumption of fresh dairy products will remain much lower in China and in Sub-Saharan Africa. Overall, only a small share of fresh dairy products is traded; hence, the strong growth in consumption will have a limited impact on international dairy prices.

In contrast with fresh dairy products, the growth in global consumption of processed dairy products is expected to slow down in the next decade to 1.7% p.a., despite renewed interest in consumption of butter and dairy fat in developed countries. Supported by a shift in consumer preference towards healthy and less processed food, and more positive health assessments of dairy fat in recent years, per capita consumption is projected to grow across all processed dairy products in developed countries. In developing countries, the level and composition of dairy consumption will remain uneven across regions, but fresh dairy products will still account for a bulk of consumption in most regions. The growth in demand for butter and WMP is expected to be driven by both income and population growth, while for the other dairy products, increase in consumption will be proportional to population growth. Due to consumer preferences and persistent limitations in the development of supply infrastructure, per capita consumption of processed dairy products will remain much lower over the outlook period in Sub-Saharan Africa, Oceania (excluding Australia and New Zealand) and Asia, while other regions such as Latin America and Caribbean, North Africa and the Near East will close the gap with some of the developed countries.

Convergence in per capita food consumption patterns remains limited

As the preceding discussion suggests, there is no global convergence in per capita consumption patterns over the outlook period. At the end of the outlook period, large discrepancies will continue to exist in terms of per capita consumption of different commodities, as well as overall calorie and protein availability. These differences are especially stark for meat and fish (Figure 1.9), where large variations in per capita consumption will persist.

Figure 1.9. **Per capita food consumption of meat and fish in 2026**

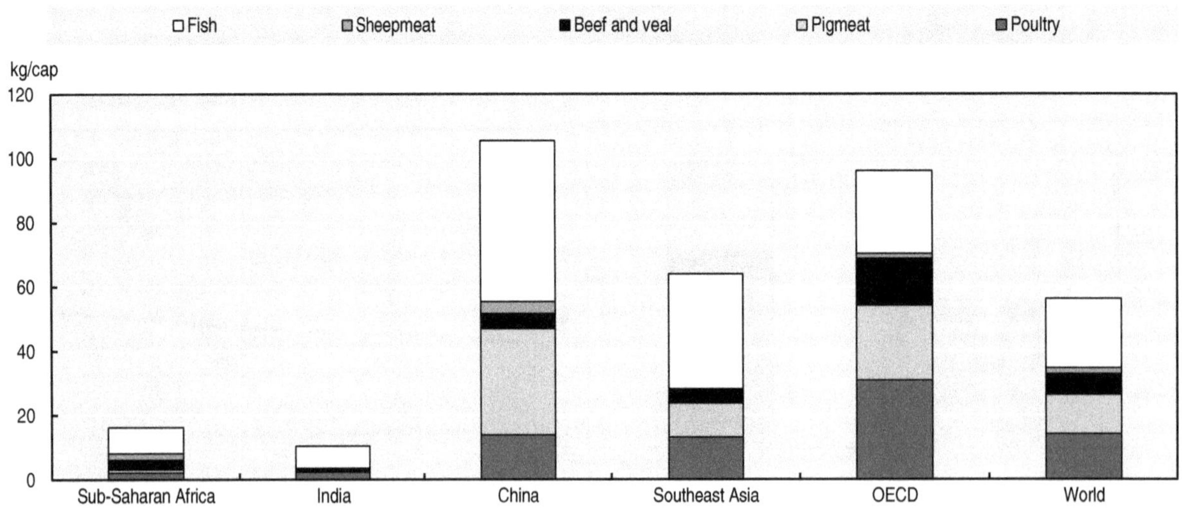

Note: Southeast Asia includes Indonesia, the Philippines, Malaysia, Thailand, Viet Nam, Lao PDR, Myanmar and Cambodia. Per capita consumption expressed in retail weight for meat; in live weight equivalent for fish.

Source: OECD/FAO (2017), "OECD-FAO Agricultural Outlook", OECD Agriculture statistics (database), *http://dx.doi.org/10.1787/agr-data-en.*

StatLink *http://dx.doi.org/10.1787/888933521066*

Compared to meat consumption, total food consumption of cereals will vary less between different regions in 2026, as cereals continue to form an important part of the diet across the world (Figure 1.10). In Sub-Saharan Africa, cereal food consumption is spread more or less equally across wheat, rice, maize and other coarse grains, whereas wheat and rice dominate in China and India. Southeast Asia has particularly high per capita cereals consumption driven by rice, while for OECD countries, wheat will continue to dominate. In the Near East, per capita rice consumption is foreseen to increase by about 6%, mainly driven by immigration from Asian countries. At a global level, wheat and rice are roughly equally important in 2026.

Figure 1.10. **Per capita food use of cereals in 2026**

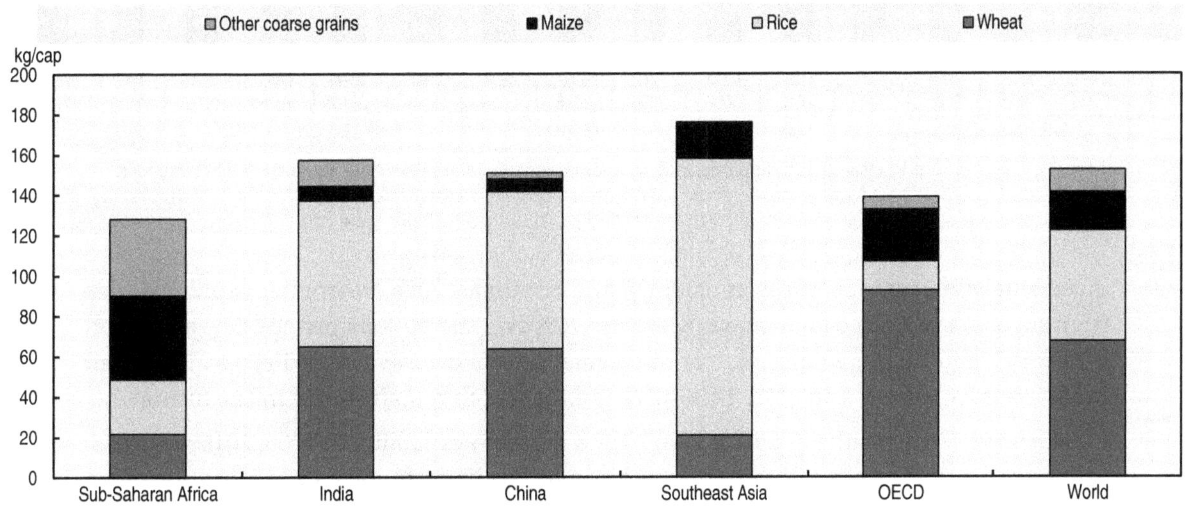

Note: Southeast Asia includes Indonesia, the Philippines, Malaysia, Thailand, Viet Nam, Lao PDR, Myanmar and Cambodia.
Source: OECD/FAO (2017), "OECD-FAO Agricultural Outlook", OECD Agriculture statistics (database), *http://dx.doi.org/10.1787/agr-data-en*.
StatLink *http://dx.doi.org/10.1787/888933521085*

Figure 1.11 shows the estimated calorie availability per capita in 2006, 2016 and 2026. The past decade saw increases in calorie availability in the developing world, especially in India, China and Southeast Asia. In OECD countries, average calorie intake decreased. These trends are projected to continue, bringing calorie availability levels in India and Southeast Asia closer to those in OECD countries. Calorie availability levels in China are currently estimated to be similar to the levels seen in OECD countries, but China would overtake the OECD countries over the outlook period.

In 2016, Sub-Saharan Africa and India show similar levels of per capita calorie availability. However, while calorie availability is expected to increase in India in the coming decade, Sub-Saharan Africa shows only limited growth. Compared to other regions, roots and tubers play a large role in Sub-Saharan Africa, accounting for 16% of total calorie availability in 2016, a share which remains constant in the coming decade.

Cereals are the most important source of calories across the world. However, Figure 1.11 also makes clear that as incomes grow, the relative importance of cereals typically decreases. In India, the contribution of cereals to calorie availability decreased from 60% in 2006 to 55% in 2016, and is projected to decrease further to 53% in 2016. This relative decline is in large part driven by the increasing calorie availability from vegetable oil, dairy and sugar. Similar trends can be seen in China (where vegetable oil and meat are

Figure 1.11. **Per capita calorie availability by food category**

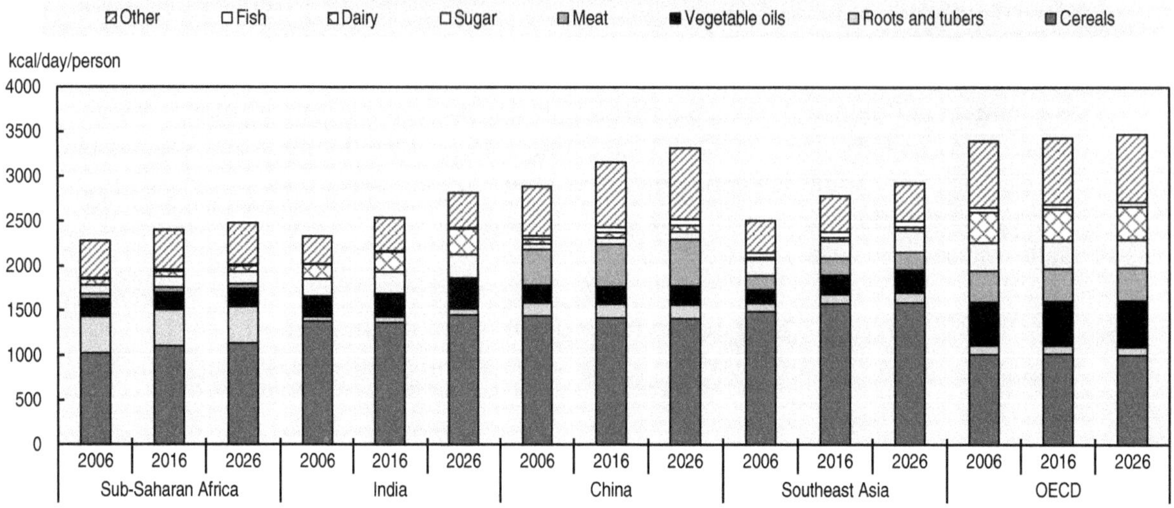

Note: Southeast Asia includes Indonesia, the Philippines, Malaysia, Thailand, Viet Nam, Lao PDR, Myanmar and Cambodia.
Source: OECD/FAO (2017), "OECD-FAO Agricultural Outlook", OECD Agriculture statistics (database), *http://dx.doi.org/10.1787/agr-data-en.*
StatLink *http://dx.doi.org/10.1787/888933521104*

increasingly important sources of calories) and Southeast Asia (where per capita calories from sugar are projected to increase by around 20% over the outlook period). One exception is Sub-Saharan Africa, where the role of cereals in total calorie availability has increased from 45% in 2006 to 47% in 2016. This share is expected to remain stable in the future.

Figure 1.12 shows the estimated per capita protein availability in 2006, 2016 and 2026. Compared to calorie availability, protein availability appears considerably more heterogeneous, with especially low levels in Sub-Saharan Africa, India, and Southeast Asia compared to China and OECD countries. A key driver of this difference is the low level of per capita animal protein consumption. In India, additional protein is coming from the fast

Figure 1.12. **Per capita protein availability by food category**

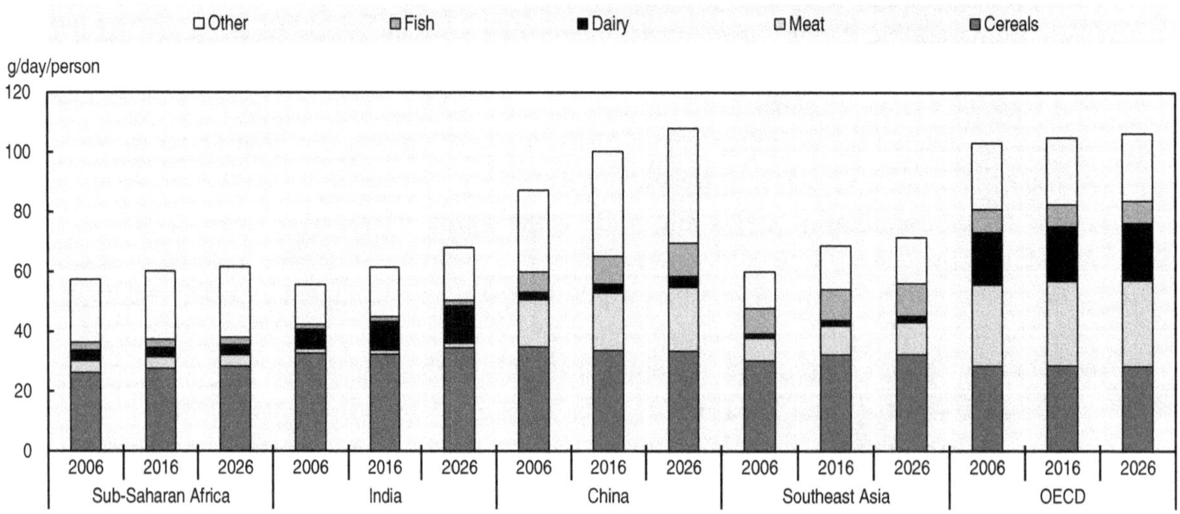

Note: Southeast Asia includes Indonesia, the Philippines, Malaysia, Thailand, Viet Nam, Lao PDR, Myanmar and Cambodia.
Source: OECD/FAO (2017), "OECD-FAO Agricultural Outlook", OECD Agriculture statistics (database), *http://dx.doi.org/10.1787/agr-data-en.*
StatLink *http://dx.doi.org/10.1787/888933521123*

expanding fresh dairy product consumption, while in Southeast Asia, high fish consumption levels form an important contribution. Limited income growth in poor rural and urban households and the slow development of a retail infrastructure for animal protein, like meat, fish and dairy, are seen as the main constraints to protein consumption growth in Sub-Saharan Africa.

Emerging economies in Asia (China, India, Southeast Asia) have thus seen strong growth in per capita availability of calories and proteins. By contrast, Sub-Saharan Africa has seen little improvement in the past decade and projections show little growth in the coming decade. Overall, then, large differences in consumption patterns and in calorie and protein availability will persist over the outlook period.

Global demand for feed to grow at a slower pace

The global use of feed reached 1.5 bln t in 2014-16. Over the course of the projection period, feed use is projected to increase further to 1.8 bln t by 2026, a growth of 18% (1.7% per year). Maize and protein meal, which together account for about 58% of total feed consumption in 2014-16, will continue to increase their share in total animal feed. However, growth will slow down compared to the last decade (Figure 1.13). Between 2004-06 and 2014-16, feed use increased by around 300 Mt. Over the next decade, the additional consumption is projected to be about 270 Mt compared to the base period (2014-16), driven by lower demand growth in China as well as in Southeast Asia. In China, feed rations have reached a plateau after a steady intensification process; growth in global livestock production is not expected to be as strong as in the last ten years.

Figure 1.13. **Feed: Regional shares in demand growth and total use**

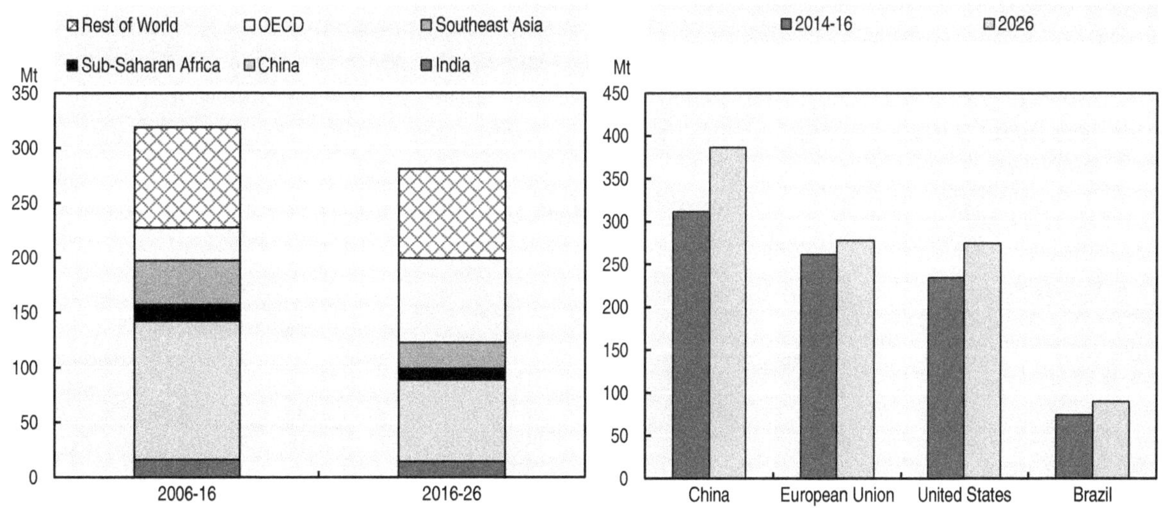

Note: Demand growth compares 2004-06 average to 2014-16 average, and 2014-16 average to 2026. Southeast Asia includes Indonesia, the Philippines, Malaysia, Thailand, Viet Nam, Lao PDR, Myanmar and Cambodia.
Source: OECD/FAO (2017), "OECD-FAO Agricultural Outlook", OECD Agriculture statistics (database), *http://dx.doi.org/10.1787/agr-data-en*.
StatLink *http://dx.doi.org/10.1787/888933521142*

The projected expansion in the Chinese livestock sector will result in a 21% increase in feed use by 2026 compared to 2016, which constitutes a significant reduction from the 70% feed consumption increase during last decade. The slowdown is caused by the transition from a period of fast commercialization and subsequent intensification of feed rations in the Chinese livestock sector, to more efficiency oriented production. Globally, China will still account for 28% of the demand increase in the coming decade. While demand for feed continues to increase in other regions (the European Union, the United States and Brazil in particular), the net effect is a marked slowdown of demand growth.

China, the European Union and the United States continue to be the leading consumers of feed, and their ranking does not change over the outlook period (Figure 1.13). Together, these three countries accounted for 53% of total feed consumption in 2014-16, a share which remains relatively stable.

Cereals are a key source for feed, especially maize (695 Mt in 2026, +21% over the outlook period), other coarse grains (182 Mt, +10%) and wheat (162 Mt, +17%). Protein meals, the second most important feed commodity, are expected to grow from 309 Mt in 2014-16 to 384 Mt in 2026, an increase of 24%. Protein meals are dominated by soybean meal, which accounts for more than two-thirds of global protein meal production.

Biofuels market slows down, reducing the demand growth for maize

In addition to food and feed, agricultural commodities are used as feedstock for biofuel production. The production of ethanol is mostly based on maize and sugarcane, and ethanol production accounts for a large share of the total demand for maize (17% in 2014-16) and sugarcane (19%); likewise, biodiesel is mostly based on vegetable oils and accounts for a considerable share of demand (13%).

As policies started to stimulate biofuel production in the second half of the 2000s, world ethanol and biodiesel production increased strongly. As a result, a rapidly growing share of global sugarcane and maize production was used in ethanol production, while biodiesel started to claim a growing share of vegetable oil production (Figure 1.14). Between 2000 and 2010, the share of global sugarcane production going to biofuel production grew from 10% to almost 20%. For maize, the share of utilization going to biofuels grew from 4% to 18% in 2011. For vegetable oil, the biofuel share in use grew from less than 1% in 2000 to between 12% and 14% in recent years.

Figure 1.14. **Growth in biofuel production, 2000-26**

(a) World ethanol and biodiesel production (left), (b) Biofuels as % of demand (right)

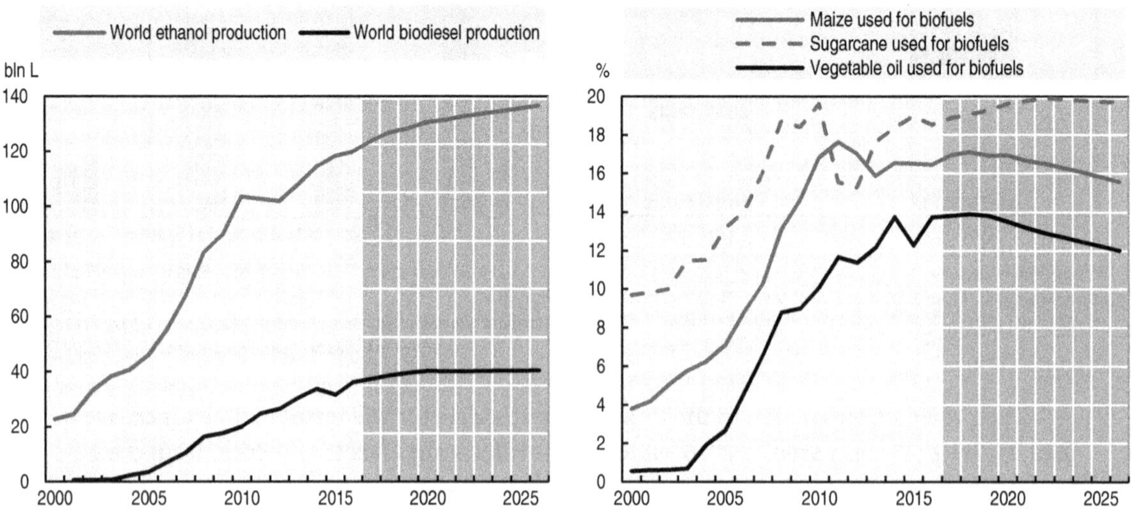

Source: OECD/FAO (2017), "OECD-FAO Agricultural Outlook", OECD Agriculture statistics (database), *http://dx.doi.org/10.1787/agr-data-en.*

StatLink *http://dx.doi.org/10.1787/888933521161*

The policy-induced expansion of biofuels was thus a major driver of increased demand for maize, sugarcane and vegetable oil over the past decade. However, growth in biofuels production is slowing down. Between 2000 and 2010, production of ethanol grew at a pace of 17% per year, more than quadrupling production in the span of a decade. After a temporary fall in 2012, growth has resumed at a slower pace of 4% per year in recent years. A similar slowdown is observed for biodiesel.

The initial growth in biofuels was heavily policy-driven, motivated by a concern for reducing greenhouse gas emissions, achieving energy security, as well as other considerations. Since the beginning, policies in key countries (United States, European Union, Brazil) have supported both the use and the production of biofuels. The evolution of biofuels markets is therefore highly sensitive to potential changes in policy, and is driven less by economic and demographic factors, which makes projections more difficult. The baseline projections are based on the best available information regarding future policies in the key regions, but projections are clearly sensitive to changes in the policy environment.

With these caveats in mind, a slowdown in growth is expected over the course of the outlook period. Annual growth in ethanol production is expected to be around 1% per year. In absolute terms, while ethanol production grew by 70 bln L between 2004-06 and 2014-16, growth is expected to be only 19 bln L in the next ten years. Similarly, biodiesel production grew 30 bln L between 2004-06 and 2014-16 but will grow by only 7 bln L over the course of the outlook period.

The slowdown of ethanol growth is driven in large part by a stagnating mandated ethanol use in the United States, whereas the demand for transportation fuels in Brazil is expected to be sustained. As a result, while demand for sugarcane (the major source of bio-ethanol in Brazil) remains relatively robust, the slowdown will be more pronounced in the growth of maize consumption, the main bio-ethanol feedstock in the United States. The stagnating ethanol demand in the United States is expected to be compensated partially by developing countries, specifically Thailand and India, where molasses is the main feedstock for ethanol production. Consumption in those two countries will continue to expand relatively fast, due to policies favouring the use of ethanol. In Thailand, demand for roots and tubers (cassava) will also continue to grow, benefitting from domestic policies in support of the ethanol industry.

Figure 1.15 shows the growth in demand for maize and vegetable oil in the last decade and over the projection period, by use. Reflecting the overall trend towards slowdown, biofuel use practically disappears as a source of demand growth over the outlook period for both commodities. For maize, the slowdown in the growth of biofuel use, together with a lower demand for feed, will account for most of the slowdown in the overall demand growth for maize. Compared to an additional consumption of 306 Mt in the last decade, use of maize is expected to grow by only 146 Mt over the next ten years, mostly driven by lower demand for biofuel use. For vegetable oil, the last decade saw an additional consumption of 64 Mt, but consumption in the next decade will only increase by 40 Mt. Most of this slowdown is explained by biofuels.

Although on a global scale biofuel use shrinks in its importance as a driver of demand growth, this net effect masks shifts among countries that reduce demand for feedstock for biofuels and others that increase their use over the outlook period. By 2026, the total use of vegetable oil for biofuels is expected to be around 26 Mt, with developed and developing countries (mostly Latin American and Asian countries) each accounting for half of the demand.

Figure 1.15. **Growth in demand for maize (left) and vegetable oil (right), by use**

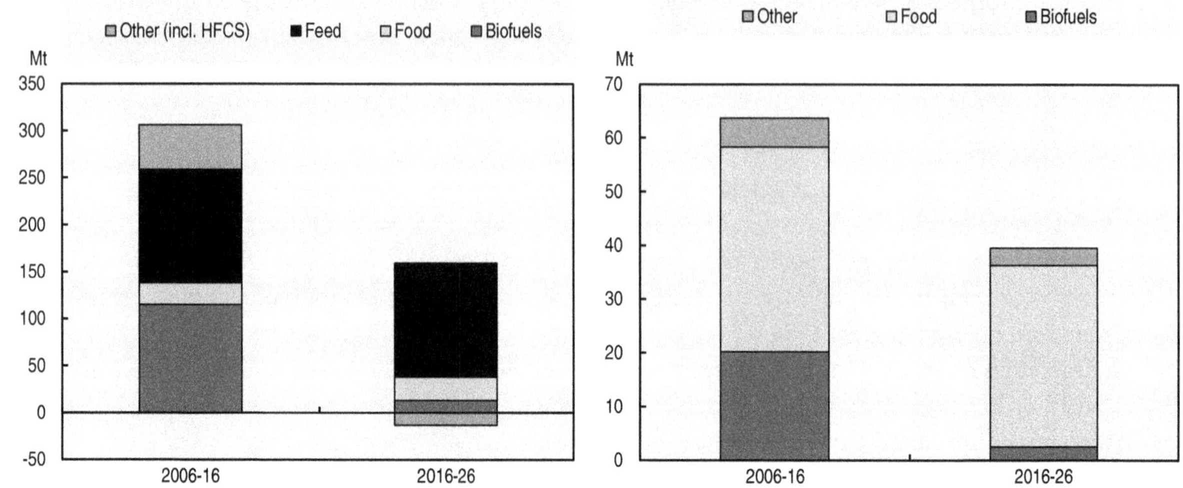

Note: Demand growth compares 2004-06 average to 2014-16 average, and 2014-16 average to 2026. Southeast Asia includes Indonesia, the Philippines, Malaysia, Thailand, Viet Nam, Lao PDR, Myanmar and Cambodia.

Source: OECD/FAO (2017), "OECD-FAO Agricultural Outlook", OECD Agriculture statistics (database), *http://dx.doi.org/10.1787/agr-data-en.*

StatLink *http://dx.doi.org/10.1787/888933521180*

In the last decade, biofuels accounted for 174 Mt of additional consumption of sugarcane. This is expected to slow down to an additional demand of 89 Mt over the next decade. Demand growth for other uses (most notably sugar production) was 355 Mt in the last decade and is expected to be 265 Mt in the coming decade. As a result, total demand for sugarcane will increase by 354 Mt in the next decade compared to a growth of 529 Mt in the last decade.

Production

Yield growth will continue to drive global crop production

Over the outlook period, global cereal production is set to grow by around 1% p.a., leading to a total increase by 2026 of 11% for wheat, 14% for maize, 10% for other coarse grains, and 13% for rice. The bulk of the additional production over the outlook period is projected to be generated through crop yield improvements.

Figure 1.16 decomposes the total increase in maize production by region into the increase due to area expansion (keeping yields constant at their regional average in the baseline period) and to higher average yields. In the case of maize, area expansion accounts for only 10% of the total increase in production, driven mainly by growth in the area under cultivation in Latin America, which increases by 6.6% from 33.5 Mha in the base period to 35.7 Mha in 2026. By contrast, the area under cultivation in North America is projected to decrease, while changes are relatively minor in the other regions.

Latin America will contribute 28% of the total increase in maize production, or 39 Mt. Of this, around one-quarter is due to the increase in area. Asia and Pacific will account for 24% or 33 Mt. In contrast with Latin America, the growth in Asia and Pacific will be driven almost exclusively by yield gains. Despite a projected decrease in the area under cultivation, North America will contribute 31 Mt or 22% of the total increase. Together, these three regions will account for 74% of the total increase, with the remainder split between the European Union, Sub-Saharan Africa and other regions. In Sub-Saharan

Figure 1.16. **Increase in maize production due to area expansion and yield growth, 2016-26**

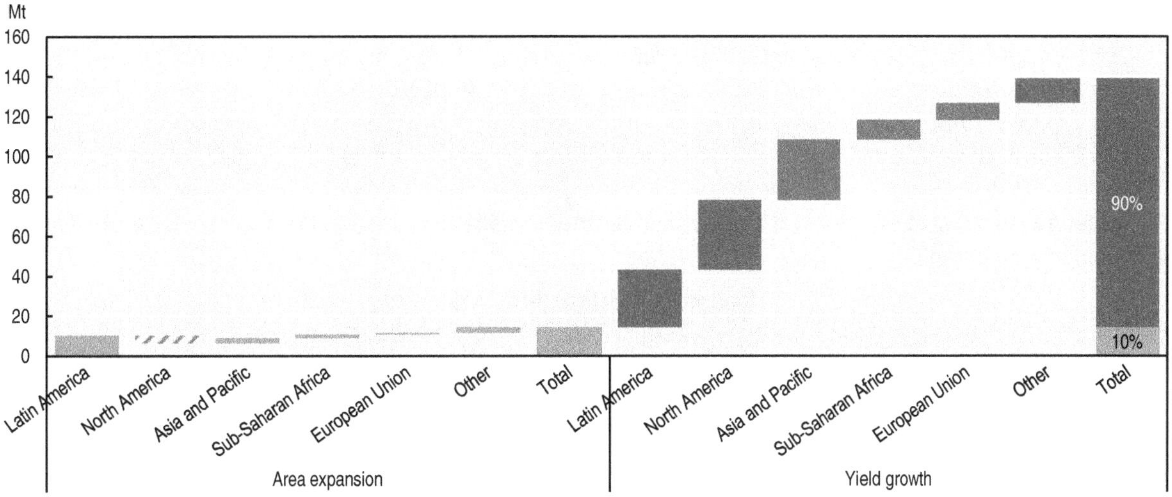

Note: Shaded areas indicate negative values. Growth compares 2026 to the baseline (2014-16) average.
Source: OECD/FAO (2017), "OECD-FAO Agricultural Outlook", OECD Agriculture statistics (database), *http://dx.doi.org/10.1787/agr-data-en*.
StatLink *http://dx.doi.org/10.1787/888933521199*

Africa, maize production is set to increase by 11 Mt. This increase is driven largely by higher yields in South Africa, Nigeria and Ethiopia, where production increases by 3.6, 1.8 and 1.8 Mt respectively over the projection period.

Global production of wheat is projected to increase by 11% over the outlook period, while the wheat area increases by only 1.8%. The increase in wheat production is therefore expected to occur through higher yields, most notably in Asia and Pacific, which will account for 46% of additional wheat production. Within the region and globally, India (15 Mt) will account for the biggest increase in production, and Pakistan (6 Mt) and China (5.5 Mt) are also expected to have significant gains. The European Union accounts for 13% of the production increase; large increases in production are also expected in the Russian Federation (9% of additional production) and Ukraine (6%).

Rice production is expected to grow by 66 Mt and will be almost exclusively driven by yield growth, which accounts for 93% of additional production. The global area dedicated to rice is expected to increase by only 1% from the base period, while global yields will increase by 12%. Major production gains are projected for India, Indonesia, Myanmar, Thailand, and Viet Nam. Yields in these countries are expected to increase by over 15%.

As yield growth will account for most of the production increase for cereals, the growth in total cereal production will have a relatively limited impact on land use. In contrast to cereals, area expansion will play an important role in the growth of oilseeds production, accounting for almost 50% of the global increase in soybean production in the coming decade. Area expansion will also remain important for growth of palm oil production. However, constraints and concerns over sustainability are expected to significantly limit growth of the cultivation area for palm oil as compared to the last decade. A global perspective on agricultural land use is provided in Box 1.1.

Yield growth is expected to satisfy most of the increasing demand for cereals over the outlook period. However, yields may show year-on-year variations depending on weather and climate conditions, such as he *El Niño* phenomenon. Figure 1.19 shows the yields of maize in the United States (the main producer) and for the world as a whole from 2000 to

Box 1.1. **Agricultural land use**

Between 1960 and 1993, global agricultural land use increased from 4.5 Bln ha to 4.9 Bln ha (FAOSTAT). Over the past ten years, however, global agricultural land use decreased by 62 Mha, a trend which is expected to continue. As shown in the first panel of Figure 1.17, more than half of agricultural land (which includes arable land and pastures) is located in ten countries, with the largest areas in China, the United States and Australia. This *Outlook* projects global agricultural land use to continue its decrease, albeit at a lower rate of 24 Mha over the coming decade. The share of the top-10 countries is also expected to decrease moderately.

Figure 1.17. **Trends of global land use of agriculture**

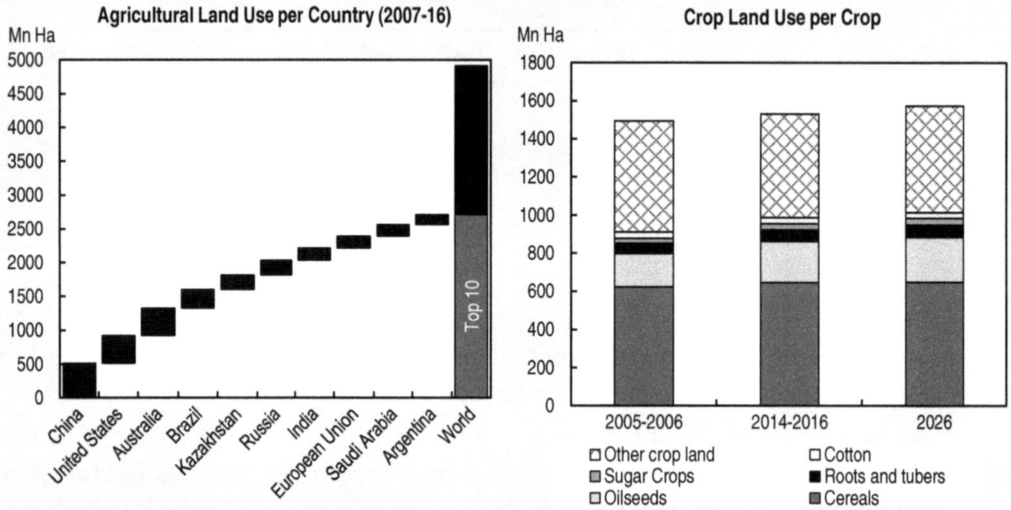

Source: OECD/FAO (2017), "OECD-FAO Agricultural Outlook", OECD Agriculture statistics (database), *http://dx.doi.org/10.1787/agr-data-en.*

StatLink *http://dx.doi.org/10.1787/888933521218*

Seventy per cent of global agricultural land is used in the form of pasture. Over the past decade, global pasture area declined at an average rate of 3 Mha per year; for the next ten years the annual reduction is estimated to be 1.7 Mha. At the same time, crop land is on an increasing trend due to the conversion between pasture and crop land. This *Outlook* assumes a continuation of the trend, with crop land projected to expand by 42 Mha, a similar increase as over the past decade. Sixty per cent of world crop land is located in ten countries, which are largely the same as the ones dominating total agricultural area, with Nigeria, Canada and Indonesia replacing Saudi Arabia, India and Kazakhstan.

As shown in the second panel of Figure 1.17, cereals are grown on about 42% of global crop land, while around 14% of cropland is devoted to oil crops. Both shares have been increasing over the past decade, but only the share of oil crops is projected to increase further over the projection period, especially due to favourable soybean production opportunities in South America. About 4% of global crop land is covered with roots and tubers, while sugar crops and cotton account for 2% each. The remainder (about 36%) is allocated to pulses, fruits and vegetables, other permanent crops, as well as set aside and fallow.

While the global picture appears quite stable, national developments are more dynamic. Agricultural land use, especially crop land use, is increasing in some countries that have potential for land expansion while decreasing in other countries due to factors that include urbanization, afforestation or desertification.

Figure 1.18 shows the average annual crop land change of selected countries where crop land use increased or decreased the most in absolute terms over the past decade, as well as the estimated annual change over the projection period. Argentina and Brazil experienced the strongest expansion in crop areas over the past ten years, adding respectively 10 Mha and 8 Mha to global crop land. For the next ten years,

Box 1.1. **Agricultural land use** *(cont.)*

crop land expansion is expected to be in a similar range for these two countries. For the other three countries in which crop land expanded over the past decade, a slowdown is expected, partly because of lower price expectations as compared to the past decade. A major reduction of crop land has occurred and is projected for the United States and for the European Union as a consequence of urbanization and afforestation as well as re-conversion of crop land into permanent grassland. In the United States, the Conservation Reserve Program (CRP) has also contributed to the reduction of crop land over the past years. Due to modifications of this programme in the 2014 Farm Bill, the projected annual crop land reduction over the next ten years is lower than during the previous decade.

Figure 1.18. **Average annual crop land change for selected countries**

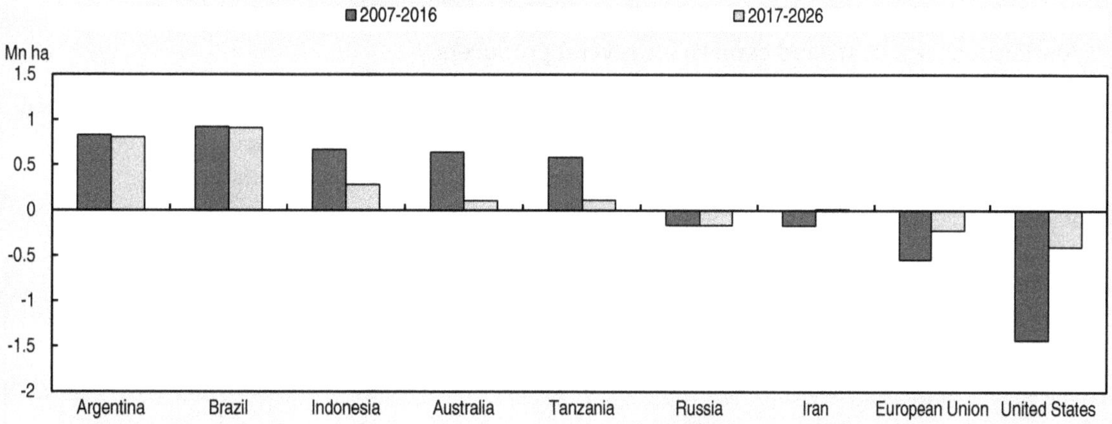

Source: OECD/FAO (2017), "OECD-FAO Agricultural Outlook", OECD Agriculture statistics (database), *http://dx.doi.org/10.1787/agr-data-en.*

StatLink *http://dx.doi.org/10.1787/888933521237*

Figure 1.19. **Maize yields in the United States and globally**

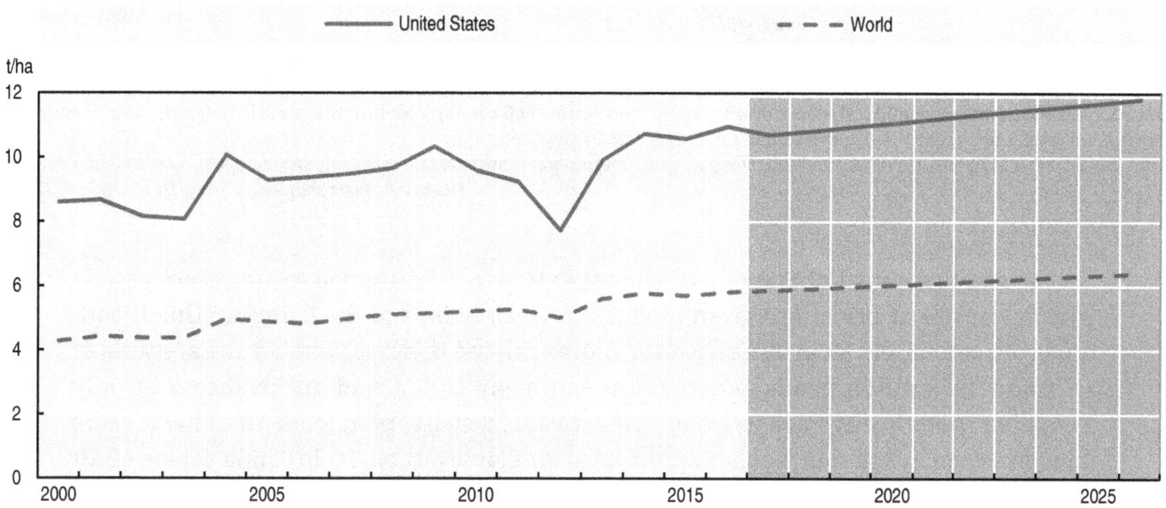

Source: OECD/FAO (2017), "OECD-FAO Agricultural Outlook", OECD Agriculture statistics (database), *http://dx.doi.org/10.1787/agr-data-en.*

StatLink *http://dx.doi.org/10.1787/888933521256*

the end of the outlook period. While the *Outlook* assumes a steady increase in yield, year-on-year variations can be considerable. In 2012, maize yields in the United States fell by 16% compared to 2011, reducing the US share in world production from 35% to 31%. Average global yields are less volatile, as yields in main producing regions are typically not strongly correlated. However, the 2012 drop in US yields still contributed to a 5% drop in global yields. By 2013, US yields had fully returned to their long-run trend, but temporary changes in yields in large producers may have a considerable impact at a global level.

Dairy: Large structural differences persist between major producing countries

For many commodities, including cereals, dairy and meat, "intensive" (high-input, high-yield) and "extensive" (low-input, low-yield) producers will continue to co-exist. Figure 1.20 illustrates this co-existence for milk production, comparing the yield (in tonnes per head) and the size of the milking animal inventory (in million heads, including cows, buffalos, sheep, goats and camels) for several producers.

Figure 1.20. **Milk production in selected countries**

(a) Yield and herd size in 2016 (left), (b) Evolution over time for major producers (right)

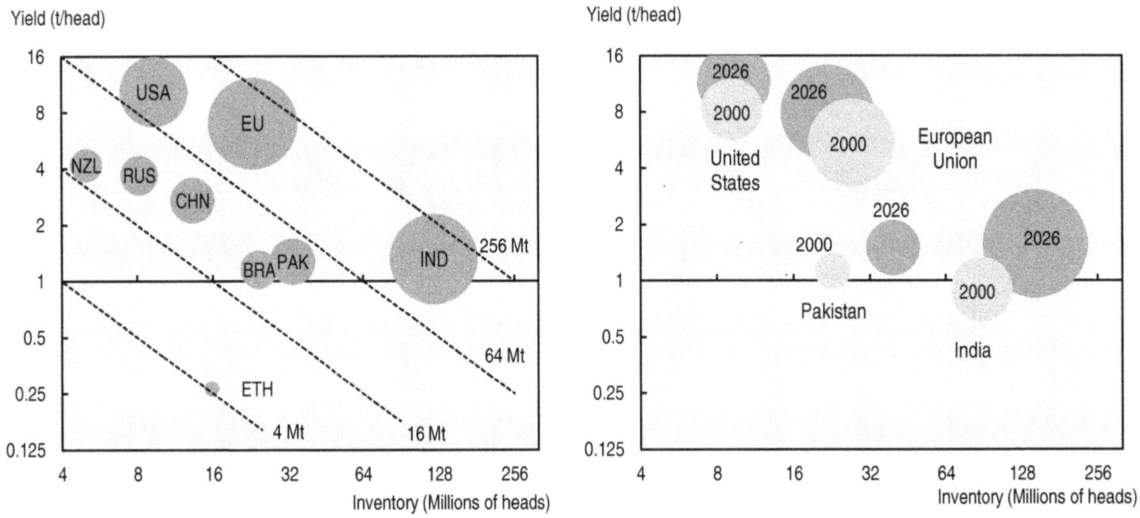

Note: Yield is milk production in tonnes per head including non-cow milk. Inventory includes non-cow herds. Both axes are shown on a logarithmic scale to allow the comparison of producers who vary considerably in scale. The size of the bubbles indicates total milk production (including non-cow milk). The downward-sloping lines connect all combinations of yields and inventories which result in the same level of production (in Mt). 'European Union' refers to EU-28 in all years.

Source: OECD/FAO (2017), "OECD-FAO Agricultural Outlook", *OECD Agriculture statistics* (database), *http://dx.doi.org/10.1787/agr-data-en.*

StatLink *http://dx.doi.org/10.1787/888933521275*

As the first panel of Figure 1.20 shows, extensive and intensive producers can be equally capable of reaching a given production level. India and the European Union both produced around 160 Mt in 2016; however, India achieved this level with an average yield of 1.3 t and 122 million heads, whereas the European Union had an inventory of only 23 million heads but average yields of 7 t per head. Likewise, production in China is more intensive than in Pakistan, yet both produce at similar levels (41 Mt in China versus 42 Mt in Pakistan in 2016). Ethiopia's dairy inventory (16 million heads) is considerably larger than the US inventory (9 million heads), yet production in Ethiopia stood at 4 Mt in 2016, only a fraction of the US production of 96 Mt. In Ethiopia, non-cow milk production plays a large role as 25% of dairy herds consist of camels, goats and sheep, which account for roughly 10% of milk production. However, even the cow inventory by itself (at around 11 million heads) exceeds that of the United States. In 2014, cow milk production in Ethiopia stood at 3.3 Mt, or 0.29 t per cow, far below US yields of around 10 t per cow.

In contrast to cereals, where up to 90% of production growth is accounted for by yield increases, a greater share of growth in milk production will be driven by increases in dairy herds. Globally, milking animal inventories will grow by 11% over the outlook period, or an increase of 79 million heads compared with the base period (2014-16). At 2016 yield levels, this would generate 48 Mt of additional production, out of a projected total increase of 178 Mt. Hence, around 27% of the projected increase is accounted for by increasing herd size.

Different regions have different dynamics over time, as shown in the second panel of Figure 1.20, which compares four large producers (the European Union, India, Pakistan, and the United States) in 2000 and in 2026, at the end of the outlook period. In all regions, yields increase over time. However, many developing countries start from a low base, so the absolute increases in productivity will remain small. In the United States, dairy herds remain roughly stable, while there is a decline in the European Union. In contrast, India and Pakistan witness both a strong increase in milking animal inventories as well as in yields, leading to strong growth in overall production. Over the first quarter of the 21st century, milk production in India will have nearly tripled. Over the course of the outlook period alone, milk production in India will grow 49%; in 2026, India will be the world's largest milk producer, with an output one-third above that of the second largest producer, the European Union. At the same time, this remarkable growth is achieved with yields below 2 tonnes per head, far below EU or US levels. Milk production in the European Union is projected to grow at 0.8% p.a. in the coming decade, which is slower than the 1.2% p.a. in the last decade, despite the end of the milk quota in 2015.

Over the course of the outlook period, the production of processed dairy products is expected to grow between 1.4% p.a. for cheese and 2.3% p.a. for skim milk powder (SMP). While the bulk of production of SMP and cheese will occur in developed countries, India will remain the top producer of butter. Given its large and expanding domestic market, however, India will not become an important player on the export market.

Continued growth in meat and fish production

Global meat production will expand by almost 40 Mt over the outlook period (Figure 1.21). Growth will continue to be driven mainly by poultry production, which increases from 117 Mt to 132 Mt (a 13% increase), and pigmeat, which grows from 116 Mt to 128 Mt (+ 10%). Beef, veal and sheep meat production are also projected to increase. Sheep meat, in particular, will register a strong growth (+21%), although it will start at a low base of 14.7 Mt in 2017 and reach 17.5 Mt in 2026.

Across the four main types of meat included in the *Outlook*, production will continue to be dominated by the "big four" meat-producing countries China, the European Union, the United States and Brazil. This dominance is especially strong for pigmeat, where these four countries account for 78% of global production in 2026. China in particular will continue to account for 47% of global pigmeat production over the course of the outlook period.

Figure 1.21. **Meat production, by type and country**

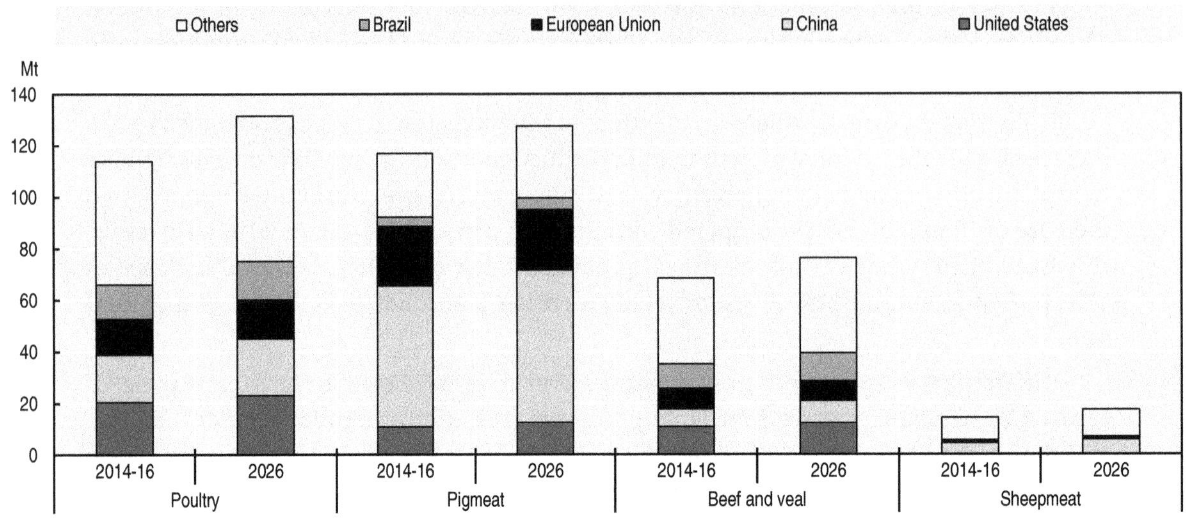

Source: OECD/FAO (2017), "OECD-FAO Agricultural Outlook", OECD Agriculture statistics (database), *http://dx.doi.org/10.1787/agr-data-en.*

StatLink *http://dx.doi.org/10.1787/888933521294*

Fish production will continue to increase to almost 200 Mt by 2026. As shown in Figure 1.22, this growth is driven exclusively by the expansion of aquaculture production. Production through capture has been flat for the last decades, with the main exceptions being the years in which *El Niño* led to a decline in fish capture in some Latin American countries. This trend is expected to continue over the outlook period. Supported by low feed prices, aquaculture production will continue to grow and most of this increase will take place in China, which accounts for 17 Mt out of the 26 Mt total increase by 2026.

Figure 1.22. **Fish production**

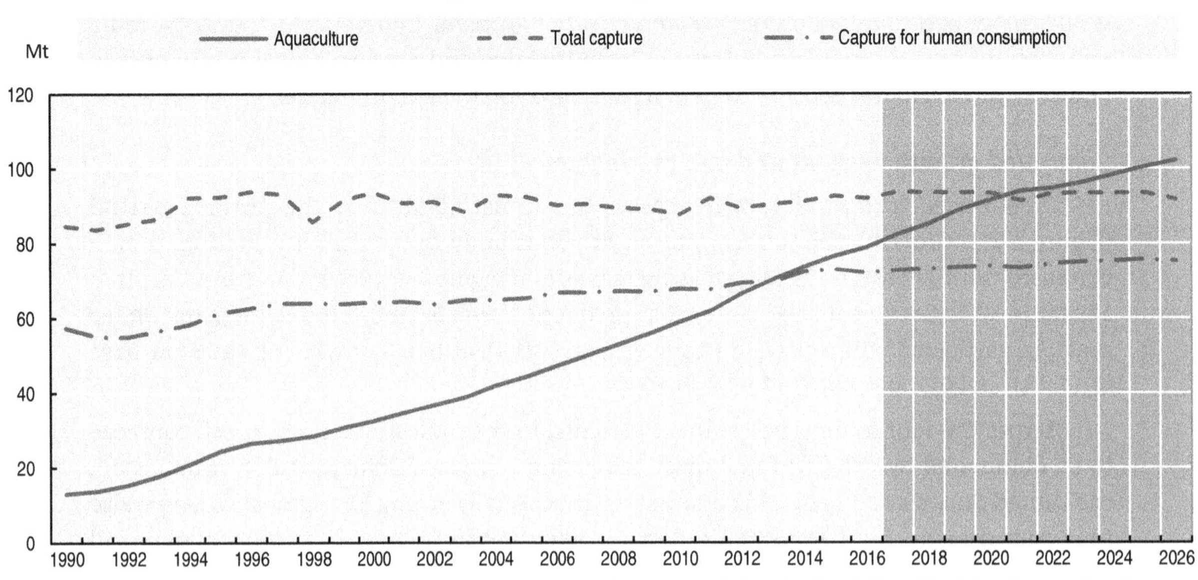

Source: OECD/FAO (2017), "OECD-FAO Agricultural Outlook", OECD Agriculture statistics (database), *http://dx.doi.org/10.1787/agr-data-en.*

StatLink *http://dx.doi.org/10.1787/888933521313*

Trade

Agricultural trade growth is slowing, more closely mirroring output growth

Agricultural trade will continue to increase, but at a slower rate than in the past. Along with global supply and demand, trade is expected to expand less over the next ten years than in the previous decade (Figure 1.23). The slower growth is most apparent for cereals and oilseeds, which together account for about 45% of the value of agricultural trade, and for pigmeat and milk powders. Trade growth in biofuels is expected to be negative in the coming decade. Modest increases in trade volume growth are expected for white sugar, sheep meat, butter, and cotton.

Figure 1.23. **Growth in trade volumes by commodity**

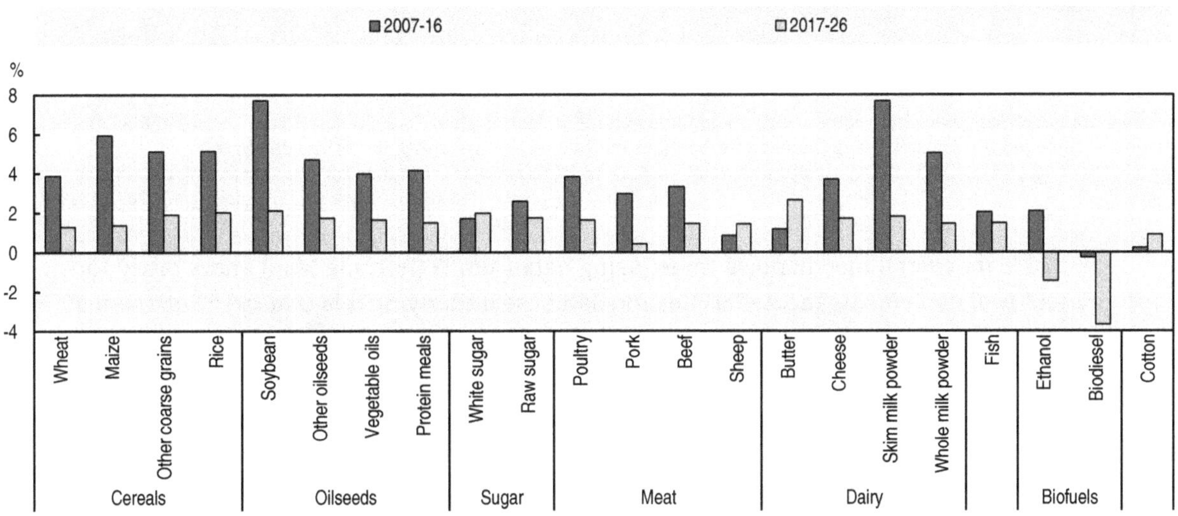

Source: OECD/FAO (2017), "OECD-FAO Agricultural Outlook", OECD Agriculture statistics (database), *http://dx.doi.org/10.1787/agr-data-en.*

StatLink *http://dx.doi.org/10.1787/888933521332*

The slowdown in agricultural trade is not an isolated phenomenon. The growth of global merchandise trade (which includes agricultural and non-agricultural goods) has been slowing down due to lower GDP growth. However, trade has also stopped growing as a share of global GDP.[1] This trend towards a lower share of trade to GDP appears to have started already before the Great Recession of 2008-09, leading some observers to question whether the trade slowdown represents "a new normal" (Hoekman, 2015).

Potential reasons cited for the slowdown in merchandise trade include: reduced demand growth; slower growth in global supply chain formation; a slowing of trade reforms; and a maturing trade sector in China (Lewis and Monarch, 2016). These factors, especially the latter two, also apply to agriculture. The effects and pace of policy reforms following the Uruguay Round have diminished, and some countries are strengthening policies to increase self-sufficiency. China's entry into the WTO in late 2001 was accompanied by a large upswing in its agricultural imports reflecting the impact of a new set of policies. However, import growth, particularly of soybeans, has slowed as demand for soymeal and oil has moderated.

Given the slowdown in agricultural trade projected in this *Outlook*, it is useful to compare the evolution of agricultural trade with the global slowdown observed in total merchandise trade. Figure 1.24 charts the evolution of trade in volume terms between 2001

Figure 1.24. **Evolution of trade volume for merchandise trade and agricultural trade**

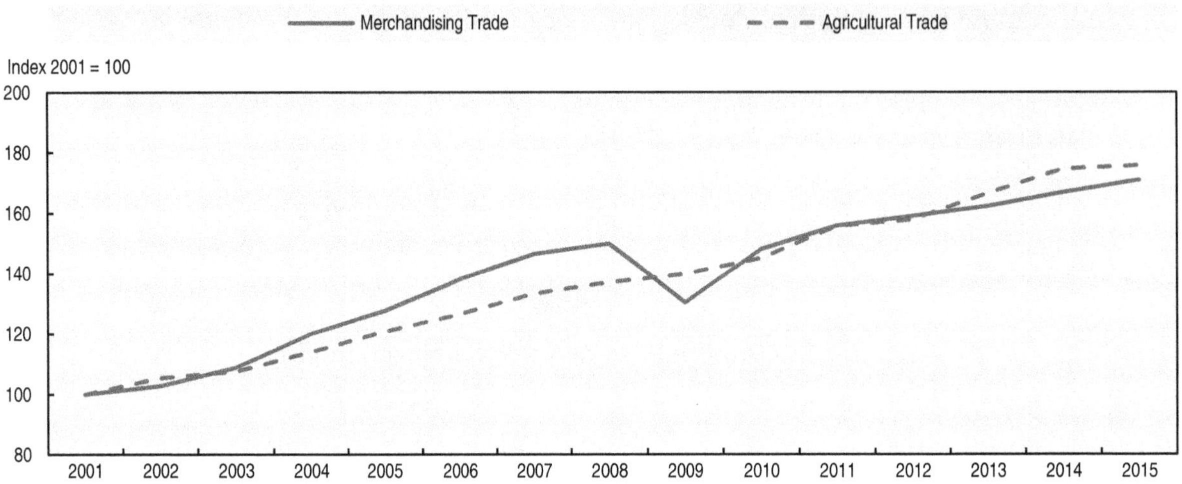

Note: Merchandise trade index calculated based on chained volume index for global merchandise trade (World Trade Organization); agricultural trade index calculated using chained volume index method on exports in Aglink-Cosimo database.
Source: OECD/FAO (2017), "OECD-FAO Agricultural Outlook", OECD Agriculture statistics (database), *http://dx.doi.org/10.1787/agr-data-en.*
StatLink *http://dx.doi.org/10.1787/888933521351*

and 2015 for overall merchandise trade (using data from ITC's Trade Map) and a proxy for agricultural trade (using the Aglink-Cosimo database underlying this *Outlook*).[2] Both series are expressed in volume terms to neutralize the effect of price changes, such as the 2007 food price increases.

During the period 2001-15, both agricultural trade and merchandise trade grew at around 4% p.a. However, the figure clearly illustrates that growth rates slowed down in both agricultural and merchandise trade towards the end of this period. Merchandise trade grew at 6.6% in 2001-07, but this rate fell to 2.3% over the 2011-15 period. Similarly, agricultural trade growth averaged 4.9% in the 2001-07 period, but fell to 3.1% in 2011-15.

While merchandise trade witnessed a strong contraction and rebound in the wake of the Great Recession, agricultural trade volume growth was considerably more robust. A possible explanation is that the trade in agri-food products is determined by deeper 'fundamentals' such as population growth and lower demand elasticities compared to most other commodities, and is thus less sensitive to income shocks.

Moreover, the growth rate of global agricultural production is generally below the real growth rate of global GDP. As a result, the lower growth rate of agricultural trade volumes remains consistent with a constant share of production traded, as discussed below. In contrast, the lower growth rate of overall merchandise trade implies a decline in trade as a share of GDP.

While the growth rate of agricultural trade is slowing down over time, removing existing trade-related and distortionary domestic production policies could stimulate trade. This is documented in Box 1.2.

Despite the slowdown in trade, the share of production that is traded will not change significantly for the commodities covered in the *Outlook*. Figure 1.26 compares the share of production that was exported during the baseline (2014-16) with the projections for 2026. Milk powders remain the most traded agricultural commodities and fresh dairy products (not depicted in the figure) will continue to be among the least traded. The trade share for vegetable oils and soybeans is also expected to remain high, with over 40% of production sold on international markets. The share of total exports of fish and fishery products (including fishmeal) will remain at about 30% of production. Despite the large volumes involved, trade in cereals is generally relatively small compared to overall production volumes. 23% of wheat production will be traded in 2026, compared to around 13% for maize and only 9% for rice.

Box 1.2. **Impacts of policies on agro-food trade**

Recent work by the OECD (2016) explores the impact of domestic support policies and trade policies (tariffs, quotas and export subsidies) of major agricultural producing regions on global agricultural production and trade, along with the effects of possible scenarios regarding the evolution of these policies in the future. The assessments were made through an application of the OECD's computable general equilibrium model, METRO, in conjunction with Aglink-Cosimo. This assessment of the impacts of policy settings as present around 2011-14 shows that agricultural support and barriers to agricultural trade still create significant distortions to world markets.

Overall, trade in all agro-food commodities would be higher in the absence of current support measures. Policies particularly limit trade in intermediate agricultural products (thus potentially hampering the development of global value chains in the agro-food sector) and industries for which demand and trade is projected to grow strongly into the future such as dairy and meat, suggesting that the costs of the status quo are likely to increase over time.

Domestic support policies may encourage national production but do not promote global production and could in fact be reducing it. For particular regions, the results also suggest that calls for increased isolation or constraints on integration in regional or global markets are likely to be counterproductive. The analysis suggests that policies that promote productivity and flexibility in production systems, enable market engagement by producers (particularly small producers), and provide safety nets for vulnerable households provide better alternatives for promoting food security than trade protection through tariffs and quotas.

Four scenarios were explored regarding the possible evolutions of policies: *Without current policies*, which represents the removal of all tariffs, quotas and export subsidies, and distortionary domestic support to agriculture; *Widespread partial policy reform*, which represents the partial removal of tariffs, quotas and export subsidies, and distortionary domestic support across all countries worldwide; *Uneven partial trade and domestic policy reform*, which sees partial removal of tariffs, quotas and export subsidies, and distortionary domestic support in developed countries with very limited changes in others; and *Policy drift*, which sees some large emerging agricultural producers increase tariffs and producer support while other countries maintain their current policies. The results of these simulations on agro-food trade are shown in Figure 1.25.

Given the negative effects of domestic support policies and associated trade policies, the largest positive impacts on trade are found for the scenario in which all current domestic support and associated trade policies are removed. However, more modest levels of reform would also generate some growth in agro-food trade, albeit to a more limited extent.

Simulations of possible policy drifts, based on current trends, show that there is also value in preventing further drifts towards more protective policies that will complement the benefits that can be achieved from further reform. Reaching a binding agreement which ensures recent positive developments in trade policies and levels of support are not compromised, therefore, is of value. The agreement reached at the November 2015 WTO Ministerial takes some steps in this direction but more are needed.

Box 1.2. **Impacts of policies on agro-food trade** *(cont.)*

Figure 1.25. **Impact on agro-food trade of policies, reforms and drifts**

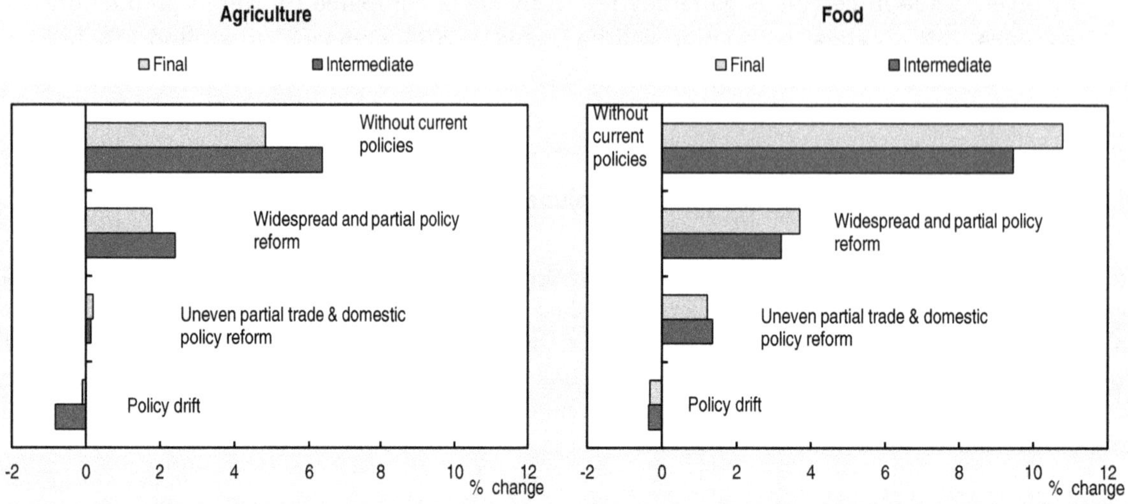

Note: Four scenarios were explored in this study: *Without current policies,* which represents the removal of all tariffs, quotas and export subsidies and domestic support to agriculture; *Widespread partial policy reform,* which represents the partial removal of tariffs, quotas and export subsidies and domestic support across all countries worldwide; *Uneven partial trade and domestic policy reform,* which sees partial removal of tariffs, quotas and export subsidies and domestic support in developed countries with very limited changes in others; and *Policy drift,* which sees some large emerging agricultural producers increase tariffs and domestic support while other countries maintain their current policies.

Source: OECD (2016).

StatLink http://dx.doi.org/10.1787/888933521370

Figure 1.26. **Share of production traded**

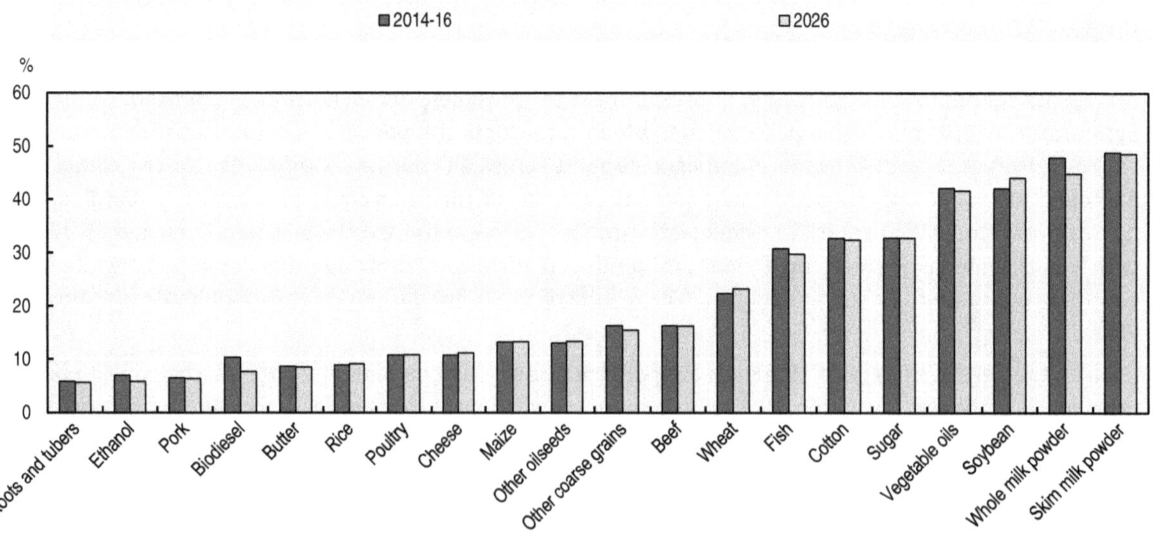

Source: OECD/FAO (2017), "OECD-FAO Agricultural Outlook", OECD Agriculture statistics (database), *http://dx.doi.org/10.1787/agr-data-en.*

StatLink http://dx.doi.org/10.1787/888933521389

While the shares of production traded do not change much for most commodities, there are some commodities where the importance of trade has undergone larger changes over the past decade. Figure 1.27 shows the evolution over time of the share of production traded for soybeans, skim milk powder, rice and biodiesel. Soybeans and skim milk powder have seen strong growth in the share in production traded between 2007 and 2016, with the share for soybeans in particular increasing by 15 percentage points over the last decade. Over the outlook period, the share of trade in production for soybeans will continue to increase albeit at a much lower rate. In contrast, the role of trade has decreased strongly for biodiesel, with the trade share dropping from 34% in 2007 to 10% in 2016, with a further drop to 8% expected by 2026.

Figure 1.27. **Share of production traded for selected commodities**

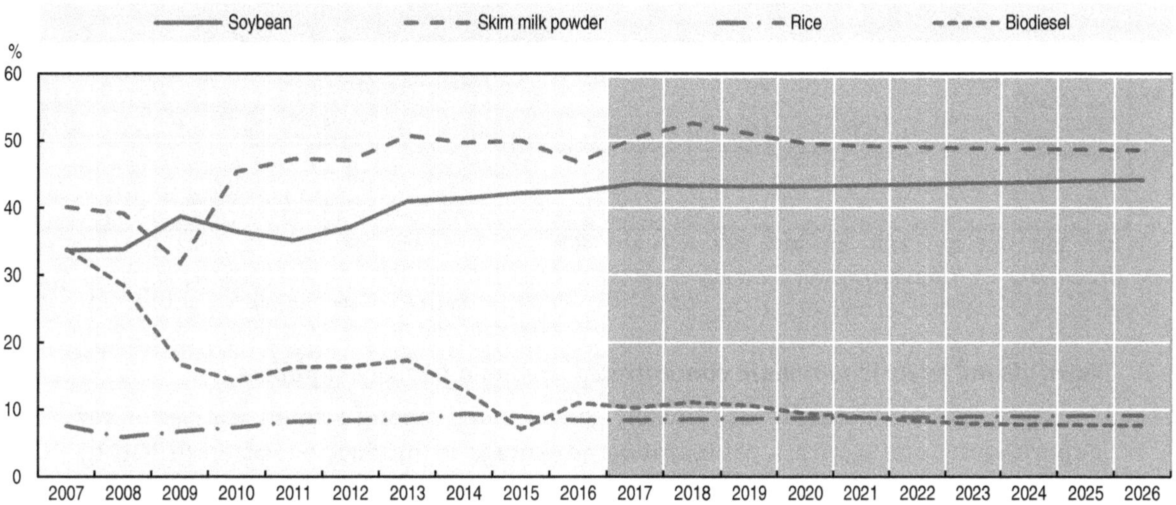

Source: OECD/FAO (2017), "OECD-FAO Agricultural Outlook", OECD Agriculture statistics (database), *http://dx.doi.org/10.1787/agr-data-en.*

StatLink *http://dx.doi.org/10.1787/888933521408*

Import dependence remains high in Middle East and North Africa

The Middle East and North Africa are heavily dependent on agricultural imports, a situation which is expected to continue. Figure 1.28 shows imports as a share of domestic demand for cereals (including feed use) for Algeria, Egypt and Saudi Arabia, as well as for Sub-Saharan Africa as a whole and three countries (Ethiopia, Mozambique and Zambia) in particular. Cereal imports in Algeria, Egypt and Saudi Arabia account for half or more of domestic demand in 2016. Saudi Arabia is almost wholly reliant on imports for its cereal consumption.

In Sub-Saharan Africa, 24% of the domestically consumed cereal was imported in 2014-16. This share is expected to increase over the Outlook period to 27%. However, this average hides important heterogeneity among Sub-Saharan African countries. Mozambique, for instance, has imported between 30% and 40% of its domestic consumption in recent years. This share is expected to increase over the outlook period, approaching that in Egypt. By contrast, import dependence for cereals is much lower in Ethiopia and Zambia. Both countries are important cereal producers in their respective regions, especially for maize, which they typically export to neighbouring countries. Ethiopia is also an important regional supplier of other coarse grains and wheat in East Africa.

However, the stability in terms of import dependence does not hold for all commodities. Over the outlook period, Sub-Saharan Africa will increase its dependency on imports to meet its food fish consumption from 40% to 44%, although this is still below the ratios of 45%-48% experienced between 2006 and 2011.

Figure 1.28. **Imports as share of domestic cereals demand in selected Middle Eastern and African countries**

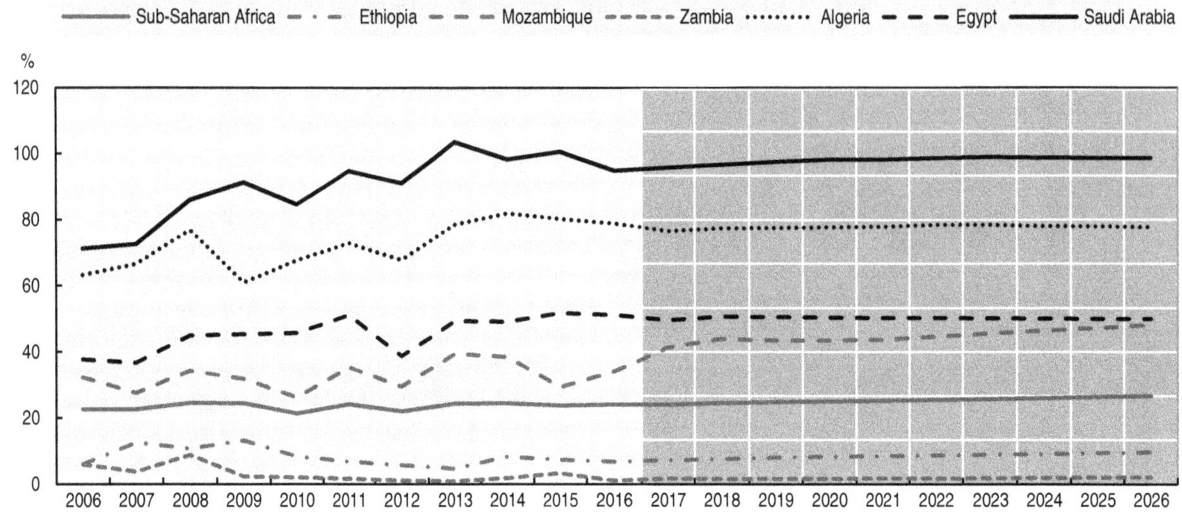

Source: OECD/FAO (2017), "OECD-FAO Agricultural Outlook", OECD Agriculture statistics (database), *http://dx.doi.org/10.1787/agr-data-en.*

StatLink *http://dx.doi.org/10.1787/888933521427*

Agricultural exports to remain concentrated among a few key suppliers

Agricultural exports are traditionally concentrated among a small number of key exporting countries with a comparative advantage in production, often driven by geographical and climatic conditions. Figure 1.29 illustrates for selected commodities the export shares of each of the top five exporters in 2026, as well as the combined export share of the top five exporters during the base period (2014-16). Among the commodities covered in the *Outlook*, the five largest exporting countries typically account for 70% or more of global export volumes. Over the course of the projection period, this concentration will persist, although some commodity-specific changes occur.

Figure 1.29. **Export shares of the top 5 exporters in 2026, by commodity**

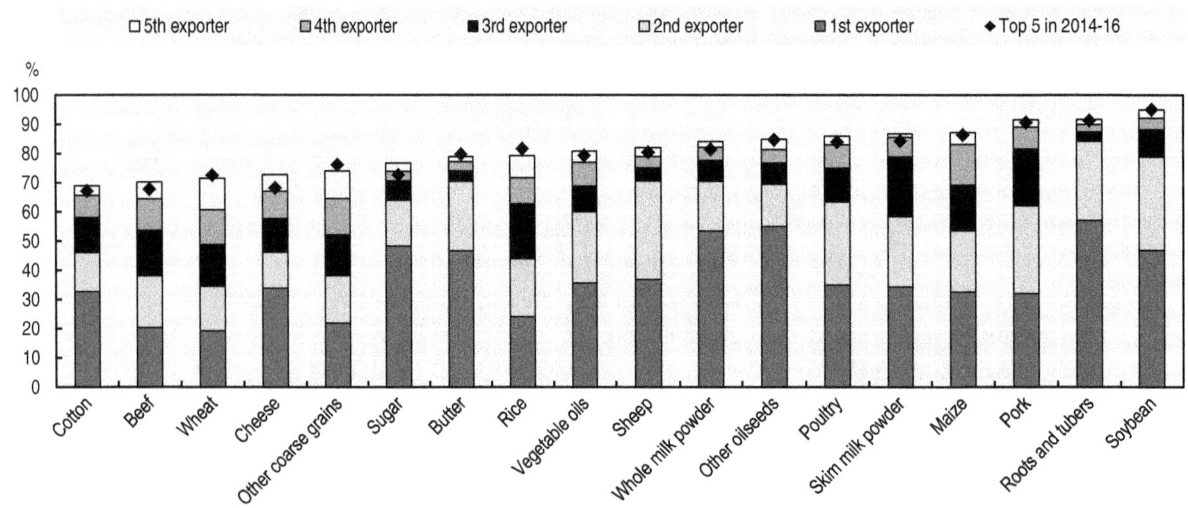

Source: OECD/FAO (2017), "OECD-FAO Agricultural Outlook", OECD Agriculture statistics (database), *http://dx.doi.org/10.1787/agr-data-en.*

StatLink *http://dx.doi.org/10.1787/888933521446*

Exports of soybeans are dominated by Brazil and the United States, which together account for nearly 80% of global exports. The top five exporters account for almost 95% of total exports, the highest five-country concentration ratio of the commodities covered in the *Outlook*. The lowest five-country concentration ratio in 2026 is found for fish, at 50% (up from 46% in 2014-16). China is the main fish exporter with 23% of the total. Over the course of the outlook period, Viet Nam will overtake Norway as the second leading exporter of fish for human consumption. The second-lowest concentration ratio is found for cotton (at slightly below 70%), although the largest exporter, the United States, by itself accounts for one-third of global exports. Although beef and wheat have similar concentration ratios to cotton, the composition of the exports of the top 5 is more diversified. The key exporter in 2026 (Brazil for beef, the European Union for wheat) accounts for 20% of global exports, the lowest values among the commodities covered here.

A small number of key exporters thus dominate most commodities. This creates a risk of potentially significant market impacts if exports are interrupted, either as a result of adverse production shocks (such as exceptionally poor harvests for cereal crops) or policy changes in the major exporting countries.

For a number of commodities, the five-country export concentration ratio will increase over the projection period. The dominance of dairy exports by suppliers in developed countries will continue as exports by the top 5 exporting countries increases for cheese (from 68% to 73%), whole milk powder (from 81% to 84%) and skim milk powder (from 84% to 87%), especially driven by export growth from the European Union. The market for meat, too, will see its concentration grow as suppliers in the Americas benefit from higher productivity and favourable local supplies of feed grain, as well as exchange rate depreciation in Brazil and Argentina. The five-country concentration ratio for poultry increases from 84% to 86% driven by growth from Brazil, the United States and the European Union. For beef, the five-country concentration ratio increases from 68% to 70%, driven by growth in Brazil and Australia. India maintains its position as third-largest beef exporter, accounting for 16% of global exports.

Imports will continue to be more widely dispersed than exports. Trade for a 'typical' agricultural commodity thus flows from a small number of key exporters to a broad group of importing countries (Figure 1.30). For some commodities, however, a relatively high share of import demand comes from just a few countries. This is particularly the case for roots and tubers and soybeans. For both commodities, China accounts for two-thirds of global imports. Global trade in roots and tubers is therefore mostly between Thailand and Viet Nam (who together account for more than 84% of exports) and China. Likewise, global trade in soybeans is mostly between Brazil and the United States (jointly responsible for 78% of exports) and China. In addition, China is also a major importer of several other commodities such as other oilseeds (mainly rapeseed), other coarse grains, cotton, and dairy products.

Risks and uncertainties around international trade

International trade in agricultural commodities is sensitive to several factors such as production conditions (such as variations in crop yields) and policy decisions in exporting countries, and macroeconomic conditions and consumer preferences in importing countries, most notably in China. China's policies and domestic demand potentially have the biggest impact for cereals, oilseeds and dairy products, as even small variations in domestic production and consumption can have a significant impact on the world market.

Figure 1.30. **Import shares of top 5 importers in 2026, by commodity**

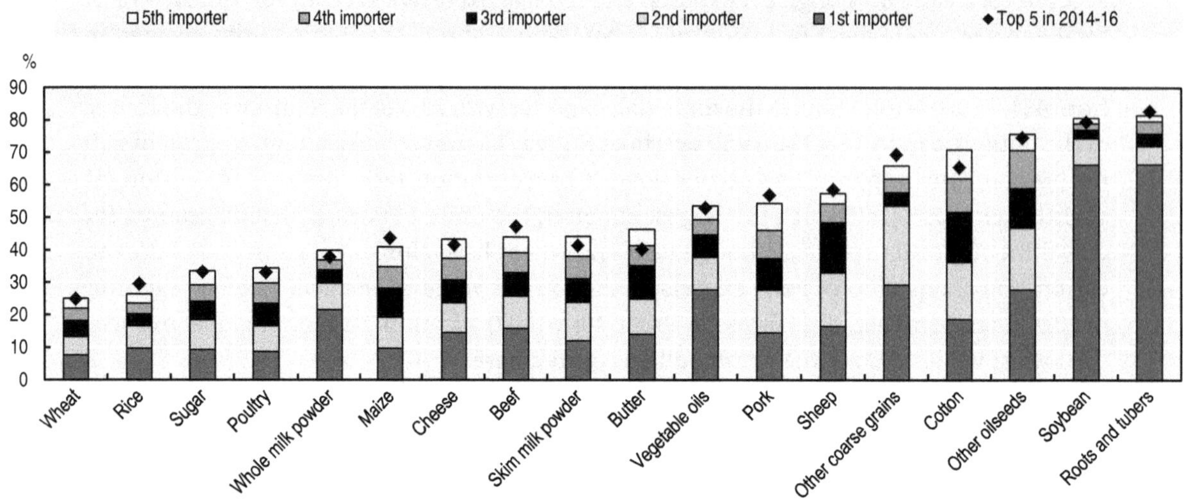

Source: OECD/FAO (2017), "OECD-FAO Agricultural Outlook", OECD Agriculture statistics (database), *http://dx.doi.org/10.1787/agr-data-en.*

StatLink http://dx.doi.org/10.1787/888933521465

Stocks of some commodities, such as maize and cotton in China, and skim milk powder in the European Union, are at relatively high levels. The decision of when and how to release these stocks can impact international prices and trade flows. The phasing-out of export taxes in Argentina will open up new opportunities for the country's soybeans, sunflower seeds and their by-products, as well as maize.

Environmental concerns may impact international trade in agricultural commodities in the coming decade if consumer awareness leads to shifts towards goods perceived as more sustainable, for instance through an increased preference for "local food". Likewise, trade may also be affected by more rigorous regulations related to environment, food safety, environmental traceability and animal welfare regulations. Another important factor that could impact the projections relates to disease risks in livestock production and aquaculture, where protective measures can have a prolonged impact on supply, demand and trade.

Prices

The *Outlook* uses prices at main markets (e.g. US gulf ports, Bangkok) of each commodity as international reference prices. Historical observations are used to describe previous developments while projected values reflect future market trends. Near-term price projections are still influenced by the effects of recent market events (e.g. droughts, policy changes), whereas in the outer years of the projection period, they are driven by fundamental supply and demand conditions only.

Prices of different commodity groups such as cereals, dairy and oilseeds are highly correlated. In the coming decade, prices for these key commodity groups are projected to remain at or somewhat below current levels in real terms (Figure 1.31). Based on the projected supply and demand conditions, prices are expected to remain below the peaks reached during the 2006-16 period but above the levels seen in the early 2000s. Meat prices have historically followed a somewhat different path, avoiding the peak of 2007 but showing strong growth post-2009, leading to a price peak in 2014. Over the coming decade, meat prices are expected to fall in real terms to levels similar to those in the early 2000s.

Figure 1.31. **Medium-term evolution of commodity prices in real terms**

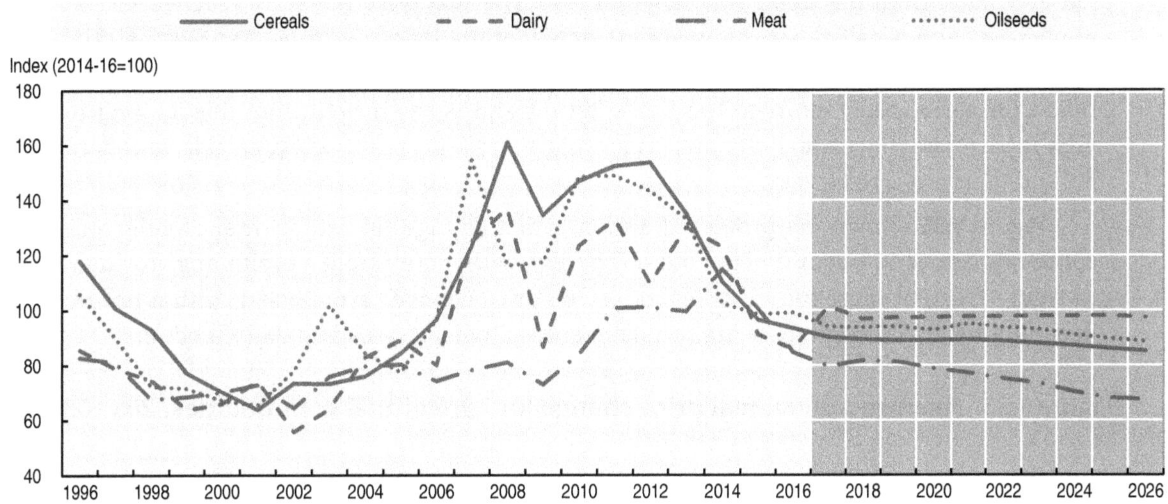

Note: Price indices for commodity groups calculated using a constant weighting of commodities within each aggregate, using the average 2014-16 production value as weights.

Source: OECD/FAO (2017), "OECD-FAO Agricultural Outlook", OECD Agriculture statistics (database), *http://dx.doi.org/10.1787/agr-data-en.*

StatLink *http://dx.doi.org/10.1787/888933521484*

While prices for cereals thus appear to reach levels above those seen in the early 2000s, the question of whether real prices are on an increasing or a decreasing trend depends on the assessment period. Figure 1.32 shows monthly real prices for maize over more than a century (1908-2016). Over the long run, prices have clearly been on a declining trend, with an average price decrease of 1.5% per year in real terms. Similar trends exist for other commodities.

However, Figure 1.32 also illustrates that prices of agricultural commodities are subject to considerable volatility and may show large deviations from their long-term trends for an extended period of time. Between 1972 and 1977, for instance, the real price of maize

Figure 1.32. **Long-term price of maize in real terms**

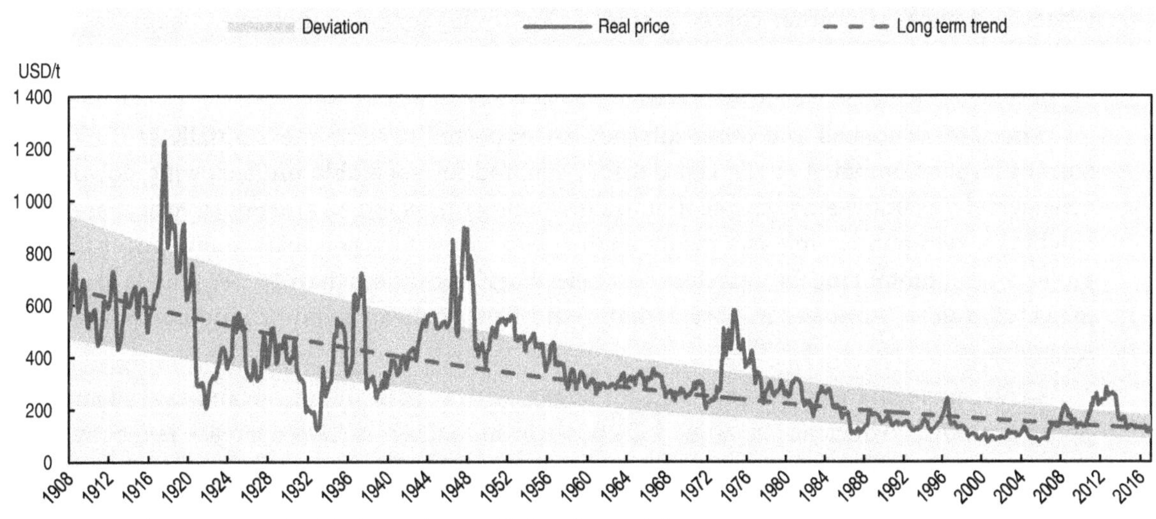

Note: Deviation refers to one standard deviation above and below the trend line.

Source: Monthly "Corn price received" from USDA Quickstats, deflated using monthly CPI data from *www.bls.gov/data.*

StatLink *http://dx.doi.org/10.1787/888933521503*

remained above trend for 56 consecutive months, under the influence of higher oil prices. The deviation from the trend was large: in 1974, the real price of maize reached levels almost two and a half times the value predicted by the long-run trend. Yet despite this deviation, which far exceeds the 2007 price peak in both magnitude and duration, the maize price eventually returned to its long-term trend. A key insight from this long-term view is therefore that commodity prices in any given year may show considerable variation around their projected levels.

Figure 1.33 shows the projected annual price change (in real terms) of selected commodities over the course of the outlook period, with more detailed evolutions provided in Figure 1.34. For most commodities, projected price changes are modest, with a flat to declining trend, although there are some increases among cereals and dairy products.

Figure 1.33. **Average annual real price change for agricultural commodities, 2017-26**

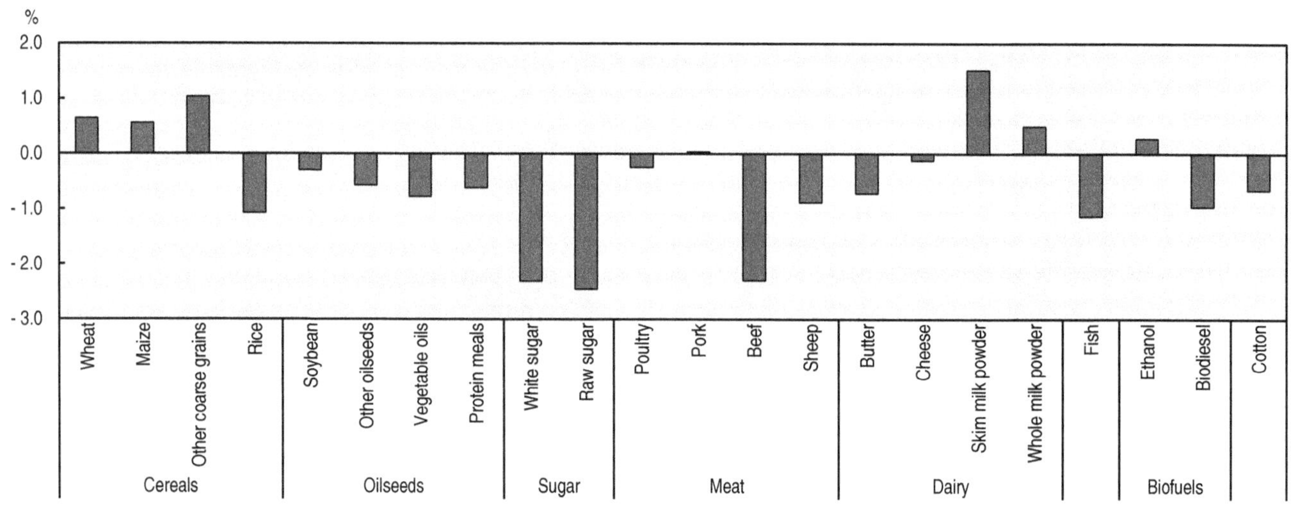

Source: OECD/FAO (2017), "OECD-FAO Agricultural Outlook", OECD Agriculture statistics (database), *http://dx.doi.org/10.1787/agr-data-en.*

StatLink *http://dx.doi.org/10.1787/888933521522*

Among **cereals**, limited real price increases of less than 1% per year are expected for wheat and maize. For other coarse grains, a slightly higher price increase is expected, sustained by growing import demand from China and Saudi Arabia. For rice, a price decrease of 1% per year is expected.

Prices for **soybeans and other oilseeds** are expected to remain essentially at their current levels. Compared to the last decade, demand for **vegetable oil** is slowing down considerably, as many emerging economies (including China, Brazil and South Africa) are reaching a saturation point; as a result, a small decrease (of 1% per year) in real prices is projected. For **protein meals**, a modest decrease in real prices (less than 1% per year) is also expected due to the lower import demand and firm soybean meal production in the Americas.

Larger price changes are expected for **sugar**, with both white sugar and raw sugar prices projected to decrease by around 2% per year in real terms. This decrease is mostly explained by the high starting point. Following a peak in 2010, sugar prices declined until 2014, but increased strongly in the following two years as consumption outstripped production. However, over the outlook period the balance is expected to be restored, leading to a gradual decrease in sugar prices.

Figure 1.34. **Evolution of individual commodity prices in real terms**

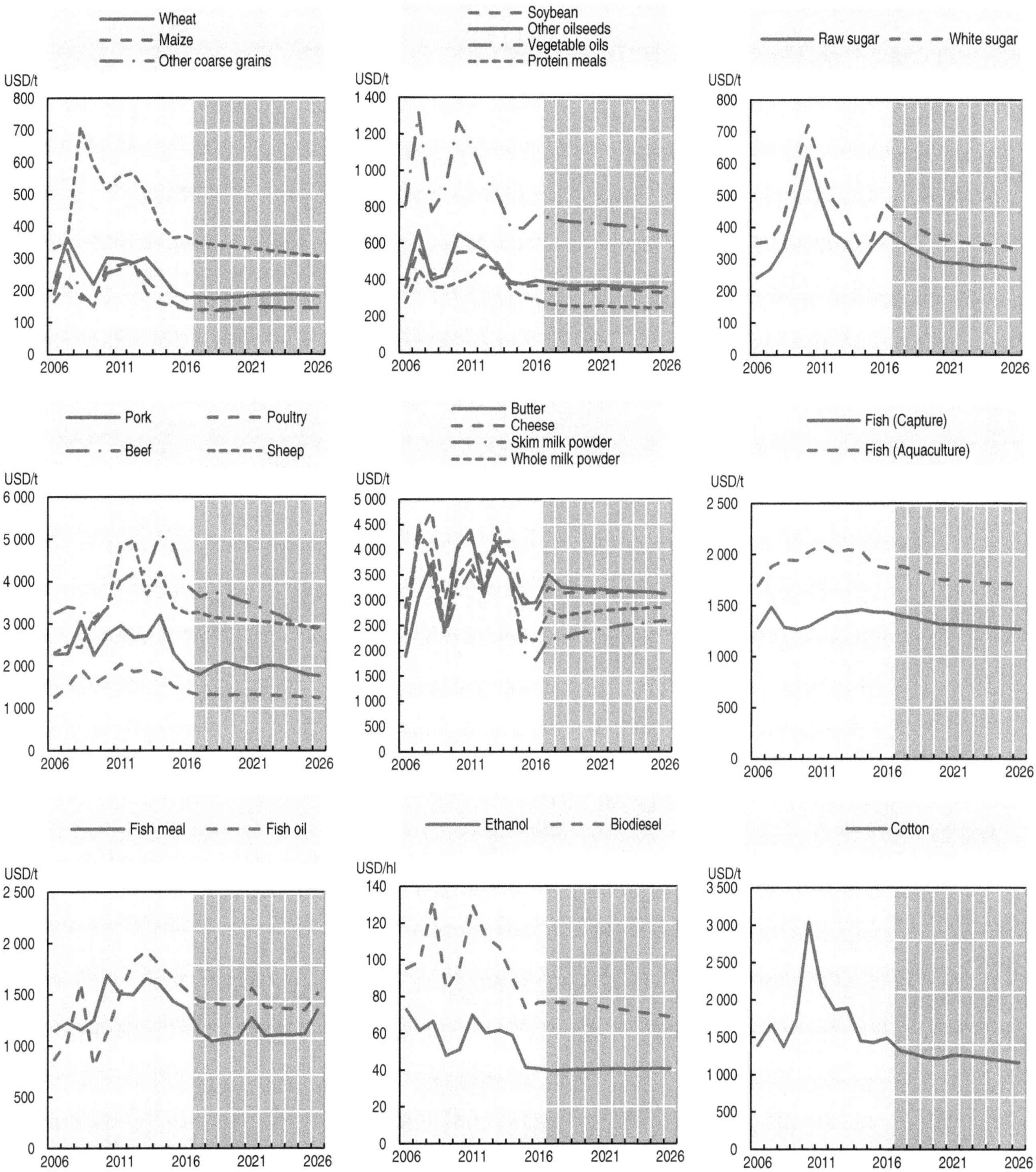

Source: OECD/FAO (2017), "OECD-FAO Agricultural Outlook", OECD Agriculture statistics (database), *http://dx.doi.org/10.1787/agr-data-en*.

StatLink *http://dx.doi.org/10.1787/888933521541*

Meat prices are expected to fall in real terms driven by production expansion through larger herds and heavier slaughter weights in key producing countries. Demand growth is limited given the slowdown in demand from China, and the absence of other developing countries as alternative sources of demand growth.

Prices for **dairy** products show a mixed picture, with a modest price decrease expected for butter, a small increase for skim milk powder and whole milk powder, and essentially flat prices for cheese.

Fish prices are expected to fall by 1% per year in real terms, given relatively high prices at the beginning of the outlook period. The decline projected in the outlook period brings the real price in 2026 below the prices observed in the 1996-2016 period. Aquaculture fish prices have been declining in real terms since 2011, a trend which is expected to continue throughout the outlook period.

For **biofuels**, ethanol prices are expected to remain at current levels in real terms while a modest price decrease is foreseen for biodiesel. The evolution of biofuels markets is heavily dependent on the evolution of crude oil prices and policy decisions, but also on the prices of feedstocks, e.g. vegetable oils for biodiesel and maize and sugar crops for bioethanol. The modest evolutions in prices for these feedstocks contribute to the relatively flat price evolutions for biofuels.

Cotton prices are set to decline by less than 1% per year. After reaching a historical peak in 2010-11, real prices fell by half. Large inventories (representing about 75% of annual consumption) will further depress prices in the early years of the outlook period. In later years, a slowdown in consumption is expected due to competition from man-made fibres.

Overall, prices are thus expected to remain at lower levels compared to the price peaks experienced in the past decade. As the higher prices of 2007-08 spurred investment in agriculture, an important question is therefore whether lower prices will lead to reduced investment. This question is explored in Box 1.3.

Box 1.3. **Will lower food prices reduce foreign agricultural investment in developing countries?**

The surge in commodity prices in 2007-08 has led to a wave of large-scale foreign investments in the agricultural sector of developing countries through several mechanisms. While developing country agriculture has traditionally been viewed as a high-risk low-profit sector, higher prices made the returns on investment more attractive for agribusiness companies. With higher prices, also agricultural land became more attractive financial investors, not least as the traditional asset classes such as equities, bonds and real estate lost their appeal amidst the financial crisis of 2007-08. Investment in farmland was supported by the expectation of further growth in global food demand, offering uncorrelated returns to bond and equity markets and providing a hedge against inflation (HighQuest Partners, United States 2010; FAO 2012).

Faced with soaring global food prices, countries dependent on food imports became increasingly concerned that international markets would no longer be an affordable and reliable source of supplies. Their fears were compounded when some food-exporting countries adopted export restrictions and outright bans to prevent a food price surge on their own market. These concerns spurred net-food-importing countries to invest in agricultural production in countries with "under-utilized" land with a view to exporting food to their home market. Finally, the rise in oil prices, which was a key driver of the food price spike, and policies promoting biofuels in major import markets led to a surge of investment in the production of feedstock crops for biofuels.

Box 1.3. **Will lower food prices reduce foreign agricultural investment in developing countries?** *(cont.)*

Almost a decade after the 2007-08 price spike, the overall market situation is decidedly different. Stocks are replenished, non-food demand has slowed, and agricultural production has risen, partly as a result of the investment surge. High outputs and slower demand growth have pushed prices lower; even in nominal terms, they are much below their peak levels of 2008. The medium-term outlook suggests that prices will remain subdued.

As investors respond to price signals, the question arises whether lower prices will result in lower investment in agriculture. Recent developments in global flows of foreign direct investment (FDI) in agriculture would seem to support this expectation. After reaching a peak of some US$35 billion in 2009, FDI in food, beverage and tobacco decreased to around USD 20 billion per year in 2013-14 (FAO 2016). However, it would be premature to conclude that foreign investment in agriculture will stop. While global agricultural FDI flows are lower than in the aftermath of the global food price crises of 2007-08 and 2011-12, they are still higher than their average levels in the early 2000s. Partly, this reflects the fact that real food prices are still higher than in the early 2000s. Partly, other factors (such as food security policies) are at play, as output prices are not the only driver of agricultural investment. It seems that countries heavily dependent on food imports continue to invest in agricultural production abroad. Short-term or medium-term market conditions have only a limited impact on policies and strategies aimed at long-term national food security.

In addition to the size of investment flows, their quality is of crucial importance both for their impacts on markets and overall development. There is growing evidence that, with adequate initial support, inclusive models that involve local farmers as business partners without transferring land rights generate more profits and developmental benefits than other models (FAO 2014). Efforts by developing country governments to promote inclusive business models that benefit local farmers will increase both the quality and quantity of foreign investment. To support these efforts, FAO has launched a global programme to enhance responsible investments in agriculture and food systems. OECD and FAO are preparing a pilot project to test the practical application of the OECD-FAO Guidance on Responsible Agricultural Supply Chains with a group of companies. These activities and other related initiatives aim to promote agricultural investment and increase its returns. Higher returns are expected to make developing country agriculture more attractive to foreign investors.

In conclusion, while lower food prices have put downward pressure on agricultural FDI flows into developing countries, countervailing factors such as food security concerns and higher returns on investment are likely to play an increasingly important role. Despite the outlook for subdued prices, it would therefore be premature to conclude that agricultural FDI flows will decline over the medium-term.

Sources: FAO (2016); FAO, IFAD and WFP (2015); FAO (2014); FAO (2012); HighQuest Partners, United States (2010).

Risks and uncertainties

The projections in the *Outlook* are based on the Aglink-Cosimo model, supplemented with, and sometimes adjusted by, expert judgment. For most commodities, this year's *Outlook* predicts relatively stable market conditions in the coming decade. However, it is important to keep in mind limitations of the methodology behind the *Outlook*.

First, the *Outlook* is based on a specific set of assumptions on, for example, oil prices, GDP, exchange rates, population growth and the evolution of yields, among others. Several of these assumptions are explained in Box 1.4. These assumptions, while based on the best available estimates, remain intrinsically uncertain. As mentioned previously, given the historical variation in some of these variables a margin of error exists around the predictions made. Moreover, such uncertainty tends to cumulate over time. Hence, over the ten-year horizon of the *Outlook*, temporary deviations from a trend may swamp the actual trend, even if the outlook projections are fundamentally sound.

The sensitivity of the projections in this year's *Outlook* is assessed using a *partial stochastic analysis*, available online at *www.agri-outlook.org*. This analysis takes historical variations in a subset of market drivers, including yields, GDP growth, the oil price and exchange rates, and assumes that the historical variability of those factors continues into the future. The projections of the *Outlook* are recalculated on the basis of multiple "draws" from a distribution of these risk factors. Each simulation leads to an alternative future "path" for prices, production and consumption.

This partial stochastic analysis shows that uncertainties tend to accumulate, so the range of confidence in the baseline projections is lower at the end of the ten year projection period. They also point to a high probability of a major price swing within the next ten years. Moreover, while there may be a broadly equal chance of prices being higher or lower than under the baseline, the potential for prices to spike upwards exceeds the degree to which they can collapse.

By construction, however, several uncertainties are not incorporated in the projections nor in the partial stochastic analysis. These include the risk of outbreaks of transboundary pests and diseases, of increased variability in yields caused by climate change, and uncertainty around policies. Policy uncertainty is especially relevant for aspects of the *Outlook* that are highly sensitive to policy decisions, such as agricultural trade and the future evolution of biofuels.

Box 1.4. **Macroeconomic and policy assumptions**

The main assumptions underlying the baseline projection

The *OECD-FAO Agricultural Outlook* provides a base scenario considered plausible given a range of conditioning assumptions. These assumptions present a specific macro-economic, policy and demographic environment which underpins the projections for the evolution of demand and supply of agricultural and fish products.

The macro-economic assumptions used in the *Outlook* are based on the *OECD Economic Outlook* (November 2016) and the IMF's *World Economic Outlook* (October 2016). A detailed overview of the macroeconomic and policy assumptions can be found in the online Statistical Appendix; an overview of key assumptions is presented below.

Sluggish economic growth

Global GDP growth remained low in 2016 at 2.9%, the slowest growth rate since 2009. After a prolonged slowdown, there are signs that growth has stabilised in the emerging economies, helped by modest recoveries from recessions in Brazil and the Russian Federation. However, hopes that advanced economies would gain momentum have been disappointing. Economic conditions have weakened in these economies, and growth continues to be subdued with only a very modest recovery expected. An equally modest increase of 3.2% in global growth rates is expected in 2017, despite low-interest rates; the growth rate for 2018 is expected to be 3.6%.

In the United States, GDP growth in 2016 was 1.5% compared to 2.6% in 2015, but an assumed fiscal easing is expected to provide additional stimulus to domestic demand over the next two years. GDP growth is projected to lower to 2.3% in 2017 and pick up to 3.0% in 2018, while medium-term growth, projected at 1.8% per annum (p.a.), is dampened by an aging population and the recent trend of low total factor productivity growth.

Growth will remain modest in the Euro area as domestic demand is weighed down by weak investment, high unemployment and political uncertainties. For EU15 members as a group, an annual average growth rate of 1.6% is expected during the projection period.

Box 1.4. **Macroeconomic and policy assumptions** *(cont.)*

GDP growth in Japan is expected to remain modest, below 1% per annum over 2017-18. The country's medium-term prospects remain weak, with an annual growth rate per annum of 0.3% during the projection period, due primarily to a shrinking population.

Among OECD countries, Turkey is expected to experience the highest growth rate over the next ten years, with an average annual rate of 3.5%, followed by Chile at 3.3%, Korea at 3% and Australia, Israel and Mexico at just under 3%. After two years of low GDP growth, Canada is expected to recover moderately in 2017-18 and maintain an annual growth rate of 2% during the projection period.

The outlook for the large Emerging Market Economies (EMEs) is uneven and generally weaker than in the past. Growth is projected to continue to slow down in China, with an average annual growth of 5.9% over the next ten years, compared to 8.5% during the last decade, while growth in India continues to be resilient at 8% p.a. on average.

A slow recovery is projected for Brazil and the Russian Federation over the next two years, averaging about 1.9% p.a. and 1.5% p.a. respectively over the projection period. Argentina should recover quickly in 2017 from its 2016 recession with growth projected to rise to 3.1% p.a. on average.

Figure 1.35. **GDP growth rates in OECD and selected developing countries**

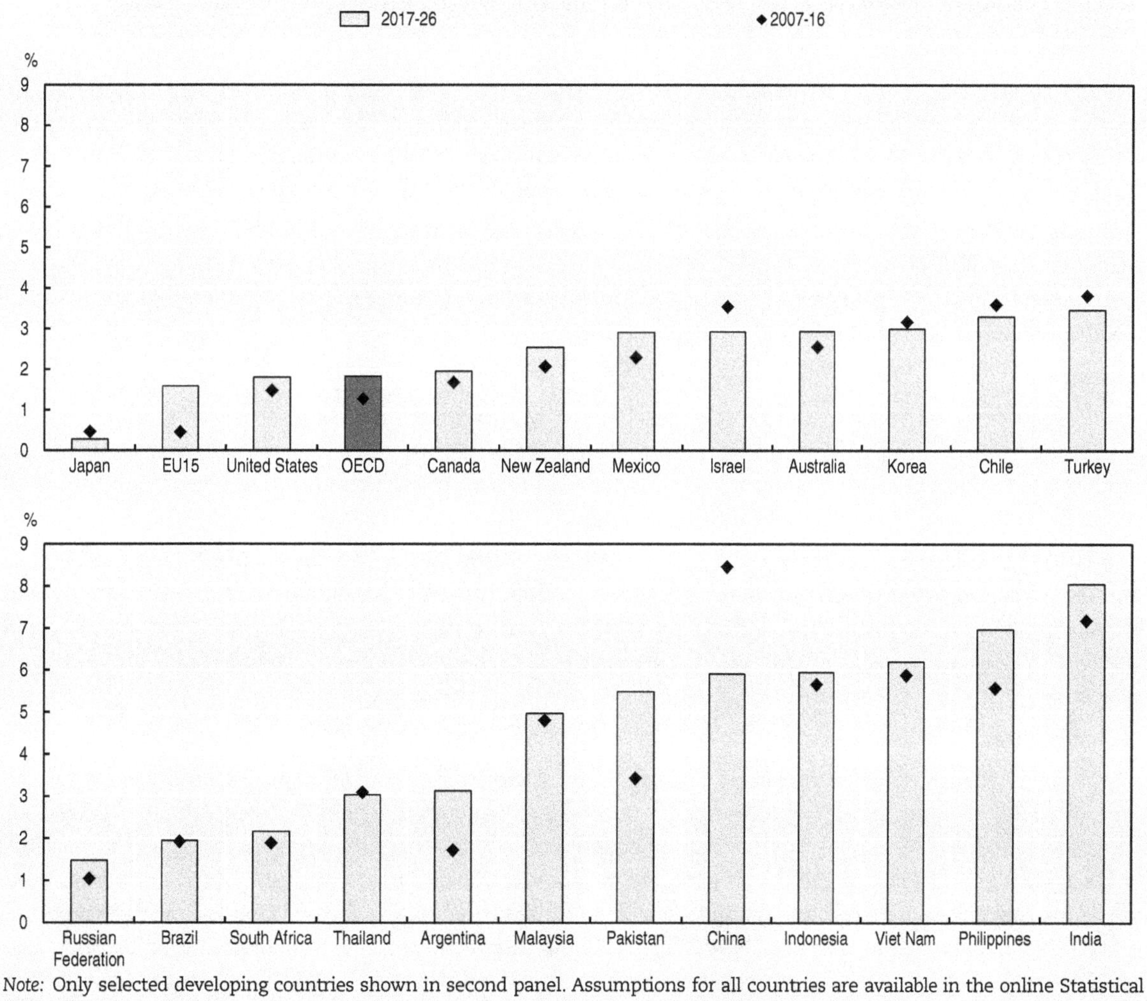

Note: Only selected developing countries shown in second panel. Assumptions for all countries are available in the online Statistical Appendix.

Source: OECD/FAO (2017), "OECD-FAO Agricultural Outlook", OECD Agriculture statistics (database), *http://dx.doi.org/10.1787/agr-data-en*.

StatLink *http://dx.doi.org/10.1787/888933521560*

Box 1.4. **Macroeconomic and policy assumptions** *(cont.)*

Over the next decade, growth prospects in developing economies are expected to remain diverse, but generally strong, across countries and regions. Myanmar, the Lao People's Democratic Republic and the Philippines are expected to lead growth in Asia, averaging 7.6% p.a., 7.1% p.a. and 6.95% p.a. respectively. Indonesia and Malaysia are expected to achieve a marginally higher growth rate than in the previous decade at 6.1% p.a. and 5.1% p.a., while growth in Thailand will remain at a similar rate as in last decade at 3.1% p.a. The picture for Sub-Saharan Africa is expected to remain uneven. In larger commodity exporting countries, such as Nigeria and Angola, growth should decelerate to 3.3% p.a., reflecting the adjustment of their economies to lower revenues from oil and other resource commodities. In contrast, several non-resource exporters, including Ethiopia, Cote d'Ivoire, Kenya and Senegal, are expected to continue expanding at a pace of more than 7% p.a., benefiting from favourable energy prices, an improved business environment, and strong infrastructure investment. Growth in North Africa and the Middle East is expected to pick up slightly to 3.8% p.a. as the slump in oil prices and ongoing conflicts continue to weigh on economic growth prospects. Growth in Saudi Arabia is expected to be weaker than in the last decade, with an average of 2.3% p.a. over the next ten years compared to 4.3% p.a. in the last decade. Benefiting from faster-than-expected increases in oil production following the removal of sanctions, growth in the Islamic Republic of Iran should pick up, averaging 4.4% p.a. Growth in Egypt is expected to average 6% p.a. The expected annual growth rate of 3.4% for Latin America over the projection period is similar to the last decade, although the Venezuelan crisis continues to weigh on the region's overall growth.

A slowdown in population growth

World population growth is expected to slow to 1% p.a. over the next decade, compared to 1.2% in the last decade. Developing countries continue to fuel this growth, particularly in Africa which is expected to have the fastest growth rate at 2.4% p.a. The Asia and Pacific region will account for more than half the world's population, and India, with an additional 149 million people by 2026, should overtake China as the most populous country.

Among OECD countries, the population of Japan is expected to decrease by nearly 4 million over the next ten years and that of the Russian Federation by 2.7 million. The population of the European Union is expected to remain stable, growing at a rate of 0.07% p.a. Australia has the highest projected population growth among OECD countries at 1.17% p.a., followed by Mexico at 1.06% p.a.

Inflation

Inflation remained weak in OECD countries in 2016, at around 1% on average; it was close to zero in the European Union, and negative in Japan after two years of slightly positive rates. Inflation in advanced economies is expected to increase over the next few years as oil prices increase modestly and output gaps gradually shrink, reaching central bank targets by around 2020.

Inflation is projected to increase from 1.1% in 2016 to 2.5% by 2019 in the United States, maintaining an average annual growth of 2.4% during the projection period. For the EU15 members as a group, the annual average inflation rate is projected at 1.8% for the next ten years. Inflation is expected to increase only slowly in Japan at 1.5% p.a. Amongst the major EMEs, consumer price inflation is projected to remain low in China and ease slowly in Brazil and the Russian Federation, facilitated by currency stabilisation.

Exchange rates

Nominal exchange rates for the period 2017-26 are mostly driven by the inflation differential in relation to the United States (with minor or no changes in real terms). Large exchange rate depreciations occurred for several advanced and emerging and developing economies in 2015. The Euro appreciated slightly in nominal terms against the US dollar in 2016, but is expected to depreciate in 2017 before appreciating again over the next ten years. Currencies are expected to appreciate in nominal terms relative to the US dollar over the next ten years in Japan, Canada, the Euro area, New Zealand, China, Islamic Republic of Iran, Malaysia, Philippines, and the Ukraine. Conversely, a strong depreciation in the currencies of Argentina, Brazil, India, South Africa, Turkey, Indonesia and Thailand is projected over the next decade. This will also be the case, but to a lesser extent, for the Russian ruble.

Box 1.4. **Macroeconomic and policy assumptions** *(cont.)*

Energy prices

World oil price assumptions to 2015 were obtained from the short-term update of the *OECD Economic Outlook* N°100 (November 2016). For 2016, the annual average monthly spot price was used, and oil prices during the projection period follow the path of the World Bank average crude oil price projected by the World Bank Commodities Price forecasts, released in October 2016.

Crude oil prices picked up at the end of 2016 after a steep drop which began in mid-2014. This increase followed an agreement by both OPEC and non-OPEC producers to reduce output by nearly 1.8 million barrels per day in the first half of 2017. The oil market will continue to rebalance itself in 2017, leading to a 32% increase of the nominal oil price, which will continue to rise moderately thereafter. Nominal oil prices are expected to increase over the outlook period at an average annual rate of 4.8%, from USD 43.8 per barrel in 2016 to USD 89.5 per barrel by 2026.

Policy considerations

Policies play an important role in agricultural, biofuel and fisheries markets, with reforms often changing the structure of markets. This *Outlook* assumes that policies will remain as they are throughout the projection period. The decision by the United Kingdom to exit the European Union is not included in the projections, as the terms of that departure have not been determined. In the current *Outlook*, projections for the United Kingdom are retained within the European Union aggregate. The Nairobi package of the World Trade Organization (WTO), especially concerning export competition, has been taken into account. In the case of bilateral trade agreements, only ratified or implemented agreements are incorporated. Thus, the North American Free Trade Agreement (NAFTA) remains unchanged throughout the *Outlook* projection while the partly implemented but not ratified Comprehensive Economic and Trade Agreement (CETA) is incorporated. The Trans Pacific Partnership (TPP) is not included as it has not been ratified. The ban by the Russian Federation on imports originating from specific countries was announced as a temporary measure and this *Outlook* assumes that the ban will be revoked at the end of 2017. The specific assumptions on biofuel policies are elaborated in the Biofuel chapter.

Notes

1. The weakness in world trade is documented and explained in recent work by the OECD. See Haugh et al., 2016.
2. As this trade measure is based on the commodities available in Aglink-Cosimo, it leaves out several important products such as fruit and vegetables or processed agri-food products. Moreover, the definition of agricultural trade here does not coincide with the definition in the Agreement on Agriculture. Nevertheless, the trade measure can serve as a useful proxy for agricultural trade more broadly, as Aglink-Cosimo covers the most important agricultural commodities.

References

FAO (2016), "Trends in foreign direct investment in food, beverages and tobacco", *FAO Commodity and Trade Policy Research Paper*, No. 51, FAO Publications, Rome.

FAO (2014), "Impacts of foreign agricultural investment on developing countries. Evidence from case studies", by Pascal Liu, *FAO Commodity and Trade Policy Research Paper*, No. 47. FAO, Rome.

FAO (2012) *Trends and impacts of foreign investment in developing country agriculture. Evidence from case studies*, FAO, Rome.

FAO, IFAD and WFP (2015). *Achieving Zero Hunger. The critical role of investments in social protection and agriculture*. FAO, Rome.

Haugh, D., et al. (2016), "Cardiac Arrest or Dizzy Spell: Why is World Trade So Weak and What can Policy Do About It?", *OECD Economic Policy Papers*, No. 18, OECD Publishing, Paris. *http://dx.doi.org/10.1787/5jlr2h45q532-en*

HighQuest Partners, United States (2010), "Private Financial Sector Investment in Farmland and Agricultural Infrastructure", OECD Food, Agriculture and Fisheries Papers, No. 33, OECD Publishing, Paris. *http://dx.doi.org/10.1787/5km7nzpjlr8v-en*

Hoekman, B. (ed.), (2015) *The Global Trade Slowdown: A New Normal?*, VoxEU.org e-book, CEPR Press, London.

Lewis, L. and R. Monarch (2016) *Causes of the Global Trade Slowdown*, International Finance Discussion Note, US Federal Reserve, November 2016.

OECD/FAO (2017), "OECD-FAO Agricultural Outlook", *OECD Agriculture statistics* (database), *http://dx.doi.org/10.1787/agr-data-en.*

OECD (2016), *Evolving Agricultural Policies and Markets: Implications for Multilateral Trade Reform*, OECD Publishing, Paris. *http://dx.doi.org/10.1787/9789264264991-en.*

OECD/FAO (2016), *OECD-FAO Guidance for Responsible Agricultural Supply Chains*, OECD Publishing, Paris. *http://dx.doi.org/10.1787/9789264251052-en*

OECD-FAO Agricultural Outlook 2017-2026

Chapter 2

Southeast Asia: Prospects and challenges

This chapter reviews the prospects and challenges facing the agricultural sector in Southeast Asia over the next decade. In line with the focus of policy makers, agriculture and fisheries issues are primarily explored with reference to trade and food security. This chapter first considers the historical performance and current state of agriculture and fisheries in Southeast Asia before presenting the market and food security projections for the medium-term (2017-26). It concludes with a discussion of the challenges and uncertainties that may influence the medium-term projections presented. Countries in Southeast Asia have experienced significant improvements in their levels of development along with strong growth in their agriculture and fishery sectors. The outlook for agriculture is broadly positive, but could be further improved by consistent policies and strategic investments, particularly in rural infrastructure.

Introduction

Southeast Asia (Figure 2.1) comprises a diverse range of countries at varying levels of development and endowments (Table 2.1). Over recent decades, the region as a whole has undergone significant development. Structural changes in many of its economies have led to significant gains, and the rise of "Factory Asia" has placed Southeast Asia central to a varied mix of manufacturing global value chains (GVCs). With this, the region has experienced strong growth in Gross Domestic Product (GDP); for most countries, real GDP growth has averaged close to 5% per year over the period 2000-16. Meanwhile, the regional population has continued to grow at close to 1.3% per year over the same period.

Figure 2.1. **The Southeast Asian region**

Southeast Asia has also made remarkable progress in terms of improving food security. In the early 1990s, undernourishment rates were the world's highest at around 31%, but these rates had fallen below 10% by 2014-16, below those seen in a number of other regions. Despite this, the varying levels of development among countries in the region means that food security remains a significant issue; in 2014-16, the region, which has a population of around 630 million (9% of world total), still contained around 60 million (or 8%) of the world's undernourished (FAO, 2017a).

The development of the agricultural and fisheries sectors[1] has contributed to the improvements in food security, and both sectors remain a key part of food security policy for regional policy makers. In this way, agricultural and fisheries policy settings are interlinked with food security objectives. This is particularly the case for policy approaches directed at the region's key staple crop – rice. However, for some countries, the use of market interventions in pursuit of food security objectives has had unintended consequences for both the development of the sectors and for food security itself.

Table 2.1. **Contextual indicators for selected countries in Southeast Asia, 2015**

	GDP per capita	Population	Rural population	Total land area	Agricultural land	Agricultural land per capita	Freshwater resources	Freshwater withdrawals agriculture	Frehswater resources per capita
		(millions)	(%)	(km^2)	(km^2)	(ha)	(billion m^3)	(billion m^3)	('000 m^3)
Cambodia	1 159	15.6	79.3	176 520	54 550	0.36	120.6	2.1	7.9
Indonesia	3 346	257.6	46.3	1 811 570	570 000	0.22	2019.0	92.8	7.9
Lao PDR	1 818	6.8	61.4	230 800	23 690	0.35	190.4	3.2	28.5
Malaysia	9 768	30.3	25.3	328 550	78 390	0.26	1003.0.	2.5	33.5
Myanmar	1 161	53.9	65.9	653 080	126 450	0.24	580.0	29.6	10.9
Philippines	2 904	100.7	55.6	298 170	124 400	0.13	429.0	67.1	4.8
Thailand	5 815	68.0	49.6	510 890	221 100	0.33	224.5	51.8	3.3
Viet Nam	2 111	91.7	66.4	310 070	108 737	0.12	359.4	77.7	4.0

Note: GDP per capita measured in current 2015 USD. Data on freshwater withdrawals and agricultural land are from 2014.
Source: World Bank (2017), World Development Indicators, *http://databank.worldbank.org/data/*.

Agricultural and fisheries sector development in Southeast Asia has also meant that it is increasingly involved in international agro-food trade. For both producers and consumers, international and regional markets are gaining importance as a source of both income and food. As such, developments in international markets, and the policies of other agro-food trading countries, are of key importance.

This chapter first considers the historical performance and current state of agriculture and fisheries in Southeast Asia before presenting the market and food security projections for the medium-term (2017-26). The chapter concludes with a discussion of the challenges and uncertainties that may influence the medium-term projections presented. In line with the focus of policy makers, agriculture and fisheries are primarily explored with reference to trade and food security. Eight Southeast Asian countries are the focus of this chapter (each are individually modelled in the *Outlook*) and include Cambodia, Indonesia, Lao People's Democratic Republic (hereafter Lao PDR), Malaysia, Myanmar, the Philippines, Thailand and Viet Nam.

Developments in agriculture and fisheries in Southeast Asia

Extensive structural changes

Agriculture and fisheries in Southeast Asian countries have undergone significant structural changes over time. The relative importance of the two sectors in GDP and employment declined in most countries between 1996 and 2014 (the earliest and latest years for which data are available) (Figure 2.2). Productivity improvements and opportunities outside agriculture have led to significant labour-shedding in several countries, but most notably in Cambodia and Viet Nam. Interestingly, the agricultural share of employment fell in Thailand even as its share of GDP rose over the period, representing a shift to relatively higher-value production along with opportunities for labour absorption in other sectors of the economy.

Figure 2.2. **Agricultural and fisheries sectors share of employment and GDP**

1996 and 2014

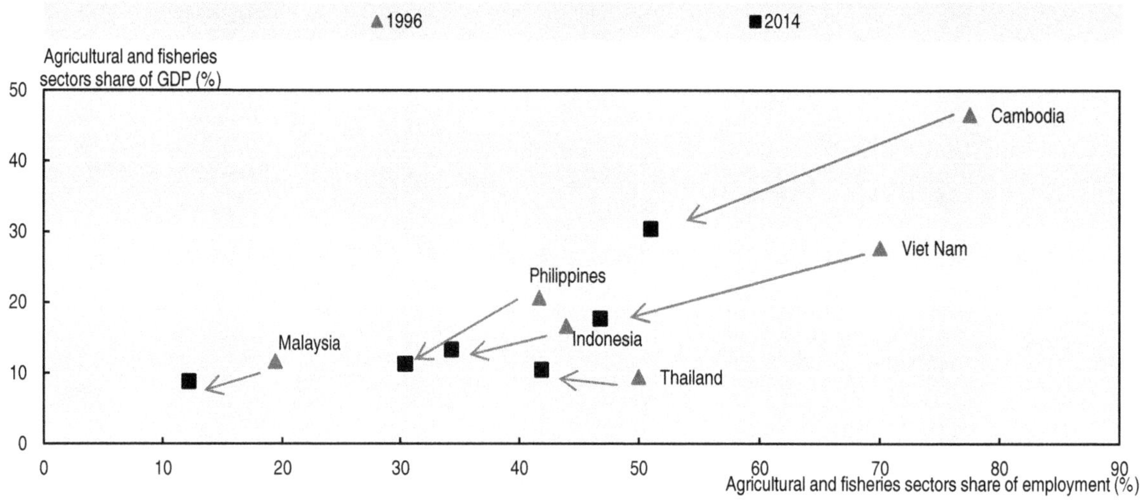

Note: Value added estimates include forestry and hunting. Data for Cambodia are for 1998 and 2012, and data for employment share are for 2013 for Thailand and Viet Nam.
Source: World Bank (2017), World Development Indicators, *http://databank.worldbank.org/data/.*

StatLink http://dx.doi.org/10.1787/888933521579

Adjustment within agriculture

While the sector overall appears to have undergone significant structural adjustment, farm sizes in Southeast Asia remain relatively small, and may remain so over the medium term (FAO, 2015). Data on farm size and its distribution are sparse. For those countries for which time series data exist – Indonesia, the Philippines and Thailand – patterns indicate a generally falling average farm size (Lowder et al., 2014). In some of these countries, changes in average land holdings can be traced to policy moves that have redistributed land, for example in the Philippines through its agrarian reform programme (OECD, 2017a). The trend of falling farm size may have broader long-term implications for agricultural productivity growth if it is also leads to a further fragmentation of production activities. In contrast, two countries appear to have exhibited trends of *increasing* farm size – Myanmar and Viet Nam. In the case of Viet Nam, land consolidation has been seen across different production activities and was found to be more visible in livestock production but only in very early stages for crops (OECD, 2015c). In terms of the distribution of farm size, although data are both limited and dated, they indicate that farms of less than 1 ha of land dominate (Lowder et al., 2014) (Figure 2.3). Indonesia and Viet Nam have the largest share of total producers who farm less than 1 ha of land. Thailand and Myanmar also stand out as countries with different patterns of ownership – both have a relatively higher number of producers who farm between 2 and 5 ha, compared with other countries.

Figure 2.3. **Distribution of farm size in Southeast Asia**

Percentage of farm holdings by size, estimates during the 2000s

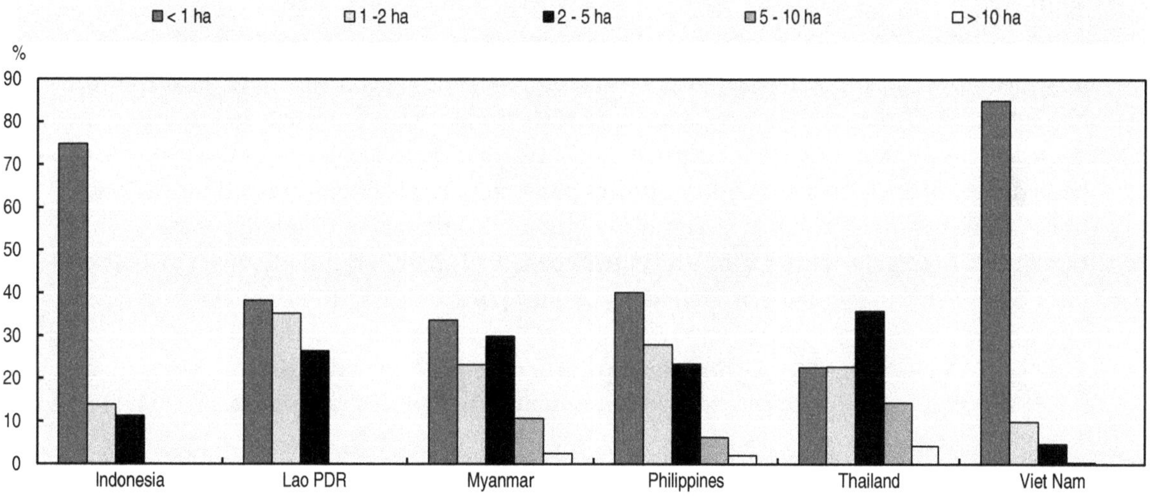

Notes: Estimates for each country relate to data collected during the 2000s. Specifically, Indonesia (2003), Lao PDR (1998-99), Myanmar (2003), the Philippines (2002), Thailand (2003) and Viet Nam (2001). No data is available for Cambodia and Malaysia.

Source: Lowder et al. (2014).

StatLink *http://dx.doi.org/10.1787/888933521598*

Structural adjustment in the sector has contributed to strong production growth over time. Since the 1960s, annual compound production growth in the Southeast Asian region as a whole has been strong (Figure 2.4).[2] However, agricultural production growth relative to population growth has been strong since the 1980s (shown as per capita growth), driven by both slowing population growth rates and increases in agricultural growth rates during the 1980s and 2000s.

Figure 2.4. **Production growth in Southeast Asia**

Decadal annual compound growth rates (%) 1960 to 2009

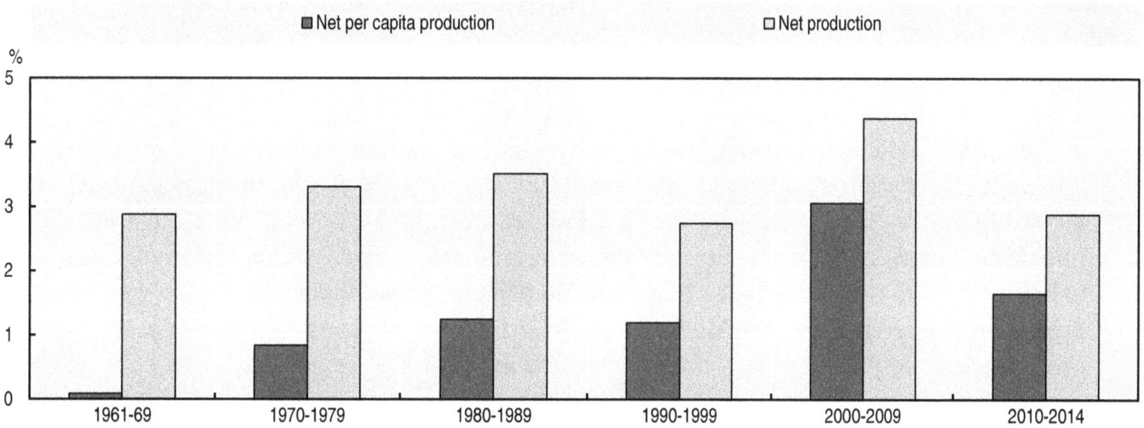

Notes: Net production refers to total production less cereal use for livestock feed. The FAO calculates net production in the form of an index; see *http://faostat3.fao.org/download/QI/*/E* for further details.

Source: FAO (2017a), FAOSTAT, *http://faostat.fao.org/*.

StatLink *http://dx.doi.org/10.1787/888933521617*

A shifting agricultural production mix centred on the key rice crop

Agricultural production in Southeast Asia remains centred around rice. Rice cultivation is the main agricultural production activity, accounting for a greater share of gross production value than any other single commodity. In general, the production shares of various agricultural activities have remained relatively stable over time; however, the contribution of rice to total gross agricultural production value has fallen since the early 1990s – from around 40% to close to 30% in 2013 (Figure 2.5). Much of the change has been driven by the increasing contribution of palm oil to total agricultural production value in the region as it represents a higher value product (combined with relative dietary shifts away from rice in some countries – discussed below). Within commodity categories, there have also been changes such as increasing poultry production within the meat sector.

Figure 2.5. **Agricultural production in Southeast Asia**

Commodity shares of gross production value in constant 2004-06 international dollars, 1963 to 2013

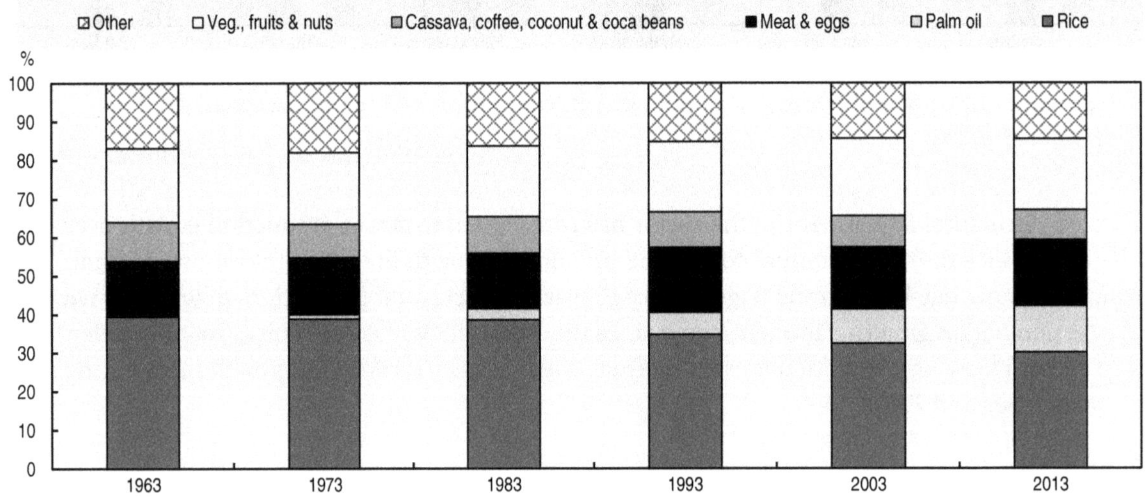

Notes: International prices are used to overcome issues in the aggregation of commodities that cannot be added up according to their physical weights. The FAO uses international prices in determining gross production value so that production trends can be seen without the influence of changes in exchange rates – see *www.fao.org/faostat/en/#data/QV* for further details.

Source: FAO (2017a), FAOSTAT, *http://faostat.fao.org/*

StatLink http://dx.doi.org/10.1787/888933521636

Across individual Southeast Asian countries, changes in the production mix are more apparent (Figure 2.6). In Malaysia, production has significantly shifted towards palm oil, crowding out both rice and other production activities. In Myanmar, there have been increases in both meat and fruit and vegetable production, and its share of production value coming from rice has fallen by around 20 percentage points over the past 50 years. Expressed as shares in constant dollar terms, in 2013, the agricultural sectors of Cambodia and Malaysia were most reliant on one production activity or sector – rice and palm oil respectively. Others are more diversified. Over the period examined, the Philippines is the only country where the share of rice in its total agricultural production value has increased.

Changes in fisheries production

Fisheries and aquaculture are important contributors to food security and nutrition, along with the livelihoods and household incomes of many living in Southeast Asia. Fish and seafood products represent the main source of animal protein for most of the

Figure 2.6. **Southeast Asia agricultural production shares by country, 2013**

Commodity shares of gross production value in constant 2004-06 international dollars

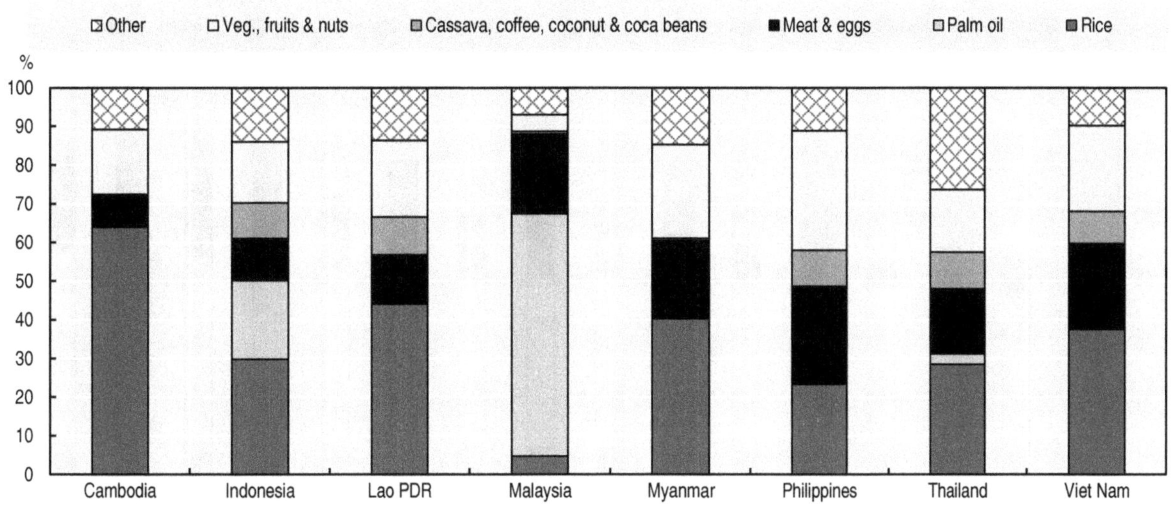

Notes: International prices are used to overcome issues in the aggregation of commodities that cannot be added up according to their physical weights. The FAO uses international prices in determining gross production value so that production trends can be seen without the influence of changes in exchange rates; see *www.fao.org/faostat/en/#data/QV* for further details.

Source: FAO (2017a), FAOSTAT, *http://faostat.fao.org/*.

StatLink *http://dx.doi.org/10.1787/888933521655*

population in the region – per capita fish consumption stands at around 36 kg, around double the world average and accounts for about 42% of total animal protein intake for individuals (FAO, 2017b).

Production from fisheries and aquaculture in the region is significant. In 2015, the region accounted for close to 17% of global fisheries production (14% for aquaculture and 19% for capture fisheries). Overall, fisheries and aquaculture production increased by around 75% over the period 2000-15. The largest increase was seen in production from inland aquaculture, where production grew by over 460% between 2000 and 2015 – growing at an average annual rate of 12.4% over the period (Figure 2.7). Over a longer horizon, the increases in fishery production are even more significant. In 1950, regional production stood at 1 Mt, rising to the 28 Mt seen in 2015. Much of this growth occurred between 1995 and 2015, over which period production doubled. During the last two decades, the fishery sector in Southeast Asia has transformed from a small-scale capture fisheries production mainly sold domestically toward a mixture of smaller-scale and larger-scale export-oriented fisheries.

For both capture fisheries and aquaculture, four of the top ten producing countries in the world are in Southeast Asia, with Indonesia the second largest producer in the world behind China. Across countries, Indonesia dominates total fishery and aquaculture production in the region, accounting for 38% of total production in 2015 (Figure 2.8). The extent of this dominance has increased over time on the back of strong production growth. At the same time, fishery and aquaculture production has also increased significantly in Viet Nam – almost tripling between 2000 and 2015 – with Myanmar reporting a similar level growth in production, moving from the sixth to third largest regional producer.

Aquaculture production is highly diversified in the region, with a large number of species cultured in fresh, brackish and marine environments targeting both domestic and

Figure 2.7. **Marine and inland fishery production in Southeast Asia**

Capture and aquaculture, 2000-15

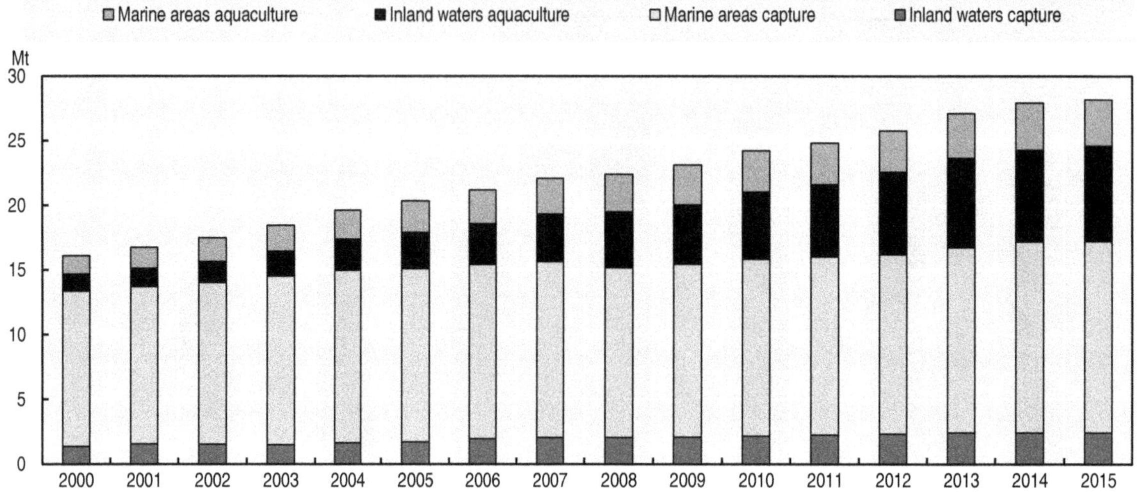

Source: FAO (2017b), Global Fishery and Aquaculture Production (database), *www.fao.org/fishery/statistics/global-production/en.*

StatLink http://dx.doi.org/10.1787/888933521674

Figure 2.8. **Contribution to fishery production by country**

Total fishery production (left); Aquaculture (right)

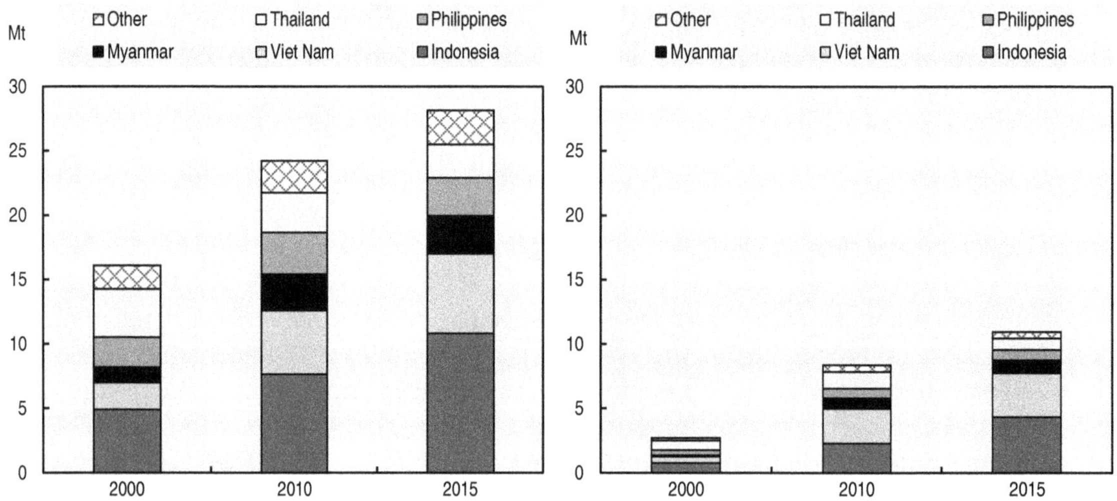

Notes: Other includes Cambodia, Lao PDR and Malaysia.

Source: FAO (2017b), Global Production Fisheries (database), *www.fao.org/fishery/statistics/global-production/en.*

StatLink http://dx.doi.org/10.1787/888933521693

export markets. For many rural areas in the region, small-scale freshwater aquaculture, often in ponds and on rice fields, plays a crucial role in providing populations with high quality protein, essential fatty acids, vitamins and minerals. Across the region, growth in aquaculture has been unequal among countries reflecting differences in local policy, management objectives and environmental factors (Figure 2.8). Indonesia and Viet Nam are the most important aquaculture producers in the region, accounting for close to 40% and 31% of the quantity produced respectively. Over the period 2000-15 production growth in Viet Nam was consistently high, only slowing towards the end of the period. In contrast, the strong growth in Indonesia took place more recently and is concentrated at the end of the period. In contrast, production in Thailand declined by 37% between 2009 and 2015 due to disease that affected shrimp production.

While much of the production growth has come from aquaculture, capture fisheries in the region remain the largest source of production – one that is also growing (by over 29% during period 2000-15). For capture fisheries in inland waters, production is reported to have increased by 79% over the period 2000-15. Unfortunately, these data are subject to a great number of uncertainties. While part of this increase has been a result of growing fishing effort to further exploit inland fisheries resources (along with a lack of resource management tools or a lack of enforcement thereof – see below), the true extent of this is unclear as the increases seen in the region might also be generated by improved statistics. Capture fisheries in inland waters play a key role in food security and poverty alleviation, sustaining the livelihoods of many rural communities. Southeast Asian countries contribute 21% of world inland capture fisheries production. Marine capture fisheries in Southeast Asia also reported production growth, but at slower rates to those reported in inland fisheries, by around 23% over the 2000-15 period (Figure 2.7).

In addition to its production of fish and other seafood species, Southeast Asia is also a major producer of seaweeds and aquatic plants, accounting for more than 43% of world production. This output is dominated by farmed tropical seaweed species from Indonesia, where farmed seaweed output increased by 5391% over the period 2000-15 (from 205 000 tonnes in 2000 to 11.3 Mt in 2015 (wet weight). At the global level, Indonesia is currently the second largest producer and the leading exporter of seaweeds, and national policy aims to maintain recently observed rates growth with a focus on export markets.

Drivers of production growth in Southeast Asia

Agriculture

Improvements in agricultural productivity have played a key role in driving agricultural output growth in the region. Although estimates are subject to measurement errors, total factor productivity (TFP)[3] for the region as a whole has increased at an average annual rate of 2.2% a year since 1991 (1.4% a year on average for the period 1961 to 2013), based on USDA (2016) data. Agricultural productivity growth has accounted for an increasing share of output growth over time (Figure 2.9). Between 2001 and 2013, productivity growth accounted for over 60% of output growth, compared with 13% in the 1980s, when increasing input use of 2.8% a year drove agricultural output growth.

Productivity growth rates in Southeast Asia also compare favourably with those observed in other regions. For the period 2001 to 2013, agricultural productivity growth in Southeast Asia exceeded growth realised in all other regions except the rest of Asia.[4] Moreover, for the same period, productivity growth accounted for a similar share of agricultural output growth (63%) to the world average.

Notwithstanding the contribution of TFP, agricultural output growth has been significantly influenced by increased input use (including land, labour capital – animals and machinery, fertiliser and feed use), which has in turn been driven by a combination of increased intensification of activities and area expansion (Figure 2.10). While data are sparse, anecdotal evidence and partial data from some countries in the region suggests

Figure 2.9. **Composition of agricultural output growth in Southeast Asia, by period (%)**

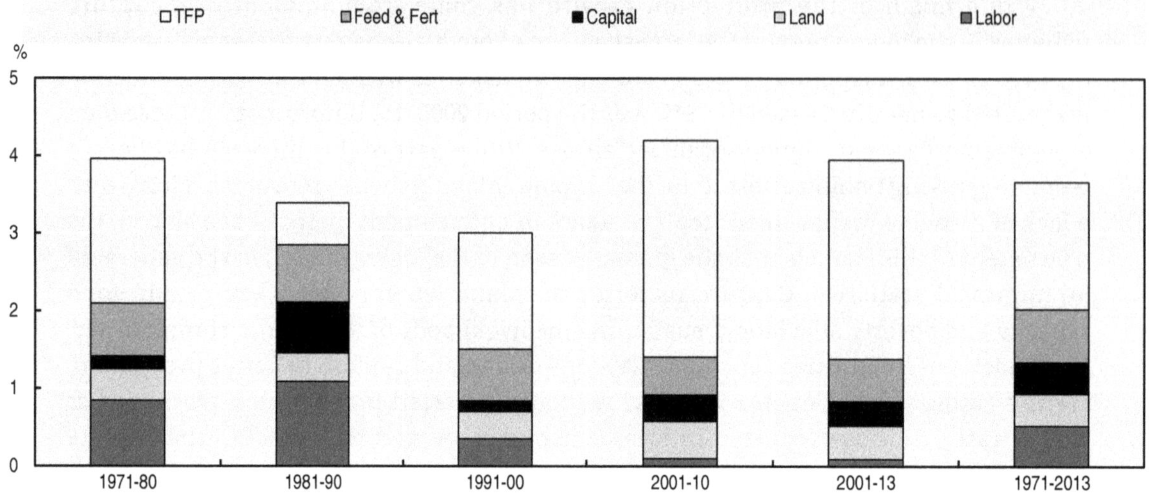

Notes: Weighted average (by output) for Cambodia, Indonesia, Lao PDR, Malaysia, Myanmar, the Philippines, Thailand and Viet Nam. Capital represents both machinery and livestock related capital. The USDA Economic Research Service methodology for measuring international agricultural TFP growth is available at *www.ers.usda.gov/data-products/international-agricultural-productivity/documentation-and-methods/*.

Source: USDA (2016), International Agricultural Productivity, *www.ers.usda.gov/data-products/international-agricultural-productivity.aspx*.

StatLink http://dx.doi.org/10.1787/888933521712

that mechanisation is occurring even on small-scale farms (FAO, 2015). USDA (2016) estimates based on FAO data suggest that while increases in labour usage dominated earlier periods, land and capital increases become more important from the 1990s onwards. Further, data on fertiliser use indicates that between 1961 and 2013, average annual growth has been around 7% for the eight countries examined since 1961, with the highest rates seen in Cambodia and Lao PDR of 13% per year on average (USDA, 2016).

A key driver of input growth has been an increase in land use. Across Southeast Asia, agricultural land has increased by close to 40% between 1980 and 2014 (FAO, 2017a). In terms of absolute expansion of agricultural land, the most significant increase has been in Indonesia, which is also the largest country in terms of total land size. In relative terms, Cambodia, Indonesia, Myanmar and Viet Nam have all seen agricultural land use expand by in excess of 50% over the period 1980-2014; the largest increase relates to Cambodia, where agricultural land has increased by over 100% (FAO, 2017a).[5] Lao PDR has also seen an increase by close to 48% over this same period.

In Indonesia and Malaysia, much of the expansion of agricultural land has been due to the conversion of forested areas to land used for palm oil production. While these changes have contributed to increasing incomes for those employed in agriculture, with positive effects on poverty and food security, this expansion has not been without significant cost or controversy. Pirker et al. (2016) cite evidence that 17% of new palm oil plantations in Malaysia and 63% of those in Indonesia came at the expense of lost biodiversity-rich tropical forest over the period 1990-2010 (Gunarso et al., 2013; Koh et al., 2011), and in addition contributed to increased carbon emissions from the sector (Carlson et al., 2012; Miettinen et al., 2012; Omar et al., 2010). These costs are not only one-off, but will have a lasting impact on the future productive capacity of the region and thus on long term income and food security. Reconciling these costs and benefits will be a key challenge for regional policy makers going forward, including demonstrating to increasingly aware consumers that palm oil production is sustainable – a challenge not viewed as insurmountable by some (Sayer et al., 2012).

Looking ahead, future area expansion is likely to be limited. Instead, increases in production of any given agricultural product will need to be driven by increases in intensification or productivity, or come at the expense of production of other products. With climate change expected to place downward pressure on yield growth of many crops (OECD, 2017b), the role of agricultural R&D and innovation systems will become increasingly important in future agricultural development over the next decade and beyond.

As part of a wider enabling environment, FAO (2015) emphasises that the public provision of education and health services will be crucial for farmers to be able to operate in an increasingly complex and knowledge-intensive industry. However, to make these investments happen, policy choices will need to change, and funding for various agricultural programmes should be reformed.

Recent analysis suggests that for countries within Southeast Asia, compared with other countries at a similar level of development, there is significant scope to increase investments in R&D and innovation systems to help safeguard future levels of productivity growth and mitigate some of the expected negative effects of climate change (Box 2.1).

Box 2.1. **Improvement of regional agricultural innovation systems is key to future productivity growth**

Public investment in agricultural R&D is essential for sustainable agricultural productivity growth. By ensuring that farmers have access to innovations that meet their diverse and complex needs, public spending on agricultural R&D is proven to be more effective at raising sustainable agricultural productivity than other public expenditures in agriculture, such as irrigation and fertiliser subsidies. Recent findings suggest that countries in Southeast Asia have scope to improve R&D and innovation systems more broadly to enhance productivity growth and to better manage future production and food security risks (OECD, 2017b). The Agricultural Growth Enabling Index (AGEI) compares the performance of selected countries – Cambodia, Indonesia, Lao PDR, Malaysia, Myanmar, the Philippines, Thailand and Viet Nam, together with a wider set of countries at a similar level of development – across the various components of the enabling environment (Figure 2.10). As such, it provides an overview of government measures and activities that potentially aid or hinder agricultural growth.

Although the performance of the ASEAN countries analysed varies significantly across the AGEI, the results reveal some common relative strengths and weaknesses. Relative strengths of the region as a whole include aspects of economy-wide policy settings – such as the broader macroeconomic environment and its structure (related to governance macro fiscal and monetary policy settings), labour market functioning and levels of human capital – and relatively abundant water resources (not shown in Figure 2.10), while common areas of relative weakness include agricultural and sustainability aspects of the enabling environment. With the exception of Malaysia, Southeast Asian countries tend to score relatively poorly with regard to public investments in agricultural R&D, land rights and access, farmer access to finance, the existence and quality of agricultural infrastructure – although Thailand also scores above average in this respect – and for the stringency and enforcement of environmental regulations (Figure 2.10). Indeed, the results suggest that, compared with other sectors, agriculture in Southeast Asian countries may actually be underprovided with public goods and other economic services.

Box 2.1. **Improvement of regional agricultural innovation systems is key to future productivity growth** *(cont.)*

Recent analysis by the OECD has recommended that Southeast Asian governments direct policy efforts towards additional investments and reforms in the enabling environment to enhance future sustainable productivity growth to help address food security and manage future risks facing the sector. These include the improvement of environmental governance; regulations on land, water and biodiversity resources; and investments in infrastructure and agricultural R&D. Governments should also persevere with reforms to improve regulatory and institutional frameworks that govern rural land market rights and access, and should consider opportunities to increase farmer access to credit, including for small-scale farmers.

Figure 2.10. **There is scope to improve a number of areas of the enabling environment**

AGEI normalised scores for each country relative to sample average

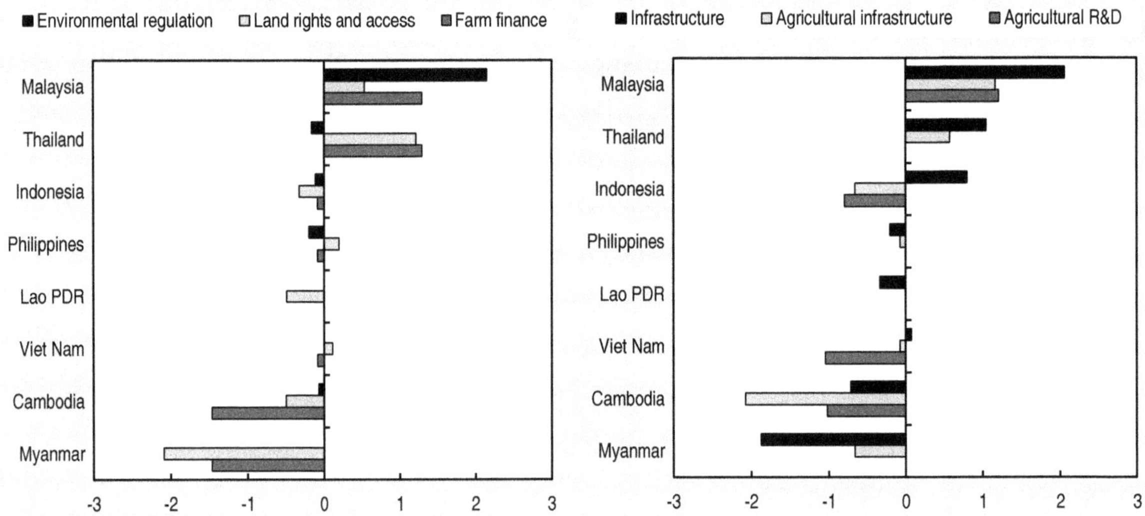

Notes: Normalised values are calculated by subtracting the average for the 32 countries covered from each country value, and then dividing the resulting country value by the standard deviation for the series. This creates a series with zero mean and unit standard error.

Source: OECD (2017b).

StatLink http://dx.doi.org/10.1787/888933521731

For some countries, additional policy reforms and investments could significantly alter future production. For Myanmar in particular, the potential for agricultural production and trade growth is potentially significant and could help drive the future development of the country (Box 2.2). This, however, will require a number of policy reforms and investments that allow producers to fulfil the opportunities they have in terms of access to regional and international markets. If Myanmar is able to make headway in this regard there are potentially significant gains in terms of poverty reduction and economic transformation.

Fisheries

In the fisheries sector, the drivers of growth relate to both productivity improvements and changes to production mix. The rapid growth of aquaculture production over the last two decades has mainly been a direct result of the sector diversifying its practices and species mix (towards exportable species) coupled with increased levels of intensification. This is particularly the case for Indonesia, Viet Nam and Thailand, the most important producers in the region. The increasing levels of intensification have created issues in

Box 2.2. **The potential role of agriculture in the future development of Myanmar**

Myanmar's economy needs to transform from an agrarian economy to one based more on a mix of activities, including manufacturing and services. Agricultural modernisation has the potential to be the catalyst for transforming the wider economy and reducing poverty wholescale.

Raising incomes in rural areas will require not only raising agricultural productivity and diversifying to high-value crops, but also expansion of agriculture's linkages to non-agricultural activities to stimulate employment in non-farm sectors. Expanding agricultural exports in a value-chain framework which can drive these linkages could be key to this transformation. This path for development is particularly relevant for Myanmar because of its natural resource endowments, its strategic location and a favourable external environment.

The OECD's *Multi-dimensional Review of Myanmar*, working through stakeholder consultations in the country, revealed a number of constraints on exports that need to be addressed:

- Poor quality infrastructure is a particular constraint in rural areas. Producers and traders often substitute the lack of public infrastructure with private, higher-cost solutions (such as fuel-based generators in place of national electricity supplies) which lowers profits and dampens incentives for investment.
- The rural sector's lack of an adequate financial system has constrained productivity. Although this is due in part to the underdevelopment of the financial system in general, the problem is particularly acute in the rural sector. Reforming the Myanmar Agricultural Development Bank (which has essentially been the only credit provider to date), providing incentives for commercial banks to operate in the sector, and expanding the variety of financial institutions and the range of services they offer will be important.
- Ambiguity in land tenure and production rights dampens production incentives. Stakeholders saw the need for an overarching law on land to overcome contradictory laws and overlapping responsibility for the laws by different ministries.
- Low levels of agronomic knowledge and skills of producers contribute to poor product quality and low productivity. Expanding agricultural extension services and farmer education, informed by solid agronomic R&D, can help spread modern farming practices using better quality inputs.
- Insufficient government support to access new markets and ensure quality and safety standards has constrained exports. The lack of government support to explore new market opportunities limits market entry potential in relation to competitors, while the lack of food safety inspection services increases production risks and limits market access. Important measures will include devoting resources to increase ISO-certified laboratories with appropriately qualified technical staff, and building the Myanmar brand through an effective export promotion agency.

Lifting these constraints will enable Myanmar to reap the opportunities offered by international markets for food products and help kick-start the country's structural transformation.

Source: OECD (2015b).

disease management and in terms of environmental impacts. For the export-oriented countries, continued growth will depend on their ability to sell aquaculture products to international buyers. This will require further adaptation to production practices that meet an increasing focus on traceability and to concerns relating to human health and potential environmental impact. Such concerns have impacted demand for selected species exports from Southeast Asia recently.

Land is also an important input for aquaculture production. The intensity of land use depends on the species; however, in general, increased production has generally depended on increasing access to land. Increasing land use will place greater pressure on an already constrained regional resource. The constraints vary across countries, but in some regions, competition exists between agricultural crops, such as rice, and aquaculture. In Viet Nam's Mekong Delta district of Tran Van Thoi, for example, from only a few ponds in 1973, by 2011 aquaculture covered around 20% of the land surface. The land occupied progressively moved from mangrove to rice paddy and then to aquaculture, with most of the latter change taking place as of 1995 to capitalise on the production of higher value shrimp (Tran et al, 2015). In contrast, Indonesia's extensive coastline and relatively undeveloped industry has meant that it has been less constrained than other countries (Phillips et al., 2015).

For marine fisheries, production growth has a number of different drivers. Growth has been fuelled by increases in fishing effort (including that displaced from more depleted coastal fisheries), and improvements in fishing technology and capacity that has allowed fishers to expand the range of their fishing activities to better access offshore stocks (Funge-Smith et al., 2012). Production growth has also been supported by fishing-induced changes to the ecosystem. For example, high rates of fishing pressure on predator species have had flow on effects on biomass levels, creating growth in biomass of prey species as falls in predation levels have allowed for catch increases in these species – fishing down the food chain effect (Funge-Smith et al., 2012). However, there are serious concerns over the sustainability of marine capture fisheries. A considerable number of fish stocks in the region are considered to be overfished – that is, fished beyond their biologically-sustainable harvest levels – and sustainable management instruments to control the level of fishing activity are often lacking (Funge-Smith et al., 2012). In Viet Nam, where coastal fishing effort is effectively unconstrained and resources are overfished, the expansion of offshore fishing operations over the last decade – targeting pelagic species such as tuna – has helped support capture fisheries growth, but there are concerns that without adequate management this development will be unsustainable. In particular, the growth in the offshore industry has predominantly come about as a consequence of government support, in the form of fuel tax credits, and is not believed to have alleviated pressure on inshore fisheries in the process (UNEP, VIFEP and WWF, 2009). Assessments, however, are limited significantly by a lack of data on a number of key regional species and true fishing pressure is often unknown due to illegal, unreported and unregulated (IUU) fishing. Given the limitations to capture fishery growth, aquaculture is expected to be the driver of production increases in the future.

Further to high levels of fishing pressure, inland, coastal and offshore waters of the region face challenges from habitat degradation, growing competition for scarce freshwater resources, reengineering of habitats by dams and other infrastructure, biodiversity loss, and industrial and urban pollution and diseases. With the region home to a large number of mostly small scale (around 90%) fishers and fish farmers – an estimated 14.5 million, of which 5.4 million are fish farmers (FAO, 2017c) – maintaining sustainable production from fishery resources will be important for the region.

Growing regional participation in world food markets

Southeast Asia is playing an increasingly important role in world agro-food trade. The region as a whole has increasingly become a net agro-food exporter, with around USD 139 billion in exports in 2014, compared with USD 90 billion worth of agro-food imports (WITS, 2017). Intra-regional agro-food trade is also an important component of food supply. The share of agro-food imports sourced from within the ASEAN group has trended upwards over time, rising from close to 21% in 2000 to 29% in 2011, but has since fallen, accounting for close to 24% of the region's total imports in 2014 (WITS, 2017). However, despite increased involvement in world markets, agro-food tariffs generally remain high and weighted average applied tariffs averaged 7.2% between 2010 to 2014.

Of the products traded, vegetable and animal fats and oils – in this case, palm oil – are the most important agro-food export, accounting for the largest share of agro-food export value – a share that has grown over time but fallen in recent years (Figure 2.11). Fisheries are also important, with exports of fish and seafood products (fish in Figure 2.11) the second-largest export earner and representing 15% of world fish exports. Since 2014, Viet Nam and Thailand have, respectively, been the third and fourth major exporters of fish and fishery products in the world. For the region, the export mix is also concentrated, with the top ten products accounting for over 75% of total export value. On the import side, there is more diversity. The top ten imported products account for just over 55% of total imports. Flours, brans and other food industry preparations and residues, dairy products, fish and seafood, and wheat are all major import products (Figure 2.11).

Rice is also a significant export and import crop. Overall, the region is a significant net exporter, with export values in 2014 that were five times greater than import values.[6] The strong net export position is primarily due to large export volumes from Thailand and Viet Nam (Figure 2.12). Recently, Cambodia also became a net exporter and Myanmar reported net exports in 2010 (but has limited reported trade data). The other countries in Southeast Asia are net importers (no data exist for Lao PDR).

With growing agro-food exports and imports, the region's producers and consumers are both more exposed to international markets and more reliant on these as a source of income and food. For Southeast Asian countries, this shift means that it is not only domestic agricultural policies that will influence outcomes for producers and consumers, but also those of other countries. The greater interactions in world markets now mean that Southeast Asian economies have more to gain from removing distortions in world agricultural markets, both those related to trade barriers and to those that distort domestic support. Recent analysis has found that multilateral reforms that reduce distortions in world agricultural markets, including those in Southeast Asian economies, can enhance the region's agricultural trade, incomes and overall welfare (OECD, 2016a). The effects are particularly strong for net exports from Indonesia, Malaysia and Thailand, primarily from higher exports of food products (processed products – for Indonesia and Malaysia in the form of palm oil, and for Thailand, in the form of sugar and processed rice). Such reforms should provide greater opportunities within the region for their agricultural sectors, ultimately helping to increase incomes in rural communities connected with agriculture and improve food security. The results indicate that it is in the region's interests that continued reforms to improve agricultural markets are made at the multilateral level. Indeed, FAO (2012) point out that with respect to food security, the gains from multilateral reforms are likely to be even greater than those from bilateral and regional agreements.

Figure 2.11. **Main agro-food export and import products**

Exports, share of total value (%) in selected years

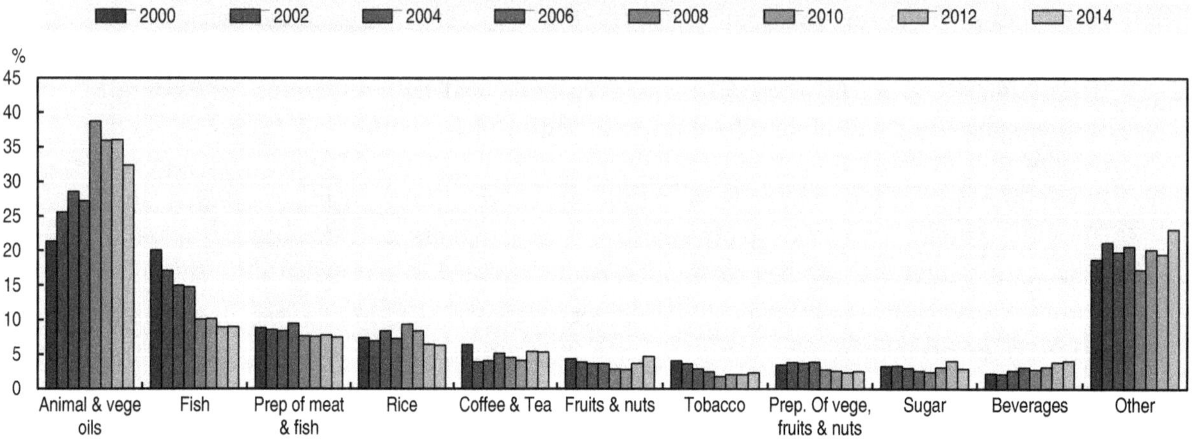

Imports, share of total value (%) in selected years

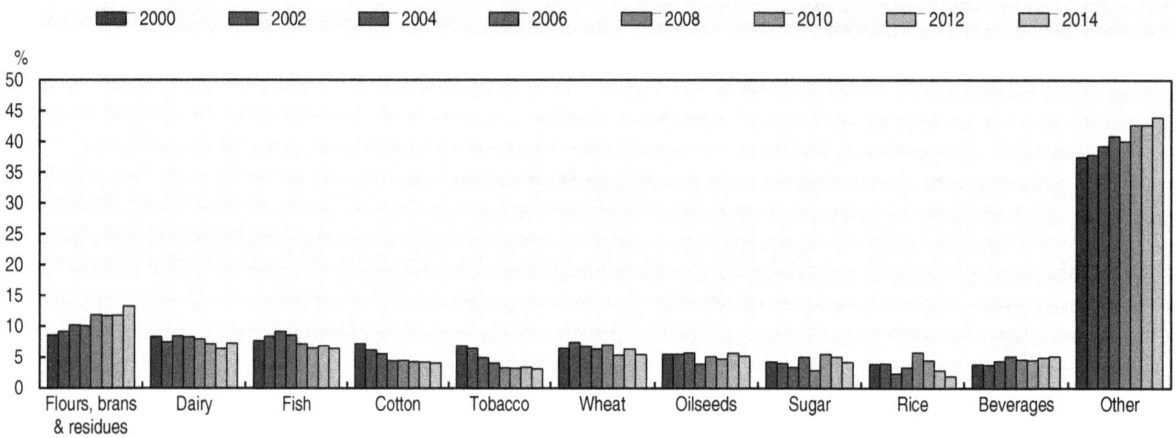

Source: WITS (2017), World Integrated Trade Solution, *https://wits.worldbank.org/WITS/WITS/Restricted/Login.aspx.*

StatLink *http://dx.doi.org/10.1787/888933521750*

Figure 2.12. **Net exports of rice**

USD billions, 2000 to 2014

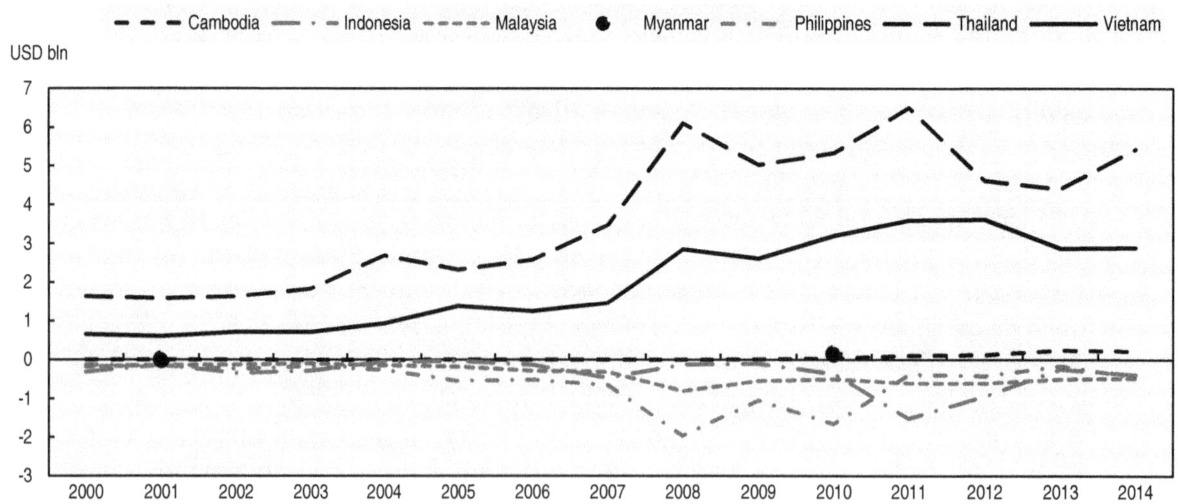

Notes: Data for Myanmar available for 2001 and 2010 only.

Source: WITS (2017), World Integrated Trade Solution, *https://wits.worldbank.org/WITS/WITS/Restricted/Login.aspx.*

StatLink *http://dx.doi.org/10.1787/888933521769*

However, for both, reform undertaken in the context of agreements needs to be accompanied by appropriate domestic policies that target labour markets, social safety nets and equity of opportunity to address the adjustment costs that will be created.

From a domestic viewpoint, the removal of trade restrictions is important for the agricultural sector to remain competitive and generate income for producers. As noted by FAO (2015), there are several dangers in excessive impediments to open trade. Distorting one commodity – usually rice in the case of Southeast Asia – affects resource allocation in general and will encourage producers to remain dedicated to rice production, reducing incentives to shift into the production of higher-value (return) crops. Beyond incomes, the influence of higher staple product prices on household budgets can impede better nutrition as access to the variety of foods needed for better nutrition is hampered. Such policies can also increase current food insecurity and the vulnerability of households to temporary food insecurity risks, as discussed below.

The rising presence in international agro-food markets is not simply a matter of exporting one commodity and importing another. Agricultural production, like that of other areas of the economy, has changed with the development of global value chains (GVCs). GVCs have arisen as both technology and changes in demand have allowed for a distribution of production so that the production of a good from raw material to final product now seldom takes place in the same location (Baldwin, 2012).

Recent data on agro-food trade in value added, as opposed to gross trade value, allows for GVC development in agricultural and food production systems to be observed (see Greenville, Kawasaki and Beaujeu, 2017). Instead of tracing individual product types across borders, the contribution of production in sectors in specific countries is observed, allowing for the value of any given trade flow to be broken up into the various contributions from sectors across the world, including in the countries in Southeast Asia.

For Southeast Asia, data on trade in value added reveals that the region is heavily integrated into world agro-food GVCs (Box 2.3). The region has strong agro-food GVC linkages to countries in other parts of Asia and to Europe. However, there appears to be significant gaps in regional inter-linkages (little trade flow of value added between countries), with the exception of some specific country links, such as Indonesia-Malaysia, and Cambodia and Lao PDR to Viet Nam.

For a number of sectors, including the large export sectors, foreign inputs form an important component of the export value. Such inputs, drawn from a diverse array of industries, help to improve competitiveness and can improve productivity within the industries that use them (Lopez-Gonzalez, 2016). For fisheries, fishery product exports from Thailand and Viet Nam rely on foreign supplied raw materials (often from within the region); these countries have higher backward integration into value chains than the ASEAN or world average (Greenville, Kawasaki and Beaujeu, 2017). These sectors also supply significant amounts of intermediate products that are used in other country exports. The important processing industries in these two countries significantly contribute to their economy through job creation and trade (FAO, 2016). The significant linkages between Southeast Asia and other countries worldwide mean that the competitiveness of agro-food exports is significantly influenced by policies that raise the cost of imported goods. Import barriers placed on agro-food products can effectively act as a tax on exports, limiting the domestic returns available from participation in agro-food GVCs (Greenville, Kawasaki and Beaujeu, 2017).

Box 2.3. **Southeast Asia a major player in agro-food GVCs**

A recent study by Greenville, Kawasaki and Beaujeu (2017) explored trade in value added data for 2011 for 20 different agro-food sectors. Examining trade in value added allows for the international trade of goods, including agricultural products, to be broken down into the various contributions from different sectors worldwide. Doing so reveals the GVC for different products.

GVCs can be characterised in a number of ways, but a common approach is to explore them from the sector-country perspective through measures of vertical specialisation – forward and backward participation. The forward indicator captures the extent to which a sector's exports form part of a production process in another country, contributing to that other country's exports (selling into GVCs), while the backward indicator indicates the extent to which imports from other countries are used in the production of a country's exports (buying from GVCs).

Southeast Asian participation in GVCs varies compared with world averages across the 20 agro-food sectors (Figure 2.13). For the oilseeds sector, there are strong linkages to ongoing GVCs largely through the vegetable oils & fats processing sector (processed palm oil). However, the vegetables oils and fats sector also has significant backward linkages, indicating that it uses a number of foreign inputs into its production processes to underpin its competitiveness – these range from imported raw palm fruit to chemical products and a significant use of imported trade and business services. Across the broader range of sectors, a large part of the differences in engagement is driven by structural factors (that is to say production possibilities due to climate and land availability, for example in the case of wheat), but not all. Globally, Greenville, Kawasaki and Beaujeu (2017) show that policy factors, such as trade policy settings, the agricultural enabling environment and policies in services are all important in explaining differences in GVC participation and domestic value added creation. In particular, they show that tariffs and other trade barriers, along with distorting forms of domestic support to the agricultural sector, act as an effective tax on value created though participation in agro-food GVCs.

Figure 2.13. **ASEAN and world GVC participation**

Backward and forward linkages, 2011

Backward (left); Forward (right)

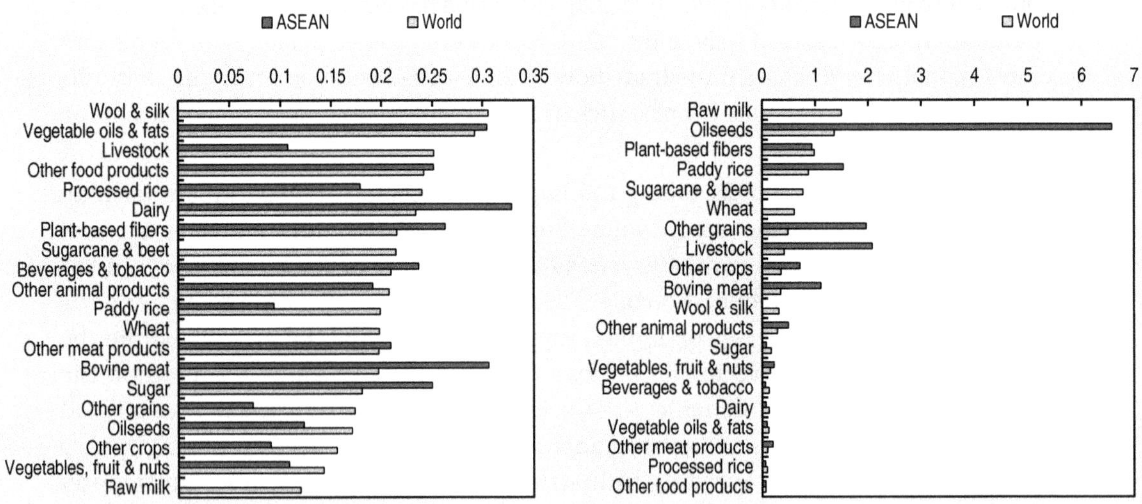

Source: Greenville, Kawasaki and Beaujeu (2017).

StatLink http://dx.doi.org/10.1787/888933521788

Agricultural policies in Southeast Asia: A focus on rice and self-sufficiency

Agricultural policy in Southeast Asia is interlinked with food security policy in a number of countries. In general, for much of the region, agricultural and food security policy can be characterised as "rice-centric", with governments employing a complex range of measures in an attempt to balance often competing objectives (Alavi et al., 2012; Dawe et al., 2014; OECD, 2017b). For both large and small rice producers, an emphasis is placed on rice production such that it is sufficient to meet domestic demand –indeed, policies oriented towards self-sufficiency are used throughout the region (Box 2.4). The policies chosen to pursue these objectives tend to vary. In general, for importing countries, they are related to attempts to spur domestic production through the use of price support, trade barriers and input subsidies. For exporting countries, governments use interventions in export markets (taxes, bans, licencing arrangements) along with attempts to "lock-in" a certain quantity of rice production (OECD, 2017b). This does not mean that other substantial investments to support agriculture have not been made. In particular, some countries have made substantial investments in the enabling environment, focusing on irrigation and other agricultural infrastructure (much of it though directed towards rice). However, the relative size of this type of expenditure suggests that these are not the main focus of policy in many countries.[7]

On the consumer side, some countries have public distribution and public stocking regimes aimed at provide subsidised rice and in some instance also at stabilising market prices. These are most notable in countries such as Indonesia, Malaysia and the Philippines (OECD, 2017b). While such regimes have stabilised prices compared to other Southeast Asian countries, as they are used in conjunction with trade barriers they have stabilised prices at much higher levels, bringing into question the net impact on food security. For example, in Indonesia domestic prices in 2012-14 were 70% above comparable world prices (OECD, 2016b) and trade and investment restrictions are reported to have placed added pressure on consumer prices for fish products (OECD, 2017b). It is worth noting, however, that much of the rice acquired for the market operations and public distribution is imported, indicating that these countries maintain an interest in having well-functioning international markets.

Stockholding policies are also seen on the exporter side, with Thailand at various points over time using government purchasing and stockholding policies as a means to influence producer incomes and influencing world prices (Permani and Vanzetti, 2014). Most notably, in 2011, the Thai Government built large stocks after it pledged to pay domestic rice producers 50% more than the market price. The Thai Government subsequently abandoned the scheme as its cost grew and world prices did not increase. Past reviews of the set of agriculture-related food security policies used in the region have pointed to shortcomings with current policy approaches, with some suggesting that opportunities exist to pursue alternative policies that can better address food security concerns in the longer term (Dawe et al., 2014; OECD, 2017b). Studies suggest that many of the interventions have created inefficiencies in resource allocation within the economies, discouraged private investment by creating greater uncertainties, and imposed significant budgetary costs on governments, and for which there are significant opportunity costs in terms of other policy priorities (OECD, 2017b). Further, large leakages and difficulties in effective targeting have characterised a number of food distribution programmes used in the region (Deuss, 2015).

Box 2.4. **Self-sufficiency policies common in Southeast Asia**

Almost all Southeast Asian countries have some form of self-sufficiency policy. The use of policies directed at achieving some level of self-sufficiency has increased since the 2007/08 food price crisis. The push towards self-sufficiency has often been framed around a desire to no longer be vulnerable to world price movements similar to those that were seen during this period – especially for rice – despite the fact that it was largely policy factors, and not global imbalances in supply and demand, that explained the food price spike (Alavi et al., 2012; OECD, 2008; Piesse and Thirtle, 2009; Naylor and Falcon, 2010; Headey, 2011).

Self-sufficiency policies are often supported by production targets for a particular commodity or set of commodities. Across Southeast Asia, almost all countries have some form of self-sufficiency related target (Table 2.2). Within this, Indonesia has the most ambitious set of targets, aiming for self-sufficiency across all main staple products. The Philippines is the only country which has coupled a drive for self-sufficiency in its two main staple crops (rice and maize) with attempts to diversify individual diets by encouraging consumption of a wider set of food products (Philippines Government, 2011).

These targets are further underpinned by a wide variety of output, input and trade-related interventions. Beyond the supply side, some countries have also sought to intervene in markets with the expressed aim of stabilising prices for the benefit of both producers and consumers. This intervention has taken the form of public stockholding policies, most notably in Indonesia, Malaysia and the Philippines.

Table 2.2. **Self-sufficiency targets of ASEAN members**

Country	Self-sufficiency target
Brunei Darussalam	Rice self-sufficiency of 20% by 2015 and 60% over the longer term (2035)
Cambodia	**No specific self-sufficiency targets**
Indonesia	Complete self-sufficiency (100% of domestic production) targets for rice, maize and soybeans by 2017 and beef and sugar by 2019
Lao PDR	Production targets for rice ~ 4.2 Mt by 2015 and rate of increase targets for other products. Absolute quantity targets of food production for some commodities
Malaysia	Self-sufficiency targets for rice of 90% of domestic consumption plus other production targets
Myanmar	**No specific self-sufficiency targets**
Philippines	Self-sufficiency in rice previously set for 2013, but later abandoned set year target. Self-sufficiency in maize production by 2013
Singapore	Increase self-sufficiency levels to 30% for eggs, 15% for fish and 10% for leafy vegetables
Thailand	**No specific self-sufficiency targets**
Viet Nam	Maintain a 2.5% rice yield increase per year until 2020, and the set aside of 3.8 m ha of land specifically for rice production

Source: Adapted from OECD (2017b).

In some instances, to spur production, policies have increased domestic prices with a view to increasing the availability of domestically-produced food. However, such policies are unlikely to be effective in helping to address food security for vulnerable consumer households. Moreover, the ineffective nature of this type of support in addressing the low farm incomes of the poorest – and in a number of cases the incidence of price support accruing to otherwise food secure households – suggests that even for poor rural producers, the long-run impacts on food security are questionable.

Beyond domestic policies, ASEAN has established a sound regional architecture to address many of the key food security challenges facing the region. ASEAN regional frameworks are developed by member states through the co-ordination of the ASEAN Secretariat, which is responsible for the organisation of the various working groups and meetings along with implementation of various ASEAN projects and activities. For agriculture and food security, the ASEAN Integrated Food Security Framework and the Strategic Plan for ASEAN Cooperation in Food, Agriculture and Forestry provide a solid platform on which ASEAN member states are pursuing policies to address long-term food security. These regional policy frameworks are underpinned by core policy areas and a number of "Strategic Thrusts", which set out actions for ASEAN member states to address food security. This regional framework is also supported by the ASEAN Plus Three Emergency Rice Reserve (APTERR) that seeks to provide food coverage across the region in times of severe short-term need and sits under the overall ASEAN Economic Community Blueprint. The general objective of these regional frameworks is to help address food security through greater regional integration. Beyond ASEAN, other regional structures exist, such as the Mekong River Commission, which are tasked to improve resource use and planning across a range of Southeast Asian countries.

Recent OECD analysis (OECD, 2017b) has indicated there are significant benefits on offer from additional efforts and policy choices that are consistent with the core policy areas identified in the regional frameworks. For example, further integration of regional rice markets, in line with the ASEAN Economic Community Blueprint, will help the region better manage food insecurity risks and, through the price effects created by integration, help to reduce regional undernourishment (Box 2.5). Rice market integration allows domestic production risk (and so price) risks to be hedged across the region, allowing individual countries scope to better manage domestic production risks that occur more frequently than international market risks. Overall, ASEAN rice market integration would reduce the undernourished population by 5% in the five countries examined (Indonesia, Myanmar, the Philippines, Thailand and Viet Nam).

However, the impact of regional integration will not be evenly felt. Both Indonesia and the Philippines would be expected to witness the largest improvements in food security, but at the same time, agricultural adjustment would take place as domestic rice production would be replaced in part by imports. For these countries, the provision of assistance specifically targeted at vulnerable households, and investments to allow producers who formerly benefited from higher prices to shift away from rice production would be required (Box 2.5). That said, even with full regional integration, for both Indonesia and the

Box 2.5. **Regional integration of rice markets good for regional food security**

The development of the ASEAN Economic Community AEC extends well beyond agriculture and aims to allow for the free flow of goods, services, investment and skilled labour across the region, along with the freer flow of capital. As such, it has the potential to significantly impact growth opportunities in the region, agricultural competiveness (within countries and for the region globally), along with important policy focuses such as food security.

Full economic integration will take time to occur. Nevertheless, in moving down this path, and through exploiting the potential benefits of developing a single market and production base, food security could be enhanced. Bello (2005) argues that free trade in rice and maize, enhanced by improved trade facilitation measures and the harmonisation of food regulations, could improve food security for each of the ten ASEAN members. Such measures would exploit the natural diversity in agricultural production systems across the region to the benefit of all members. Others have explored further integration specifically in the area of rice. Rice has remained a product which has only seen little steps taken to regional integration. Hoang and Meyers (2015) found that for the importing countries of Indonesia, Malaysia and the Philippines, integration of rice markets could lead to falls of around 30-40% in prices, whereas price rises on world markets were around 30%. It is noted, however, moves to integration are best realised through shared actions over time. In this way, the disruptions to world markets are minimised and time is allowed for adjustments in both exporting and importing countries, avoiding pressures on world markets.

Box 2.5. **Regional integration of rice markets good for regional food security** *(cont.)*

Recent OECD analysis supports findings on the potential positive links between regional rice market integration and food security. The analysis explored both tariff reductions but more importantly further reforms that see full integration and the convergence of producer prices across the region. The analysis shows that there is much to be gained – in terms of managing risk and improving food security – from moving towards regionally integrated rice markets. For the economies involved, the analysis suggests that regional integration of rice markets could increase total welfare by around 2.8 billion USD annually (once full integration is achieved in 2025). Of this, USD 1 billion accrues to the Philippines with the remaining gains spread more evenly across countries. Where integration occurs, fall of between 25 and 45% in prices are seen in importing markets (Indonesia, Malaysia and the Philippines), with prices rising in the other regional markets by between 9 and 17%. Underlying these estimates, however, are a range of winners and losers from the reforms and it is important to deal with the adjustment this entails, in particular, it is important to provide new opportunities for displaced rice farmers and safety nets for households put at risk in both importing and exporting countries.

At the household level, the impact of ASEAN rice market integration was explored using individual household level data; it was found that integration would reduce undernourished populations by 5% in the five countries examined (Indonesia, Myanmar, the Philippines, Thailand and Viet Nam). The 5% fall in undernourishment accounts for both the benefits from price falls in some countries and costs from price rises in others. Of these five countries, undernourishment in two rice-importing countries – Indonesia and the Philippines – would fall the most due to the resulting decreases in domestic prices (in Indonesia, Malaysia and the Philippines prices are projected to fall by 39%, 26% and 45% respectively). The integration of regional rice markets also helps to mitigate the otherwise large impact of weather risks in the region. In particular, increased consumer access in both Indonesia and the Philippines could offset the food insecurity impact of a regional *El Niño* or of domestic crop failure, which are identified as the largest risks to food security for these two countries. While the regional *El Niño* scenario increases the undernourished population in five ASEAN member states by 49% under the current rice trade regime, integrating the regional rice market could mitigate the impact to a 11% increase. However, integration will have negative impacts on producers in importing countries and poor consumers in exporting countries due to the price effects. While safety nets can help to mitigate the potential negative effects of these, it is also likely that the gradual integration of the regional rice market would actually prevent a sharp increase in consumer rice prices in exporting countries.

Regional integration will also have an impact on world markets as there would be some diversion of trade. In total, integration would see an increase in regional trade by 10 Mt, about half of which would come from a diversion of exports that would have gone to the rest of the world (with the difference attributable to higher production growth and lower consumption growth in exporting countries). Reduced supply to the world market would cause international prices to rise by approximately 8%, thus impacting on food security in countries outside the region.

In addition, greater involvement of the private sector in regional rice trade could help to facilitate the necessary market integration, as well as providing benefits in terms of greater efficiency, reduced distortions and greater potential for growth. Viet Nam could, for example, allow its private exporters to play a greater role in the export market, while in the Philippines, Malaysia and Indonesia; the role of state agencies in imports could be restricted to the neutral management of emergency stocks to enable the greater involvement of private traders.

Source: OECD (2017b); Furuhashi and Gay (2017, forthcoming).

Philippines, despite a shift to larger import volumes, 89% and 73% of their respective domestic consumption would continue to be provided by local production (compared with current levels of 99% to 86% respectively). This highlights that in both countries, regional integration and a vibrant and internationally competitive rice sector can indeed co-exist.

Regional integration will also have impacts outside Southeast Asia. Rice trade is concentrated to a few large exporters globally, and as such, the shift in supplies to other Southeast Asian countries will influence world prices and supplies in other regions. In particular, the out-of-region effects would see world prices rise by 8%.

Fisheries policies in Southeast Asia: The sustainability and food security challenge

Like agriculture, the fishery sector in Southeast Asia is dominated by small-scale producers. Coupled with difficulties in managing often open access resources, this presents a number of challenges for regional policy makers as they seek to ensure that production is sustainable. In conjunction with this, like for agriculture, fishery policies are often interlinked with food security objectives. Less information is available on a consistent basis across the region on fisheries management policies, however; in general all countries recognise the sustainability challenges facing their fisheries sectors, but have taken differing steps to address them.

In Indonesia, for example, the main objective underpinning fisheries sector policy relates to increasing domestic production in order to increase the availability of seafood in the country, as well as supporting the livelihoods of artisanal fishers and aquaculture producers (OECD, 2017b). An ambitious programme to achieve this objective has been put in place that combines attempts to address illegal industrial fishing; promoting the development of the artisanal fleet through modernisation; encouraging the expansion of artisanal aquaculture production by supporting the creation of artisanal cooperatives; restricting imports to protect domestic producers and fishers from competition; and improving value creation by investing in infrastructure and attracting foreign investment to the processing sector. Fisheries policies in the Philippines also feature food security objectives linked to production, employment and poverty reduction (FAO, 2017d).

Malaysia, the Philippines and Thailand, along with Indonesia, all have policies targeting illegal, unreported and unregulated (IUU) fishing but to varying degrees (FAO, 2017d). These policies ultimately seek to reduce fishing pressure and better allocate the returns from fishery resources to domestic fishers. Malaysia also has in place a series of spatial management tools implemented through marine protected areas. Such measures have been argued to help improve fishery management outcomes in instances where more direct and efficient policy measures cannot be implemented (Greenville and MacAulay, 2007) – in this case due to the small scale nature of producers.

Policies in both Cambodia and Viet Nam are heavily focused on the development of the aquaculture sector (FAO, 2017d). For Viet Nam, there has been a focus on developing new varieties to expand access to international markets while at the same time attempting to better comply with a number of market requirements related to product safety and production techniques. Increasing the competitiveness of Vietnamese producers, by improving domestic transport links within the country and facilitating the movement of product from production sites to export hubs, is also a priority. For Cambodia, policy efforts are seeking to exploit production synergies with rice cultivation, and so have a small-scale production focus.

Medium-term outlook

The previous two decades have witnessed substantial changes within the agriculture, fishery and food sectors of the Southeast Asia region. The ongoing policy environment and changes in international markets, coupled with the continued evolution in the region's economies and societies and growing environmental issues, all form important driving influences over the next decade. The key questions facing the Outlook include not only how food security in the different countries of the region will evolve, but also whether and how the region's trade profile may change in a way that may affect international markets.

Key economic and social factors underlying the agricultural outlook for the region

The region has developed considerably over the past 15 years, a trend that is expected to continue. Going forward, key influences on the medium-term outlook will include continued relatively high levels of economic growth, consumption changes (both regionally and globally) and population growth.

Economic growth for Southeast Asia the outlook is relatively optimistic (Figure 2.14). For four of the countries examined in the region, per capita GDP growth is projected to be higher than that experienced over the past 15 years (2002-16). Furthermore, growth rates are expected to exceed those seen in developed countries – exceeding OECD and EU averages – but for all but Myanmar, per capita growth is expected to be below that of the People's Republic of China (hereafter "China").

Figure 2.14. **Past and projected GDP per capita growth in Southeast Asia**

Average annual per capita growth rates (%), selected periods

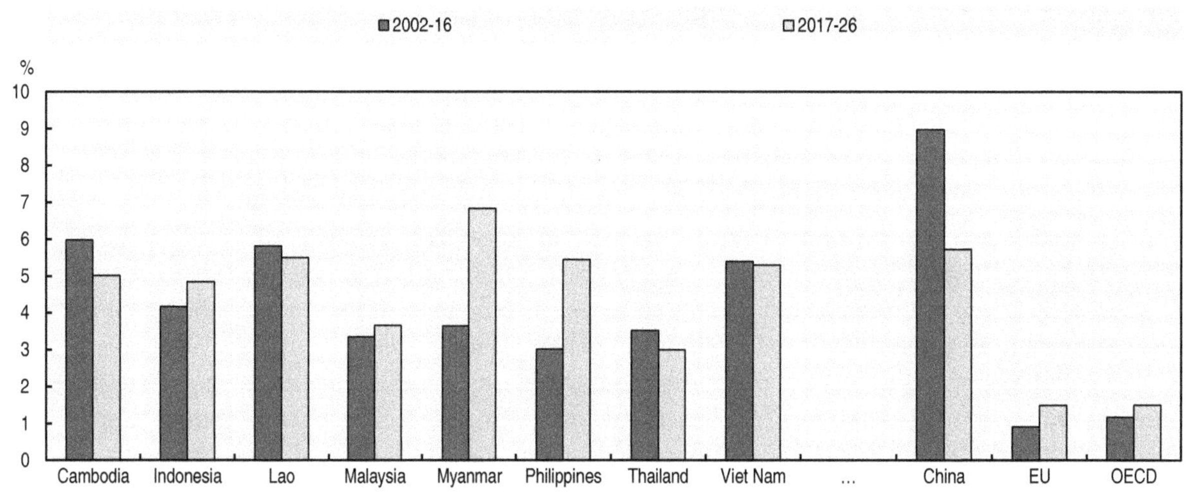

Source: IMF (2016); OECD-FAO (2017), "OECD-FAO Agricultural Outlook", OECD Agriculture statistics (database), *http://dx.doi.org/10.1787/agr-data-en*.

StatLink http://dx.doi.org/10.1787/888933521807

The expected high levels of growth in the Southeast Asian region will have effects on agro-food markets. First, higher growth should reduce poverty levels, which will in turn contribute to increases in demand and the reduction of undernourishment. Second, higher incomes will also change the *nature* of demand. As incomes grow, there will be a substitution away from some staple crops, such as rice, to other products, particularly animal products. Third, the changes in economic growth are occurring alongside population growth. Higher population levels will lift demand across the board for agro-food products, augmenting the abovementioned income effects for some products.

Continued shifts in consumption away from cereals

As the region develops, income levels rise; and as people move to urban settings, consumer buying patterns will also change. With rising incomes, the general transition from staple cereal consumption to protein based diets is expected to occur over the medium term in Southeast Asia. For this region, the key changes will revolve around shifts in demand for rice. Since the early 1960s, countries in Southeast Asia have seen drops in the relative importance of rice in meeting total caloric consumption. The rates of change have been most significant for both Thailand and Malaysia (which have the highest per capita income), indicating that diets have diversified most in these countries compared with the 1960s. In contrast, the importance of rice in the average diet has increased in the Philippines due to rising incomes of the poorest (Lantican, Sombilla and Quilloy, 2013), and in Brunei Darussalam more recently, albeit to a lesser extent and from a much smaller base. Nevertheless, data on household consumption in five Southeast Asian countries (Indonesia, Myanmar, the Philippines, Thailand and Viet Nam) reveals the income effect; in other words, wealthy households consume less rice than poorer households (OECD, 2017b). Similar effects are likely to be seen at the global level, with demand for rice expected to fall relative to that of other products (Sharma, 2014). Despite this, income and population growth will see total demand for rice and other products increase over the medium term.

In terms of expenditure shares, the most notable change in consumption (expressed as shares of total expenditure) relates to the continued fall in rice's share of total consumption – from nearly 30% in 2001 to 21% in 2016, falling further to 20% in 2026 (Figure 2.15). For the other major consumption items – those of meat and eggs and fish, shares are expected to remain stable over the projection period.

Figure 2.15. **Changes in consumption in Southeast Asia**

Food expenditure shares (%)

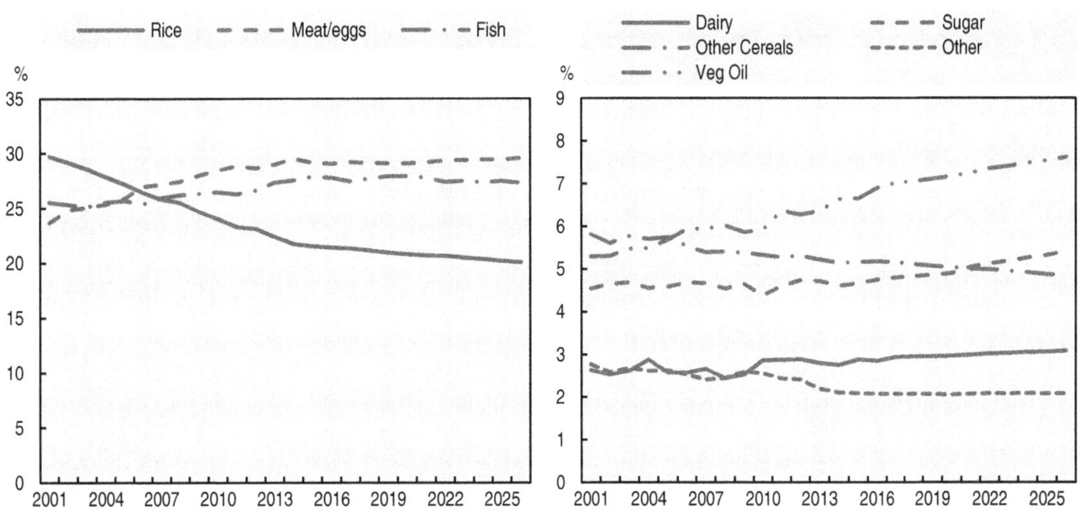

Note: Apparent food consumption of modelled products valued at estimated retail prices in USD in 2010.

Source: OECD-FAO (2017), "OECD-FAO Agricultural Outlook", OECD Agriculture statistics (database), *http://dx.doi.org/10.1787/agr-data-en.*

StatLink http://dx.doi.org/10.1787/888933521826

Of the other commodities, both sugar and vegetable oils are products which experience more significant changes in demand. For both of these, the projected changes in income are associated with an increase in consumption expenditure share of close to 1% per year between 2016 and 2026.

Slowing population growth

Population is expected to continue growing but at slower rates than observed in the past. Over the projection period, total population growth in Southeast Asian countries (excluding Myanmar) is projected to fall from the 1.3% annual growth experienced in the period 2001-16 to 0.9%. This overall growth masks large differences across countries – Lao PDR is projected to experience annual growth of around 1.5% compared to close to zero growth in Thailand. Population projections also indicate that, over the next 10 years, the rural population within the region will start to decline. Continued strong growth in the urban population will mean that urban populations will exceed rural populations by 2020.

With continued strong GDP growth and falling population growth rates, per capita incomes are likely to rise faster than in the past. Such changes will accelerate shifts in demand as highlighted above. However, for food security and poverty alleviation, it is important that the projected growth is *inclusive* and that Southeast Asian countries are able to avoid the widening of income inequalities.

The outlook for production and prices in Southeast Asia

Production

The changes in production within Southeast Asia projected over the medium term are a combination of both domestic supply and demand effects along with feedback from international markets. The relative influence of domestic and international impacts will depend on the relative exposure to international markets by different sectors. For example, production of vegetable oils in the region will be more influenced by international markets under current policy settings than many other sectors as 70% of production is exported (in 2016).

For individual countries, projected growth rates vary (Figure 2.16). Highest growth rates are projected for the least developed countries – Lao PDR, Myanmar and Cambodia. However, strong growth rates are also observed for Viet Nam and Thailand, two of the region's biggest agricultural exporters.

For the region as a whole, while agriculture and fishery production is expected to grow, slowing growth rates in a number of countries will mean that the growth of regional production will slow relative to world production growth. This means the region's share in total world production is expected to remain relatively stable over the medium term. Rising land and environmental factors will play a role in these changes. Net agriculture and fish production is projected to grow at the rate of 1.8% per year over the next decade, down from a robust rate of 2.7% per year experienced over the previous ten years (Figure 2.17).

The slow-down in production in the region is mostly due to reduced growth in fishery production which is projected to fall to a growth rate of 1.2% per year, down from annual growth of over 3.6% seen over the past 15 years (Figure 2.18). With the high share of fishery production in total production, the effect of this slow-down is significant. Most of the slow-down in production is derived from the slowing of growth in aquaculture as past expansion in activities are projected to be limited by land availability, environmental constraints and

Figure 2.16. **Net agriculture and fish production across Southeast Asia**

Index values

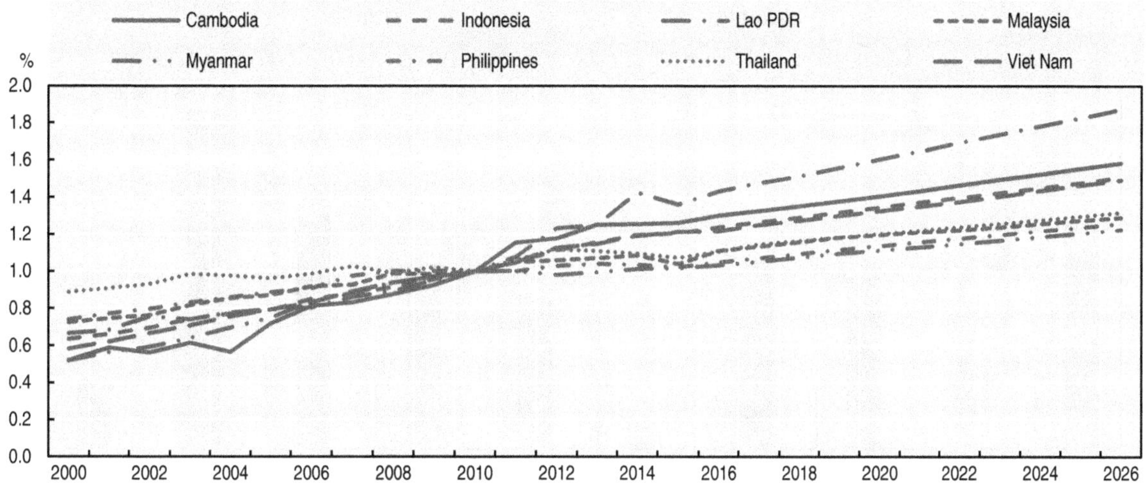

Source: OECD-FAO (2017), "OECD-FAO Agricultural Outlook", OECD Agriculture statistics (database), *http://dx.doi.org/10.1787/agr-data-en.*

StatLink *http://dx.doi.org/10.1787/888933521845*

Figure 2.17. **Southeast Asian versus world agriculture and fish production**

Average annual growth rates and share of world trade (%)

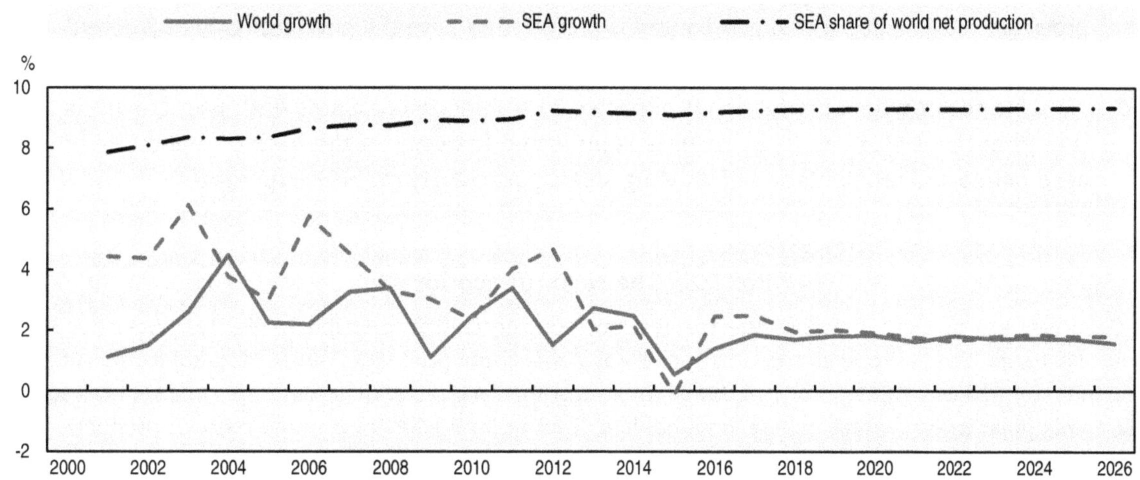

Source: OECD-FAO (2017), "OECD-FAO Agricultural Outlook", OECD Agriculture statistics (database), *http://dx.doi.org/10.1787/agr-data-en.*

StatLink *http://dx.doi.org/10.1787/888933521864*

market opportunities. Similarly, the past expansions in capture fishery production, driven through inland capture fisheries, are not projected to continue as pressure on already exploited stocks is expected to cap production at current levels, Indeed, there is a risk that production could fall if management practices are not improved.

The region's other major crop, palm oil (captured through vegetable oils), is also projected to slow in growth (Figure 2.18). Past expansion in production has been driven by both yield improvements but importantly by area expansion. Production is projected to fall from a growth rate of close to 6.5% over the past 15 years to around 2% over the next ten years. For rice, the third largest production activity in value terms, the region is projected to grow at a rate of around 1.6% per year, slightly higher than that seen in the past decade but lower than the growth rate observed over the past 15 years. At the regional level, commodities anticipated to

Figure 2.18. **Changes in major production activities in Southeast Asia**

Average annual growth rates (%)

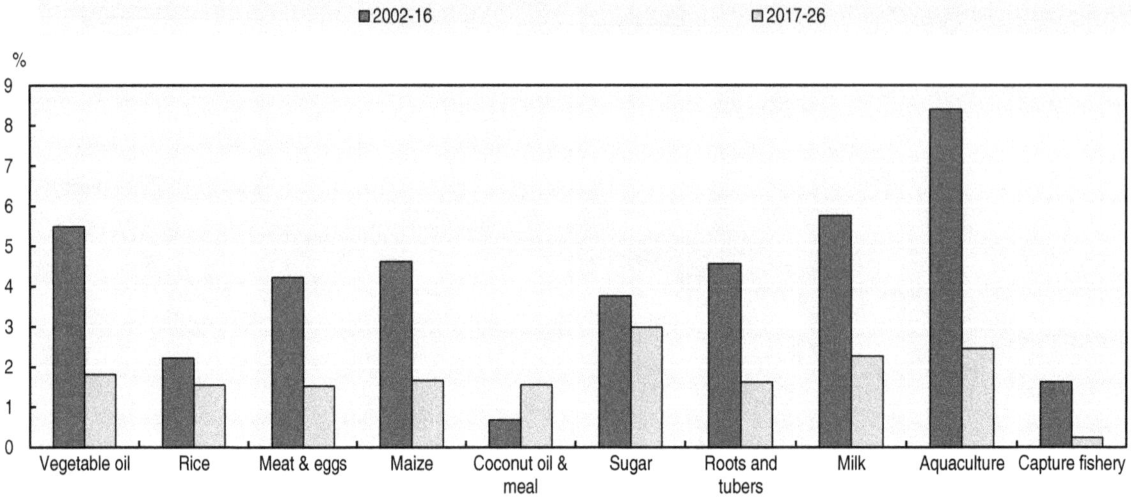

Source: OECD-FAO (2017), "OECD-FAO Agricultural Outlook", OECD Agriculture statistics (database), *http://dx.doi.org/10.1787/agr-data-en.*

StatLink *http://dx.doi.org/10.1787/888933521883*

grow most strongly include are sugar (3.0%/yr) and milk (2.3%/yr), albeit at slower rates than in the past. For meat and eggs, production growth is similarly projected to slow and there are projected compositional changes. Poultry is projected to have the strongest growth (1.8%/yr) and strengthening its lead over pig meat as the largest meat sector in the region.

One sector where production is expected to accelerate compared with past growth is that of coconut (Box 2.6). This increase is projected to occur on the back of replanting of aged palms and rehabilitation of growing areas, particularly in the Philippines.

Box 2.6. **The coconut economy**

Coconuts are cultivated across the tropics, but commercial production is highly concentrated in Southeast Asia. The Philippines accounts for 44% of global copra production and Indonesia follows at 28%. The industry makes significant contributions to the agri-food sectors of these countries and is also a socio-economic pillar in rural areas, where smallholders account for 80-90% of primary coconut production. In the Philippines alone, an estimated 25 million people depend on the coconut industry.

Despite 1 Mha of new coconut plantings during the last decade, global coconut production stagnated as a result of declining productivity. This downward trend was due to aged palms, insufficient access to inputs, underdeveloped institutional capacity and numerous pests and diseases. The situation has also been intensified by the devastation of large coconut-producing regions by increasingly frequent severe weather events, such as typhoon Yolanda in 2014.

Palm kernel oil and coconut oil are the main raw materials of the vegetal oleo chemical industry. The small-scale structure of the coconut plantations and processing plants, combined with the rapid expansion of the highly concentrated and industrialised palm oil industry, have caused many processors to shift to more competitive palm kernel oil. Despite challenges, the global demand for certain coconut products has increased substantially in recent years – notably for high-value added products such as coconut water, coconut sugar and virgin coconut oil. Further investments into productivity and competitiveness of the sector are needed, allowing farmers to take full advantage of these opportunities to improve and stabilise their incomes.

Box 2.6. **The coconut economy** *(cont.)*

In the Philippines (and India), government efforts are now underway to improve coconut production and productivity. Ongoing replanting and rehabilitation programmes are expected to increase the productivity of the aged palms going forward, supporting the projected recovery in production over the next ten years (Figure 2.19). About 70% of the 1.1 Mt production increase in copra by 2026, will originate from improved yields. While planted area has remained largely fixed in the recent past, the outlook foresees additional planting of coconut palms in Indonesia, the Philippines and Viet Nam over the next decade.

Figure 2.19. **Global copra production by region**

Total production, Mt

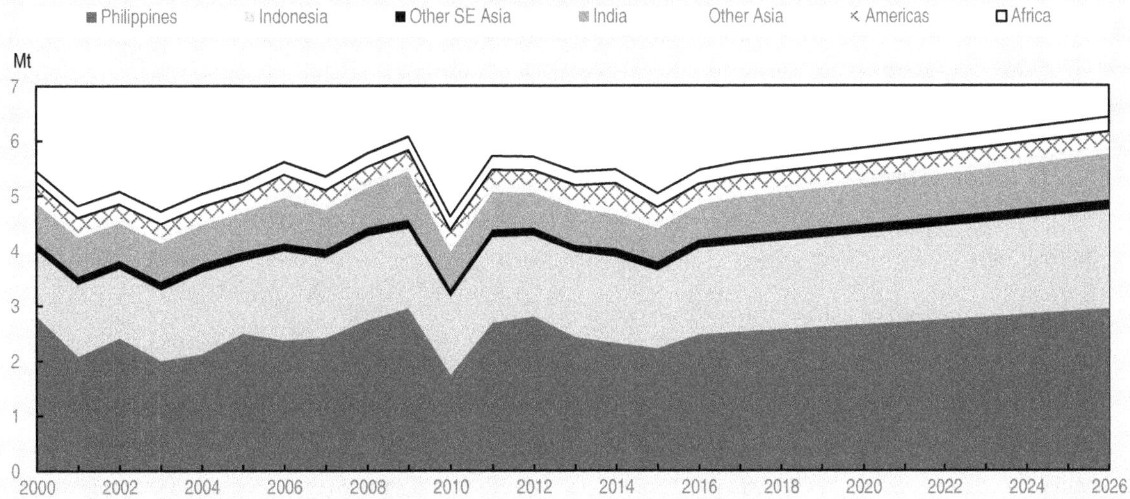

Source: OECD-FAO (2017), "OECD-FAO Agricultural Outlook", OECD Agriculture statistics (database), *http://dx.doi.org/10.1787/agr-data-en.*

StatLink *http://dx.doi.org/10.1787/888933521902*

For individual countries within the region the changes in production vary along existing lines of relative production levels and comparative advantages (Figure 2.20). For example, the growth of vegetable oil is concentrated in Indonesia and Malaysia, with sugar production growth concentrated in Thailand. Similarly, fishery production growth mainly flows from increased production in Indonesia and Viet Nam. The story for rice is more mixed. All countries are seen to increase production with large volume changes seen in both the large exporting countries of Thailand and Viet Nam, along with significant increases in the more populous countries such as Indonesia. However, uncertainties exist over the rice production increases in these countries, and in particular in Viet Nam due to concerns over water salinization (Box 2.7).

Improvements in productivity of agricultural production systems, through both the closing of yield gaps and the intensification of production processes, are projected to be the most significant drivers of production growth (Figure 2.21). The region as a whole has only limited scope for increases in production to be created through increases in land use, as both existing lands are already exploited and due to rising land competition for other uses (such as for urban or industrial purposes). Across major crop production activities in the region, total area harvested is projected to increase by only 4% over the next decade compared with a 16% increase in area seen in the ten years prior to the 2014-16 base period. Increased area allocated for sugar cane, palm and coconut production account for

Figure 2.20. **Changes in major production activities in Southeast Asia**

Increase in production across major production activities, 2017-26

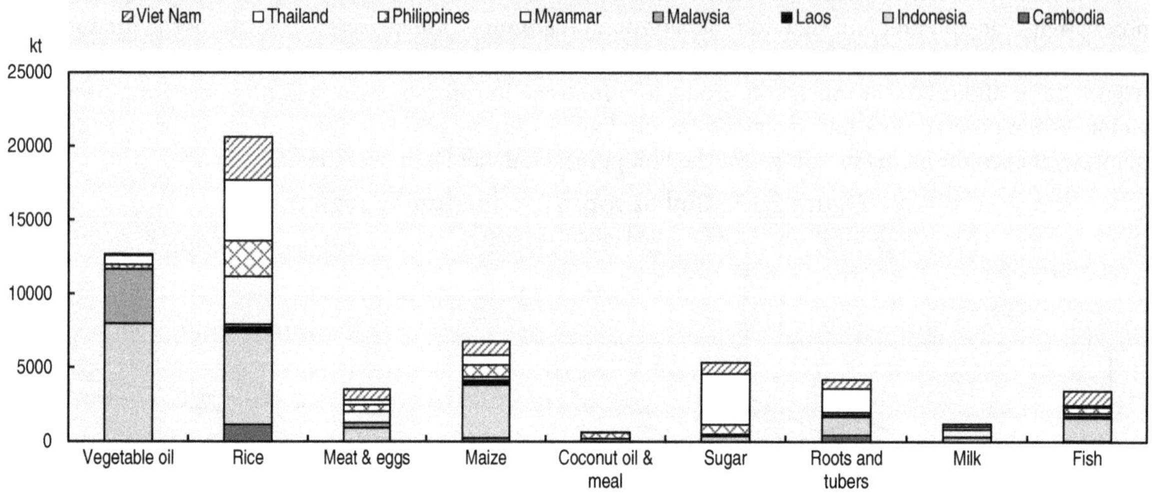

Source: OECD-FAO (2017), "OECD-FAO Agricultural Outlook", OECD Agriculture statistics (database), *http://dx.doi.org/10.1787/agr-data-en.*

StatLink *http://dx.doi.org/10.1787/888933521921*

Box 2.7. **The impact of water salinization on Viet Nam's rice sector**

Viet Nam's agricultural sector plays an important role in the country's economy. Following the introduction of the overall policy package of *doi moi* in the late 1980s, rice output rose rapidly to a level that remains substantially above domestic needs. This success story, however, is now in jeopardy, above all due to climate change and the growing problem of soil salinization.

Problems of soil salinization

Salinity can cause problems for rice production in both irrigated and rain-fed areas. Rice is highly sensitive to salt stress in its early growth stage. Transplanted seedlings can die and establishing a sufficient crop stand becomes very difficult. Salinity in coastal areas evolves during the season: it is high in both the soil and water during the dry season, but decreases after the monsoon rains begin. However, the salt concentration increases once again during the dry season when most fields are left barren. Salinity problems are also encountered in some inland areas due to improper irrigation.

During the 2015/16 cropping season, severe and prolonged dry weather associated with *El Niño* caused the worst salinity problems in almost a century. In 2016, the high concentration of salt in the soil resulted in severe crop damage, reducing the harvest by 4%, nearly 2 Mt below the 2015 level.

How many areas of croplands are vulnerable to salinity problems?

Soil and water salinization in the dry season is a major problem in the coastal Mekong Delta (Tuong et al., 2003; Carew-Reid, 2007), with around 1.8 Mha subject to dry season salinity annually (Carew-Reid, 2007; MRC, 2010). During the low flow months of March and April, saline water intrudes 40-50 km inland from estuaries via the main river systems (White, 2002; Sam, 2006). Salinity can damage both high-yielding rice (in double or triple rice cropping systems) and traditional rice (in rice-shrimp rotational farming system) paddies. According to a report by the Vietnamese Ministry of Agriculture and Rural Development (MARD, 2011), 100 000 ha of the 650 000 ha of high-yielding paddies in the Mekong delta are at a high risk of dry-season saltwater intrusion.

Box 2.7. **The impact of water salinization on Viet Nam's rice sector** *(cont.)*

Impact on the rice production projection and food security

The medium-term outlook suggests that Viet Nam will continue to expand its rice production, securing its position as a leading rice exporter. Production is expected to shift towards a superior rice, allowing the country to compete with Thailand, the world's premier rice exporter. These baseline projections, however, assume that Viet Nam will be able to confront the challenges that are arising from climate change and the growing salinization of its paddy fields. Failing this, there is evidence that salinization will result in a serious drop in production, thus jeopardising the country's export position, as well as compromising the income and food security of its smallholder farmers. Some authors even suggest that Viet Nam could become a net importer if the problem of salization is not adequately addressed (Dijk et al., 2014; Chen, 2012), which in turn would affect the overall food supply situation in Southeast Asia. To address these challenges, the Vietnamese government has developed a national strategic plan for 2008-20 (MONRE, 2008).

most of the growth in area. Rice area is projected to increase by less than 1% by 2026 compared to the 2014-16 base period. However, strong yield growth is projected for all commodities, particularly for palm and coconut, where yields fell in the last decade due to new investments in area expansion.

Figure 2.21. **Area and yield changes for major production activities in Southeast Asia**

Changes in area and yield across major production activities (%)

Area (left); Yield (right)

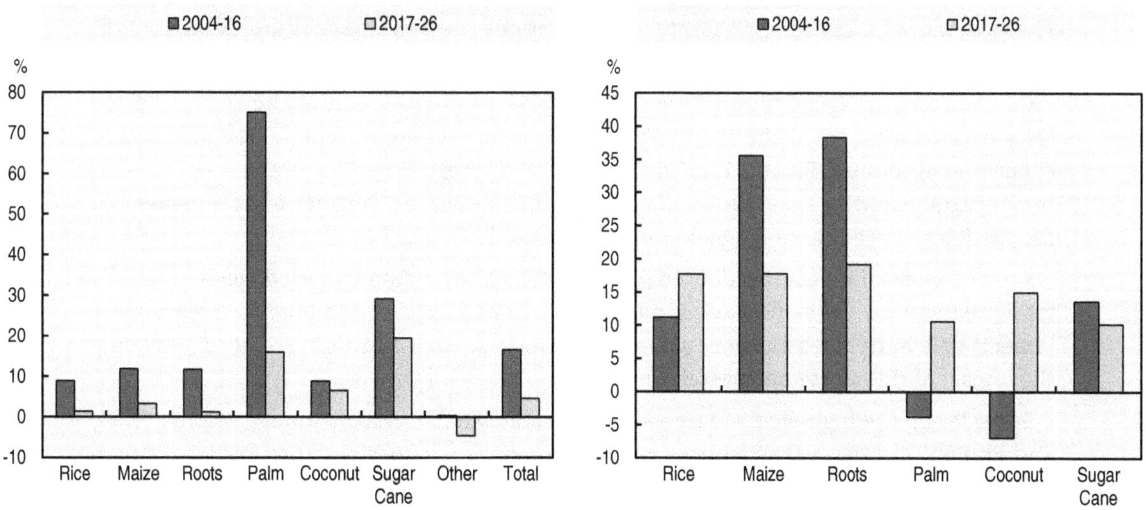

Source: OECD-FAO (2017), "OECD-FAO Agricultural Outlook", OECD Agriculture statistics (database), *http://dx.doi.org/10.1787/agr-data-en.*

StatLink *http://dx.doi.org/10.1787/888933521940*

Production within the region will also become increasingly affected by changes in climatic conditions brought about from climate change. While over the medium term such impacts are difficult to project, the region has been identified as one of the most affected regions worldwide. In the last few decades, sea levels in the region have been reported to have risen by between 1 and 3 mm per year (ADB, 2009). The number of floods, cyclones and periods of drought has also increased, leading to a decline in water, soil and land resources, with further increases expected in the future (Cruz et al., 2007). These changes have implications for both terrestrial and marine-based production systems and due to the pressures created are likely to lead to further conflicts between environmental outcomes and food production (Box 2.8).

Box 2.8. **Mangroves and land use change: The case of Southeast Asia**

Mangroves are immensely important ecosystems, harbouring rich aquatic and terrestrial biodiversity. They offer multiple ecosystem services including providing fish habitat, supporting nutrient cycling, carbon storage, and salinity regulation. Currently, mangrove forests cover around 14 Mha, of which around one-third are in Southeast Asia (FAO, 2007). Losses of between 30 to 50% are estimated to have occurred over the last five decades due to land-use change for aquaculture, agriculture and infrastructure development (Donato, 2011). The degree of mangrove loss has varied by region, with hotspots in Myanmar, particularly in Rakhine state, in Indonesian Sumatra and Borneo, and in Malaysia. By comparison, the rate of mangrove deforestation was considerably lower in Thailand, Viet Nam, and the Philippines.

Policies to promote food security and local development, coupled with limited protection of open access mangrove resources, were the main forces behind mangrove land-use change in coastal mangrove areas from 2000 to 2012 (Richards and Friess, 2016). Conversion of forest area into aquaculture (30% of total mangrove area loss), was particularly dominant in Indonesia, Cambodia, and the Philippines. Over the coming decade, Indonesia's aquaculture production is expected to expand by about 37%, the Philippines by 25%, and Cambodia by 47%. At least some of this is expected to take place in the coastal margins, therefore, pressure on the mangrove areas will continue. However, policies encouraging intensification rather than expansion have now been implemented. These, along with tighter environmental regulations for new aquaculture development, mean the impact on mangroves is expected to decline.

Conversion to rice agriculture from 2000 to 2012, was important at the regional scale (22% of total area) with the main concentration in Myanmar, where rice production expansion accounted for much of the mangrove deforestation. The Outlook projects no further expansion in the country's rice area in the coming decade, with increases in production achieved thorough yield improvements.

Palm oil plantations also accounted for a significant part of mangrove conversion (16% of total area) during the same period, particularly in Malaysia and Indonesia. This *Outlook* projects only minor area expansion of oil palm in these two countries up to 2026, reducing the impact of this sector on coastal forests.

Considering the high biodiversity value of mangroves for carbon storage (Alongi, 2014) and climate mitigation, as well as the other ecosystem services they provide, much stronger environmental safeguards are required. One option to ensure that their utilisation is carried out sustainably, would be the introduction of payments for environmental services (carbon storage) targeted at local communities that derive their livelihoods from mangroves and its multiple services.

Increases in agricultural production are also likely to place further pressure on the environment. Palm oil is one production activity where environmental trade-offs have been identified. The effects of increases in production of palm oil on the environment in the region, however, will be heavily influenced by both of the environmental policies directed at the sector but also the policies that directly influence production – such as biofuels policies and other domestic support measures. Indonesia, Malaysia and Thailand all have biofuels policies targeting the use of palm oil. In Thailand, the government has set up targets for ethanol and biodiesel use of 4.1 Bln L and 5.1 Bln L by 2036. Indonesia similarly has targets, currently set at 10% (biodiesel mandate) but targeted to reach 30% by 2020 (however, at present, current usage is around 6%). For the region, biofuels production is projected to increase by around 4% year, helping to stimulate demand for palm oil production.

Prices

Across Southeast Asia's major production crops, world prices are expected to decline slightly over the medium term (see Chapter 1). For example, real prices for rice and vegetable oils, the region's largest export items, are projected to fall. A similar picture is seen for the region's main import products. These shifts at the global level are driven by the projected changes in productivity and input use counterbalanced against growth in demand. For most commodities, output growth is expected to exceed demand growth placing downward pressure on real prices over the medium term.

The extent to which regional prices will vary in line with world prices will depend on the trade exposure of each of the individual countries within the region. For rice, Indonesia, Malaysia and the Philippines have in place border controls (tariffs and licensing arrangements) along with domestic support policies that limit price transmission. Indeed, in these countries rice prices are considerably higher (more than would be expected to arise from transport costs) and less variable (OECD, 2017b). However, even for these countries, the underlying drivers of price falls; that of rising productivity levels, are expected to hold and would place downward pressure on domestic prices if current policy settings are maintained. For others, such as the larger exporters of Thailand and Viet Nam, trends in world rice prices are expected to follow similar patterns.

The outlook for trade in the region

Over the medium term, the increase of production along lines of already established comparative advantages, coupled with rising incomes and demands for a wider variety of food products leads to a deepening of existing trade across commodity groups. In other words, the region is projected to increase the volume of products it currently exports while also increasing the volume of the products it currently imports (Figure 2.22). The largest changes in this deepening of trade balances are seen for vegetable oil and rice, where the trade surplus is increasing, and wheat and maize where the trade deficit is increasing. The trade deficit for dairy powders grows to some 1.1 Mt, which is a significant in size relative to world markets, at over 17% of global imports

Across these individual products, the contribution to the changes in the net trade balances flow along the pre-exiting trading patterns (Figure 2.23). For vegetable oils, rising net exports are driven by increased exports from Malaysia and Indonesia, while for rice increased net exports are driven by rising exports from Viet Nam and Thailand. For sugar, the region shows differing patterns with Thailand increasing exports while a number of other countries in the region increasing their net imports.

Implications of market developments for food security

The projected changes in production, trade, incomes and prices over the medium term across Southeast Asia will have a significant impact on food security. These changes will

Figure 2.22. **Changes in the trade balance of major commodities in Southeast Asia**

Net trade balance (exports less imports)

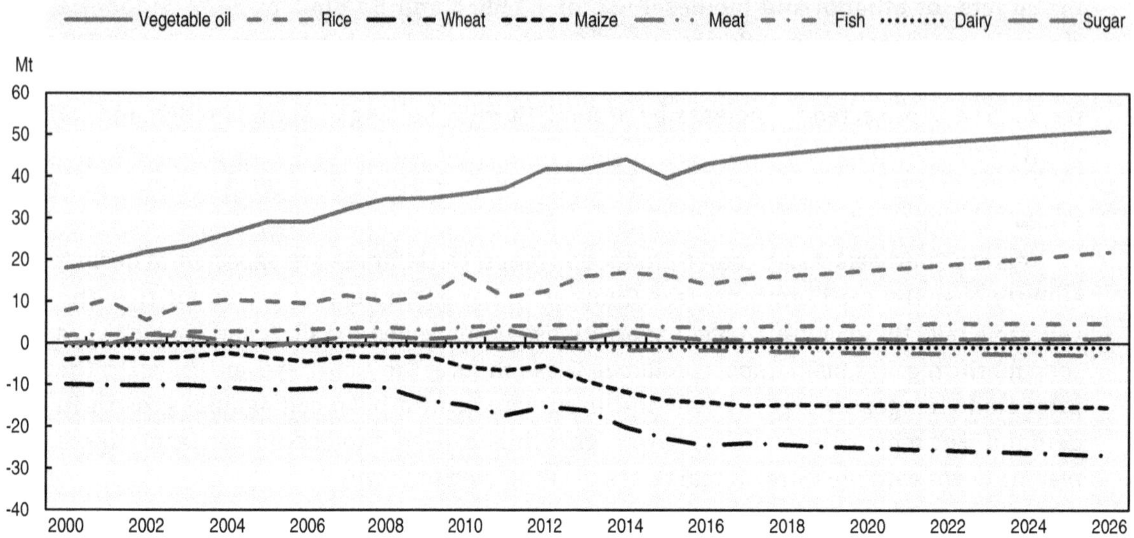

Source: OECD-FAO (2017), "OECD-FAO Agricultural Outlook", OECD Agriculture statistics (database), *http://dx.doi.org/10.1787/agr-data-en*.

StatLink *http://dx.doi.org/10.1787/888933521959*

Figure 2.23. **Contributions to changes in the trade balance of major commodities in Southeast Asia**

Changes in net trade balance (exports less imports), 2017-26

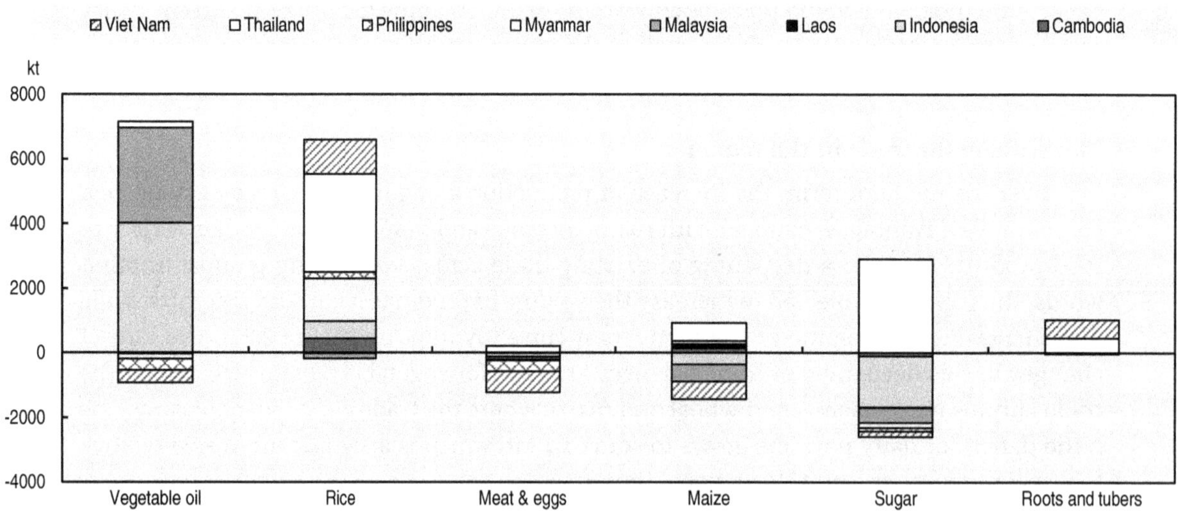

Source: OECD-FAO (2017), "OECD-FAO Agricultural Outlook", OECD Agriculture statistics (database), *http://dx.doi.org/10.1787/agr-data-en*.

StatLink *http://dx.doi.org/10.1787/888933521978*

have an impact not only availability and accessibility of food but also are likely to influence its utilisation and stability. While impacts of the two former elements are difficult to project in the context of the *Outlook*, by examining the changes in undernourishment based on the observed aggregates of food supply and income growth over the projection period an insight can be gained into the possible changes in in food security over the medium term.

For Southeast Asia, while the projections suggest that overall the region will see continued falls in the number of undernourished individuals, the improvements witnessed will not be sufficient to overcome food insecurity. All countries individually make progress in reducing undernourishment over time, with Indonesia, Thailand and Viet Nam all on target to achieve Sustainable Development Goal (SDG) number 2 by 2030 (less than 5% of the population being undernourished). However, for the remaining countries, and for the region in aggregate, the projected changes over the medium term will not be sufficient to overcome food insecurity. With current high levels of food insecurity, Cambodia, Lao PDR and Myanmar are projected to be furthest away from meeting the SDG2 target, and for the Philippines, the current stagnation in undernourishment improvements is projected to continue.

The changes over the medium term will not only influence aggregate calorie consumption but also its composition. Most of the increase in calorie intake over the medium term is due to crops other than rice, particularly vegetable oil and sugar (Figure 2.24). However, increased rice consumption is still a contributor to higher calorie intake in all countries but Viet Nam and Myanmar. Meat, dairy and fish consumption is responsible for higher protein intake in all countries, particularly Myanmar, Indonesia and Viet Nam.

Figure 2.24. **Sources of changes in calorie and protein intake in Southeast Asia**

Calorie (left); Protein (right)

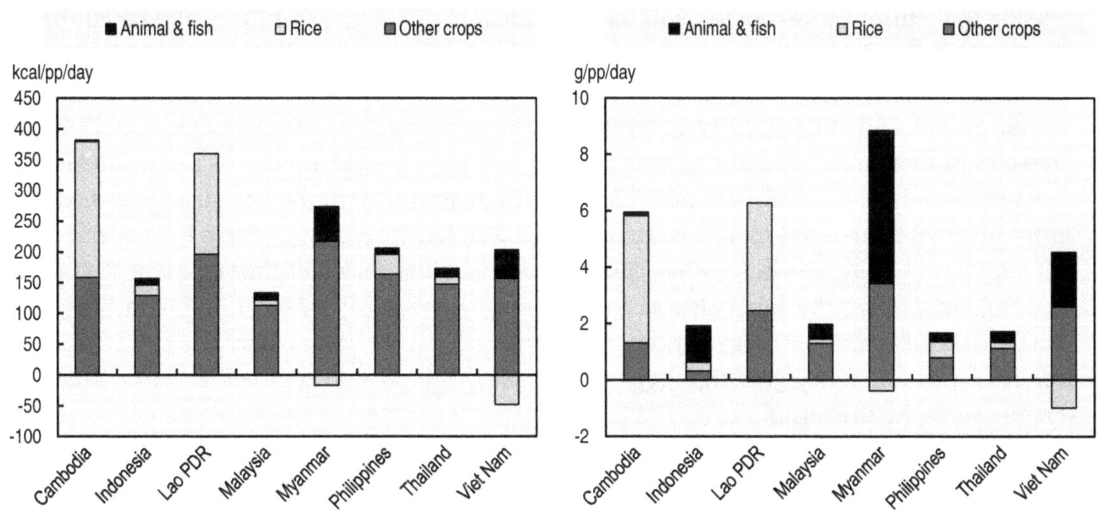

Source: OECD-FAO (2017), "OECD-FAO Agricultural Outlook", OECD Agriculture statistics (database), *http://dx.doi.org/10.1787/agr-data-en.*

StatLink *http://dx.doi.org/10.1787/888933521997*

The medium term results on undernourishment indicate that further policy effort will be required in the region is to overcome food insecurity. Policy makers have a number of policy levers that they could employ to help address these, but in the context of having markets deliver better food security outcomes, a key factor will be removing distortions to agricultural and food markets. As discussed earlier, realisation of the AEC Economic Blueprint with respect to rice market integration has the potential to yield significant improvements in reducing the rates of undernourishment in the region. Furthermore, actions taken to improve access of poorer households to food, through measures such as social safety net payments, have been found to be able to significantly reduce projected rates of undernourishment over the medium term (OECD, 2017b). These results indicate that, for the region, it is not a lack of available food that is the fundamental problem behind food insecurity, but rather effective access to that food.

Challenges and uncertainties in the medium-term outlook

The medium term outlook for Southeast Asia points to a number of strengths of the agricultural and fisheries sectors yet challenges and uncertainties exists. These relate to the region's ability to meet the projected productivity improvements, particularly in the face of climate change risks and challenges. Further, the region has placed significant pressure on its natural resource base – its natural capital – during its past development, and so finding ways to sustainably produce will important. Lastly, with the continued interactions in international markets, continued global uncertainty over actions to reduce market interventions and to prevent new ones from arising will impact the region. Each of these is discussed briefly here.

The baseline presented in this chapter requires a continued push to realise the projected productivity gains. Embodied in the projections are assumptions around continued policy reform and investments that will drive future growth. Within the region, as globally, investments in R&D are low and in some cases already declining. R&D plays a role through both past investments in R&D (the stock) and the rate of new investments (the flow) (Sheng, Mullen and Gray, 2011; Smeets Kristkova, Van Dijk and Van Meijl, 2016). In any given year, productivity performance is influenced by both these factors. However, this means that current investments will have a cumulate effect on the future, and so falling R&D spending will have lasting impacts that will be hard to correct if they persist. Smeets Kristkova, Van Dijk and Van Meijl (2016) demonstrate that if this relationship between R&D investments and productivity growth continues to hold, current declines in R&D investments will mean that the assumption of yield growth that underpins many models, ranging from long term climate projections to the medium term models such as the one presented here, are likely to be overly optimistic. For Southeast Asia, where R&D spend is already low in comparison to other countries at a similar levels of development (OECD, 2017b), improving the agricultural innovation systems represent a key challenge. Furthermore, beyond R&D, fragmentation in farm size, if it continues, may also create risks for future productivity growth, suggesting issues in land markets will become a key challenge facing the region.

A key uncertainty facing the region's productive capacity relates to climate change. As noted, climate change is expected to have a significant impact of the region. This will require the sector to adapt and adjust to changes over the medium and longer term. Even with R&D to help in adaptation actions (OECD, 2017b; Ignaciuk and Mason-D'Croz, 2014), current policies may put at risk adaptation responses and could potentially compound the impact of climate change. In the Philippines, for example, support policies oriented to rice work against incentives for adaptation and can increase producers exposure climate risks (OECD, 2017a). Similarly, for the region as a whole, current trade distortions have the potential to amplify the global price effects from climate change (OECD, 2017b). Furthermore, the agriculture sector, as a large greenhouse gas emitter, will also need to be involved in efforts to mitigate the effects of climate change. While there are likely to be synergies for some sectors in terms of efficiency gains and practice change that reduces greenhouse emissions – including efforts related to soil carbon sequestration such as the "4 in 1000" initiative – there will be instance where these do not exist. Much of the ultimate impact will once again depend on the discovery of new and innovative solutions, putting the innovation system at the forefront of required policy focus.

Allied to the pressure that will be created by climate change is the need to better manage the region's natural resources and make agricultural and fisheries production more sustainable. The region has experienced significant environmental costs from area expansion already, and while limits to further expansion exist, the management of this land along with fresh water and marine resources will be a key challenge for regional policy makers. Having in place systems that better inform producers about more sustainable practices and having regulations that ensure externalities are controlled will be critical. For aquaculture, a further consideration is the need to avoid undue administrative burdens on the industry whilst ensuring that environmental requirements are met (OECD 2016c). In capture fisheries, sector reducing or redirecting policy support such as fuel tax exemptions, which contribute to overcapitalisation and the overexploitation of resources, towards more effective management will be an important component of achieving sustainability (OECD 2017c).

For Southeast Asia, achieving continued economic growth in a time of global uncertainty with respect to international markets will also be a key challenge. This extends beyond the agriculture and fisheries sectors. The region has been one of the major beneficiaries of globalisation and the development of GVCs. For the region, global value chain participation across all industries has been associated with productivity growth and higher incomes (measured as domestic value added creation) (Lopez-Gonzalez, 2016). Further, the development of GVCs has meant that domestic trade restrictions effective act as a tax on exports (Greenville, Kawasaki and Beaujeu, 2017; Lopez-Gonzalez, 2016; OECD, 2015d), harming the development of several sectors (Jouanjean, Gourdon and Korinek, 2017 forthcoming). A more distorted international market place will work against the region's future growth, for agricultural and non-agricultural sectors alike. For regional policy makers, taking steps to ensure market distortions are reduced, both regionally and multilaterally, will be important if future growth projections are to be realised.

Conclusions

Countries in Southeast Asia have experienced significant improvements in their levels of development along with strong growth in their agriculture and fishery sectors. Production growth in agriculture and fisheries has been brought about by productivity growth along with significant increases in the use of both intermediate and natural inputs. However, the medium term projections point to a slowing of this growth, suggesting that for continued development of agriculture and fishery sectors, policy makers must look to a new wave of reforms to ensure strong and sustainable productivity growth.

While the scope for change inevitably varies across the region given its diversity, key next steps will be to create an environment where agricultural and fishery innovation can take place and which is conducive to sustainable productivity growth. This will entail addressing a number of the environmental challenges facing the agriculture and fishery production. It will also entail better integration in regional and global markets, which will require steps to address and improve the efficiency of the service markets that support the agriculture sector – a policy sphere that often lies outside the remit of agriculture and fishery ministries.

Policies need to focus on creating a more robust enabling environment for the region's producers and avoid distorting incentives along the food chain. This will allow adjustment to take place and allow the region to realise efficiency gains in its production systems. Taking these steps should also better equip the region to combat food insecurity and malnutrition in all its forms to achieve SDG2.

Notes

1. For this chapter, the fisheries sector is taken to mean both capture and aquaculture production.
2. The Southeast Asian region includes the ten ASEAN members and Timor-Leste.
3. Total factor productivity (TFP) is an indicator for measuring agricultural productivity. It takes into account all of the market inputs used in agricultural production (labour, land, livestock, machinery and intermediate inputs) and compares these with the total market outputs produced (crop and livestock commodities).
4. Excluding West Asia.
5. Agricultural land refers to the FAO's category of agricultural area, which includes is the sum of areas under "Arable land", "Permanent crops" and "Permanent pastures".
6. Net exports of rice are calculated as total exports to all partners less total imports from all partners.
7. See OECD (2017) for a more detailed description of current agricultural policies in the region.

References

ADB (2009), *The economics of climate change in Southeast Asia: A regional review*, Asian Development Bank, Manila.

Alavi, H., A. Htenas, R. Kopicki, A. Shepherd and R. Clarete (2012), *Trusting trade and the private sector for food security in Southeast Asia*, World Bank, Washington, DC.

Alongi, D.M. (2014), "Carbon cycling and storage in mangrove forests", *Annual Review of Marine Science*, vol. 6, pp. 195-219.

Baldwin, R. (2012), "Trade and industrialisation after globalisation's second unbundling: How building and joining a supply chain are different and why it matters", in *Globalization in an Age of Crisis: Multilateral Economic Cooperation in the Twenty-First Century*, R. Feenstra and A. Taylor (eds.), University of Chicago Press.

Bello, A.L. (2005), "Ensuring food security – A case for ASEAN integration", *Asian Journal of Agriculture and Development*, Vol. 2/1&2, Southeast Asian Regional Center for Graduate Study and Research in Agriculture, Philippines, pp. 87-108.

Carew-Reid J (2007), "Rapid assessment of the extent and impact of sea level rise in Viet Nam", *Climate Change Discussion Paper*, no. 1, International Centre for Environmental Management, Brisbane.

Carlson, K.M., L.M. Curran, G.P. Asner, A.M. Pittman, S.N. Trigg, J.M. Adeney (2012), "Carbon emissions from forest conversion by Kalimantan oil palm plantations", *Nature Climate Change*, Vol. 3/3, pp. 283-287.

Chen, C.C., B. McCarl and C.C. Chang (2012), "Climate change, sea level rise and rice: global market implications", *Climate Change*, Vol. 110/3, pp. 543-560.

Cruz, R.V., H. Harasawa, M. Lal, S. Wu, Y. Anokhin, B. Punsalmaa, Y. Honda, M. Jafari, C. Li and N. Huu Ninh (2007), "Asia" in *Climate Change 2007: Impacts, Adaptation and vulnerability*. Contribution of Working Group II to the Fourth Assessment Report of the Intergovernmental Panel on Climate Change, M.L. Parry, O.F. Canziani, J.P. Palutikof, P.J. van der Linden and C.E. Hanson (eds.), Cambridge University Press, Cambridge, United Kingdom, pp. 469-506.

Dawe, D., S. Jaffee, and N. Santos (2014), *Rice in the shadow of skyscrapers: Policy choices in a dynamic East and Southeast Asian setting*, Food and Agriculture Organization of the United Nations, Rome.

Deuss, A. (2015), "Review of the performance and impacts of recent stockholding policies", in *Issues in Agricultural Trade Policy: Proceedings of the 2014 OECD Global Forum on Agriculture*, OECD Publishing, Paris, *http://dx.doi.org/10.1787/9789264233911-5-en*.

Donato, D.C. (2011), "Mangroves among the most carbon-rich forests in the tropics", *Nature Geoscience*, vol. 4, pp. 293-297.

FAO (2017a), *FAOSTAT* (database), Food and Agriculture Organization of the United Nations Statistics Division, Rome, *http://faostat3.fao.org/home/E (accessed on 16 January 2017)*.

FAO (2017b), Fishery and Aquaculture Statistics. Global production by production source 1950-2015 (FishstatJ). In: *FAO Fisheries and Aquaculture Department* [online]. Rome. Updated 2017. *www.fao.org/fishery/statistics/software/fishstatj/en (accessed on 12 March 2017)*.

FAO (2017c), "Fishery and Aquaculture Statistics", Statistics and Information Branch of FAO Fisheries and Aquaculture Department. Personal communication (10 March 2017).

FAO (2017d), *FAOLEX Database*, Food and Agriculture Organization of the United Nations, Rome, *www.fao.org/faolex/en/*.

FAO (2017e), *FAOSTAT agriculture emissions database*, Food and Agriculture Organization of the United Nations, Rome, *www.fao.org/faostat/en/#data/GT*.

FAO (2017f), *FAOSTAT land use emissions database*, Food and Agriculture Organization of the United Nations, Rome, *www.fao.org/faostat/en/#data/GL*.

FAO (2016), *The state of world fisheries and aquaculture 2016: Contributing to food security and nutrition for all*, Food and Agriculture Organization of the United Nations, Rome.

FAO (2015), *Agricultural transformation of middle-income Asian economies: Diversification, farm size and mechanization*, by David Dawe, ESA Working Paper No. 15-04, Food and Agriculture Organization of the United Nations, Rome.

FAO (2014), *The state of world fisheries and aquaculture: Opportunities and challenges 2014*, Food and Agriculture Organization of the United Nations, Rome.

FAO (2014), *Regional trade agreements and food security in Asia*, Food and Agriculture Organization of the United Nations Regional Office for the Asia Pacific, Bangkok.

FAO (2007), *The world's mangroves 1980-2005*, FAO Forestry Paper 153, Food and Agriculture Organization of the United Nations, Rome.

Funge-Smith, S. M. Briggs and W. Miao (2012), *Regional overview of fisheries and aquaculture in Asia and the Pacific*, Asia-Pacific Fishery Commission, Food and Agriculture Organization of the United Nations Regional Office for Asia and the Pacific, Bangkok.

Furuhashi, G. and H. Gay (2017, (forthcoming), "Market implications of the integration of Southeast Asian Rice Markets", *OECD Food, Agriculture and Fisheries Papers*, forthcoming.

Giri C, J. Long, S. Abbas, R.M. Murali, F.M. Qamer, B. Pengra and D. Thau (2015), "Distribution and dynamics of mangrove forests of South Asia", *Journal of Environmental Management*, Vol. 148, pp. 101-11.

Greenville, J., K. Kawasaki and R. Beaujeu (2017), "How policies shape global food and agriculture value chains", *OECD Food, Agriculture and Fisheries Papers*, No. 100, OECD Publishing, Paris, *http://dx.doi.org/10.1787/aaf0763a-en*.

Greenville, J. and MacAulay (2007), "Untangling the benefits of protected areas in fisheries", *Marine Resource Economics*, vol. 22/3, pp. 267-85.

Gunarso, P., M.E. Hartoyo, F. Agus, and T. Killeen (2013), *Oil palm and land use change in Indonesia, Malaysia and Papua New Guinea*, Round Table on Sustainable Palm Oil (RSPO), Singapore.

Headey, D. (2011), "Rethinking the global food crisis: The role of trade shocks", *Food Policy*, Vol. 36, Elsevier, Amsterdam, pp. 136-146.

Hoang, H. K. and W.H. Meyers (2015), "Price stabilization and impacts of trade liberalization in the Southeast Asian rice market", *Food Policy*, Vol. 57, Elsevier, Amsterdam, pp. 26-39.

Hooijer, A. S. Page, J. G. Canadell, M. Silvius, J. Kwadijk, H. Wosten, and J. Jauhiainen, (2010), "Current and future CO2 emissions from drained peatlands in Southeast Asia", *Biogeosciences*, Vol. 7, pp. 505-1514.

Ignaciuk, A. and D. Mason-D'Croz (2014), "Modelling adaptation to climate change in agriculture", *OECD Food, Agriculture and Fisheries Papers*, No. 70, OECD Publishing, Paris, *http://dx.doi.org/10.1787/5jxrclljnbxq-en.*

IMF (2016), *World economic outlook October 2016: Subdued demand, symptoms and remedies*, International Monetary Fund, Washington D.C.

Jouanjean, MA., Gourdon, J. and Korinek, J. (2017), "GVCs: Sectoral analysis of developing countries", OECD Trade Policy Papers, OECD Publishing, Paris, forthcoming.

Koh, L.P., J. Miettinen, S.C. Liew, and J. Ghazoul (2011), "Remotely sensed evidence of tropical peatland conversion to oil palm", *Proceeding of the National Academy of Sciences of the United States of America*, Vol. 108, pp. 5127-5132.

Lantican, F.A, M.A. Sombilla and K.P. Quilloy (2013), *Estimating the Demand Elasticities of Rice in the Philippines*, Southeast Asian Regional Center for Graduate Study and Research in Agriculture (SEARCA), Los Baños.

Lopez-Gonzalez, J. (2016), "Using Foreign Factors to Enhance Domestic Export Performance: A Focus on Southeast Asia", OECD Trade Policy Papers, No. 191, OECD Publishing, Paris, *http://dx.doi.org/10.1787/5jlpq82v1jxw-en.*

Lowder, S.K., J. Skoet and S. Singh (2014), "What do we really know about the number and distribution of farms and family farms worldwide?", Background paper for *The State of Food and Agriculture 2014, ESA Working Paper* No. 14-02, Food and Agriculture Organization of the United Nations, Rome.

MARD (2011), *Rice Production Evaluation for 2010 and Work-Plan for 2011 for Southern Vietnam*, Agricultural Publishing House. pp. 129-146.

Miettinen, J., A. Hooijer, C. Shi, D. Tollenaar, R. Vernimmen, S.C. Liew, C. Malins, and S.E. Page (2012), "Extent of industrial plantations on Southeast Asian peatlands in 2010 with analysis of historical expansion and future projections", *GCB Bioenergy*, Vol. 4/6, pp. 908-918.

MRC (Mekong River Commission) 2010, *Impacts of Changes in Salinity Intrusion. Assessment of basin-wide development*, Technical Note 8, Vientiane.

Naylor, R.L. and W.P. Falcon (2010), "Food security in an era of economic volatility", *Population and Development Review*, Vol. 36/4, New Jersey, United States, pp. 693-723.

OECD (2017a,), *Agricultural Policies in Philippines*, OECD Publishing, Paris, *http://dx.doi.org/10.1787/9789264269088-en*

OECD (2017b), *Building Food Security and Managing Risk: A Focus on Southeast Asia*, OECD Publishing, Paris, *http://dx.doi.org/10.1787/9789264272392-en..*

OECD (2017c), *Informing Fisheries-Related Trade Negotiations*, OECD Publishing, Paris.

OECD (2016a), *Evolving Agricultural Policies and Markets: Implications for Multilateral Trade Reform*, OECD Publishing, Paris, *http://dx.doi.org/10.1787/9789264264991-en.*

OECD (2016b), *Agricultural Policy Monitoring and Evaluation 2016*, OECD Publishing, Paris, *http://dx.doi.org/10.1787/agr_pol-2016-en.*

OECD (2016c), *Aquaculture Licensing*, OECD Publishing, Paris, *https://one.oecd.org/document/TAD/FI(2015)11/FINAL/en/pdf.*

OECD (2015a), *METRO v1 Model Documentation*, OECD Publishing, Paris, *www2.oecd.org/oecdinfo/info.aspx?app=OLIScoteEN&Ref=TAD/TC/WP(2014)24/FINAL.*

OECD (2015b), *Multi-dimensional Review of Myanmar: Volume 2. In-depth Analysis and Recommendations*, OECD Publishing, Paris, *http://dx.doi.org/10.1787/9789264220577-en.*

OECD (2015c), *Agricultural Policies in Viet Nam*, OECD Publishing, Paris, *http://dx.doi.org/10.1787/9789264235151-en.*

OECD (2015d), *Participation of Developing Countries in Global Value Chains: Implications for Trade and Trade-Related Policies*, OECD Publishing, Paris, *http://dx.doi.org/10.1787/5js33lfw0xxn-en.*

OECD (2008), "Rising food prices: Causes and consequences", *OECD Policy Brief*, OECD Publishing, Paris, *www.oecd.org/trade/agricultural-trade/40847088.pdf.*

Omar, W., N. Abd Aziz, A. Tarmizi, M.H. Harun, and A. Kushairim (2010), *Mapping of Oil Palm Cultivation on Peatland in Malaysia*, MPOB Information Series No. 529, Kuala Lumpur.

Pendleton L, D.C Donato, B.C. Murray, S. Crooks, W.A. Jenkins, S. Sifleet, C. Craft, J.W. Fourqurean, J. B. Kauffman, N. Marbà, P. Megonigal, E. Pidgeon, D. Herr, D. Gordon, A. Baldera, (2012), "Estimating global 'blue carbon' emissions from conversion and degradation of vegetated coastal ecosystems", *PLoS One*, vol. 7(9):e43542.

Permani, R. and D. Vanzetti (2014), "Rice Mountain: An Assessment of the Thai Rice Pledging Program", Contributed paper prepared for presentation at the 58th AARES Annual Conference, Port Macquarie, New South Wales, 4-7 February 2014.

Philippines Government (2011), "Briefer on the Food Staples Self-Sufficiency Roadmap 2011-16" (webpage), *Official Gazette*, Manila.

Phillips M, P.J.G Henriksson, N. Tran, C.Y. Chan, C.V. Mohan, U-P. Rodriguez, S. Suri, S. Hall and S. Koeshendrajana (2015), *Exploring Indonesian aquaculture futures*, WorldFish. Penang, Malaysia.

Piesse, J. and C. Thirtle (2009), "Three bubbles and a panic: An explanatory review of recent food commodity price events", *Food Policy*, Vol. 34, Elsevier, Amsterdam, pp. 119-129.

Pirker, J., A. Mosnier, F. Kraxner, P. Havlík and M. Obersteiner (2016), "What are the limits to oil palm expansion?", *Global Environmental Change*, Vol. 40, September, pp. 73-81.

Richards, D.R. and D.A. Friess (2016) "Rates and drivers of mangrove deforestation in Southeast Asia, 2000-12", *Proceedings of the National Academy of Sciences USA*, vol. 113/2, pp. 344-349.

Rutten, M., M.van Dijk, W. van Rooij, and H. Hilderink, "Land Use Dynamics, Climate Change, and Food Security in Vietnam: A Global-to-local Modeling Approach", *World Development*, Vol. 59, July 2014, pp. 29-46.

Sam, L., (2006), *Saline Water Intrusion in the Mekong Delta*, Agricultural Publishing House (in Vietnamese).

Sayer, J., J. Ghazoul, P. Nelson, A.K. Boedhihartono (2012), "Oil palm expansion transforms tropical landscapes and livelihoods", *Global Food Security*, Vol. 1/2, pp. 114-119.

Sharma, R. (2014), "Outlook for Rice Demand, Supply and Trade" in Dawe, D., Jaffee, S. and N. Santos (eds) *Rice in the Shadow of Skyscrapers: Policy Choices in a Dynamic East and Southeast Asian Setting*, Food and Agriculture Organization of the United Nations, Rome.

Sheng, Y., Mullen, J.D. and Gray, E.M. (2011), *Public investment in agricultural R&D and extension: An analysis of the static and dynamic effects on Australian broadacre productivity*, ABARES Report to the Grains Research and Development Corporation, Canberra.

Smeets Kristkova, Z., M. Van Dijk and H. Van Meijl (2016), "Projections of long-term food security with R&D driven technical change – A CGE analysis", *NJAS – Wageningen Journal of Life Sciences*, Vol. 77, Elsevier, Amsterdam, pp. 39-51.

Tran, H , T. Tran., M. Kervyn (2015), "Dynamics of Land Cover/Land Use Changes in the Mekong Delta, 1973-2011: A Remote Sensing Analysis of the Tran Van Thoi District, Ca Mau Province, Vietnam", *Remote Sensing*, vol. 7, pp. 2899-2925.

Tubiello, F.N., M. Salvatore, J. Ferrara, J. House, S. Federici, S. Rossi, R.Biancalani, RD. Condor Golec, H. Jacobs, A. Flammini, P. Prosperi, P. Cardenas-Galindo, J. Schmidhuber, M.J. Sanz-Snachez, N. Srivastava, and P. Smith, (2015), "The Contribution of Agriculture, Forestry and other Land Use activities to Global Warming, 1990-2012", Global Change Biology, 10 January 2015.

Tuong, T.P., S.P. Kam, C.T. Hoanh, L.C. Dung, N.T. Khiem, J. Barr and D.C. Ben (2003), "Impact of seawater intrusion control on the environment, land use and household incomes in a coastal area", *Paddy Water Environment*, vol. 1, pp. 65-73.

UNEP, VIFEP and WWF (2009), *Fisheries subsidies, supply chain and certification in Vietnam: Summary Report*, September 2009, *http://unep.ch/etb/areas/fisheries%20country%20projects/vietnam/Final%20Summary%20Report%20Vietnam.pdf*.

USDA (2016), *International Agricultural Productivity* (database), United States Department of Agriculture Economic Research Service, *www.ers.usda.gov/data-products/international-agricultural-productivity.aspx* (accessed on 17 August 2016).

WITS (2017), *World Integrated Trade Solution* (database), World Bank, Washington D.C., *http://wits.worldbank.org/default.aspx* (accessed on 16 January 2017).

World Bank (2017), *World development indicators* (database), World Bank, Washington D.C., *http://databank.worldbank.org/data/* (accessed on 25 November 2016).

OECD-FAO Agricultural Outlook 2017-2026

Chapter 3

Commodity snapshots

This chapter describes the market situation and highlights of the latest set of quantitative medium-term projections for world and national agricultural markets, for the ten-year period 2017-26. It provides information on prices, production, consumption, trade and main uncertainties for cereals, oilseeds, sugar, meat, dairy products, fish, biofuels and cotton. The quantitative projections are developed with the aid of the partial equilibrium Aglink-Cosimo model of world agriculture. The printed version of this chapter only includes the projection highlights for each commodity whereas further details and an extensive statistical annex are available online.

CEREALS

Market situation

Global supplies of major cereals continued to exceed overall demand, leading to a significant build-up of inventories and much lower prices on international markets as compared to the previous decade. In 2016, world cereals production reached a new high, exceeding the previous peak of 2014. Wheat and maize outputs increased the most, driven by record high crops in several countries, especially among the world's leading exporters. Given the continued large surplus of cereals, downward pressure on world prices is unlikely to be relieved over the coming months.

Projection highlights

Prices will likely remain under pressure in the short term due to low prices during the base period (2014-16), sluggish economic growth conditions, large stocks, low oil prices, and a strong US dollar. Over the course of the medium term, however, cereal prices are projected to increase in nominal terms, but not by enough to keep pace with inflation, which indicates a slight decline in real terms. The decline in real terms is more pronounced for rice since human consumption is its only relevant use category while prices of the remaining cereals are also supported by feed and other uses. Prices of all cereals, even in nominal terms, are projected to be lower on average than in the previous decade, although well above the levels of before 2007.

Global cereal production is projected to expand by 12% between the base period and 2026, mainly driven by yield growth. Compared with the base period, production of wheat in 2026 is projected to be 11% higher (78 Mt), with most of the increase in India (15 Mt), followed by the European Union (10 Mt), the Russian Federation (7 Mt), Pakistan (6 Mt), and the People's Republic of China (hereafter "China") (5.5 Mt). Rice production is set to increase by 13% (66 Mt), with most of the increase (58 Mt) concentrated in Asian countries, led by India (20 Mt), Indonesia (7 Mt), Bangladesh, Thailand (6 Mt each), Viet Nam (4 Mt), and China (3.5 Mt). Maize production is projected to rise by 14% (138 Mt), led by United States (29 Mt), the Brazil (22 Mt), China (14 Mt), Argentina (11 Mt), the European Union (9 Mt) and India (6 Mt). Production of other coarse grains is projected to increase by 10% (30 Mt), with the biggest increases in Ethiopia (4 Mt), India (3.5 Mt), Argentina (2 Mt), the Russian federation (1.9 Mt), and Nigeria (1.8 Mt).

Global cereal use is projected to grow by 13% or 338 Mt, to reach 2 863 Mt by 2026. Wheat consumption is expected to increase by 11% compared to the base period, and will continue to be largely used for human consumption (67% of total use throughout the projection period). The use of wheat for feed is projected to increase, primarily in China, Pakistan and Viet Nam in relative terms, while the use of wheat for the production of biofuels will account for only 1.2% of global use in 2026. Maize use for animal feed is projected to increase to 121 Mt, increasing its overall share over total use from 56% during the base period to 60% in 2026, largely on account of fast expanding livestock sectors in developing countries. Maize for human consumption is projected to grow by 19% (24 Mt), mainly in developing countries also, especially those in Africa where white maize is a main staple in several countries. The use of other coarse grains is also set to grow by 12% (34 Mt), driven by feed demand (17 Mt) followed closely by food demand (16 Mt). The expansion of food use is mainly in Africa (13 Mt), while the European Union and the Russian Federation have the highest expansion for feed. Direct human consumption

Figure 3.1. **World cereal prices**

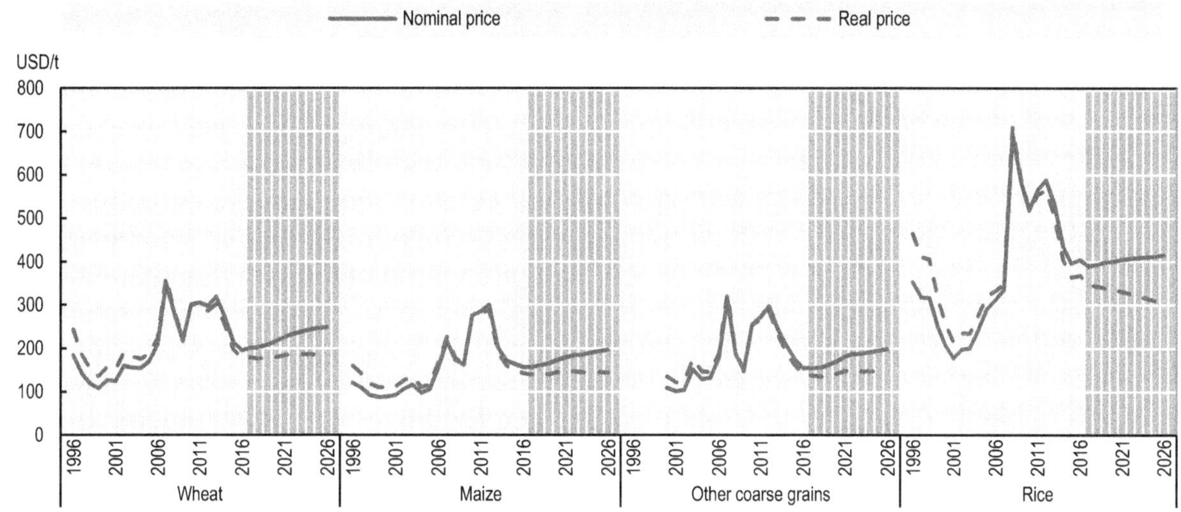

Note: Wheat: US wheat No.2 Hard Red Winter (fob), maize: US Gulf maize, No.2 Yellow (fob), other coarse grains: Barley (feed Rouen), rice: Thailand, 100% B, 2nd grade.
Source: OECD/FAO (2017), "OECD-FAO Agricultural Outlook", OECD Agriculture statistics (database), *http://dx.doi.org/10.1787/agr-data-en*.
StatLink *http://dx.doi.org/10.1787/888933522016*

remains the main end-use of rice, a major staple in large parts of Asia, Africa, Latin America, and the Caribbean. Total consumption is predicted to rise from 494 Mt in the base period to 560 Mt by 2026, principally due to population growth. Given the expected demographic changes, Asian countries are expected to account for close to 80% of the projected increase in global rice consumption.

World trade in cereals by 2026 is projected to increase to 448 Mt, up 14% from the base period. At this projected level, global trade would expand at a slightly faster rate than production (1.5% p.a. *vs.* 1.2% p.a.), increasing the share of global production that is traded to 15.6%. For wheat, this share is expected to reach 23% by 2026, compared with 13% for maize and 15% for other coarse grains. The Russian Federation has started to play a major role on international markets for wheat and maize in the past few years. It was the fifth largest exporter of wheat on average over the past decade and is projected to become the second largest exporter over the projection period, contributing 15% to global trade. Developed countries are expected to continue to be the main exporters of wheat and coarse grains to developing countries, while rice is mostly traded between developing countries. The global players on international rice markets are expected to remain the same, although Cambodia and Myanmar are projected to increase their shares of the international market over the next decade.

Continued lower cereal prices, as compared to the previous decade, will impact planting decisions and hence supply responses. Prices relative to other crops, such as oilseeds, are therefore an important factor as lower prices might lead to a more vigorous reallocation towards other crops. On the demand side, developments in the fastest growing economies will have profound implications for trade. Changes in demand in China and the timing with which they release their maize stocks are the main uncertainties during the projection period.

The expanded cereals chapter is available at
http://dx.doi.org/10.1787/agr_outlook-2017-7-en

OILSEEDS AND OILSEED PRODUCTS

Market situation

Global soybean production increased strongly in 2016, with the United States and Brazil registering record crops. The aggregate world production of other oilseeds (rapeseed, sunflower seed and groundnuts) increased for the first time in three years. Increased sunflower production, mainly in the Russian Federation and Ukraine, helped offset the decreased production of rapeseed in the European Union. This has brought some relief to a relatively tight market situation.

Vegetable oil production declined in the 2015 marketing year for two reasons. First, palm oil yields decreased in Southeast Asia (Chapter 2) due to *El Niño*, and secondly, the market share of soybeans, which contain less oil than other oilseeds, increased, resulting in a stagnation of oilseed oil production. This led to a sharp decline in world stocks and although vegetable oil production recovered in 2016, this will not be sufficient to relieve the relatively tight market in view of the demand growth for vegetable oils to produce biodiesel in 2016, especially in Indonesia and the United States. Per capita food use of vegetable oils also continued to grow both in developed and developing countries.

The growing demand for protein meals, especially in China, has been the main driver behind the expansion of global oilseed production. This has increased the share of protein meals in the returns from the crushing of oilseeds, in particular for soybeans due to their higher protein content.

Projection highlights

In nominal terms all oilseeds and oilseed product prices are projected to increase slightly over the outlook period. Due to saturated per capita food demand, stagnation in the biodiesel sector and ongoing livestock intensification in many emerging economies, vegetable oil prices will decline further than protein meal prices in real terms over the outlook period. Prices for soybeans and other oilseeds are also projected to decline in real terms. Nevertheless, volatility should be expected due to market uncertainties.

During the outlook period, global soybean production is expected to continue to expand, but at 1.9% p.a., which is well below the growth rate of 4.9% p.a. of the last decade. This slowdown is due mainly to a decrease in additional area planted. Brazil soybean production is expected to grow at 2.6% p.a., the fastest of the major producers as more additional land is available, compared to Argentina (2.1% p.a.) and the United States (1.0% p.a.). Consequently, Brazil is projected to overtake the United States as the largest soybean producer. Production of other oilseeds increases by 1.0% p.a. over the next decade, considerably below the 3.4% p.a. growth rate of the previous one. Crushing of soybeans and other oilseeds into meal (cake) and oil are the dominate usage and will increase faster than other uses, in particular direct food consumption of soybeans, groundnuts and sunflower seeds as well as direct feeding of soybeans. Overall, 90% of world soybean production and 86% of world production of other oilseeds are projected to be crushed in 2026.

Vegetable oil includes oil obtained from the crushing of soybeans and other oilseeds (about 55% of world vegetable oil production), palm oil (35%), as well as palm kernel, coconut and cottonseed oils. Growth in demand for vegetable oil is expected to be slower in the coming decade due to reduced growth in per capita food use in developing countries (1.1% p.a. compared to 3.1% in the previous decade) and to the stable demand for vegetable oils that are used to produce biodiesel. Despite a slowdown in the expansion of the mature oil palm area, there will be significant production growth in Indonesia (2.0% p.a. vs. 7.0% p.a. in the previous decade) and Malaysia (1.5% p.a. vs. 1.2% p.a.).

Protein meal production and consumption is dominated by soybean meal. Compared to the past decade, consumption growth of protein meal (1.7% p.a. vs. 4.1% p.a.) will be limited by slower growth in global livestock production and by the fact that the protein meal share in Chinese feed rations has reached a plateau. Chinese consumption of protein meal is projected to grow by 2.3% p.a. compared to 7.9% p.a. in the previous decade, a rate which still exceeds the growth rate of animal production.

Vegetable oil has one of the highest trade shares (42%) of production of all agricultural commodities. This share is expected to remain stable throughout the outlook period, with global vegetable oil exports reaching 91 Mt by 2026. Vegetable oil exports will continue to be dominated by Indonesia and Malaysia (Figure 3.2), which are strongly export-orientated: about two-thirds of Indonesian and more than 80% of Malaysian vegetable oil production is exported. While the share will remain unchanged in the latter over the outlook period, in Indonesia it is expected to decrease as more vegetable oil will be used as feedstock for biofuels. Indonesian exports will grow at 1.5% p.a. compared to 6.1% p.a. in the last decade.

Soybean, other oilseeds and protein meal exports are dominated by the Americas. The phasing-out of export taxes in Argentina opens new opportunities for its soybean and sunflower production and their products, although there could be some reallocation of land in favour of competing grain crops that benefit from immediate export liberalisation. Growth in world trade of soybeans is expected to slow down considerably in the next decade, a development directly linked to the projected slower growth in soybean crushing in China.

Figure 3.2. **Exports of oilseeds and oilseed products by region**

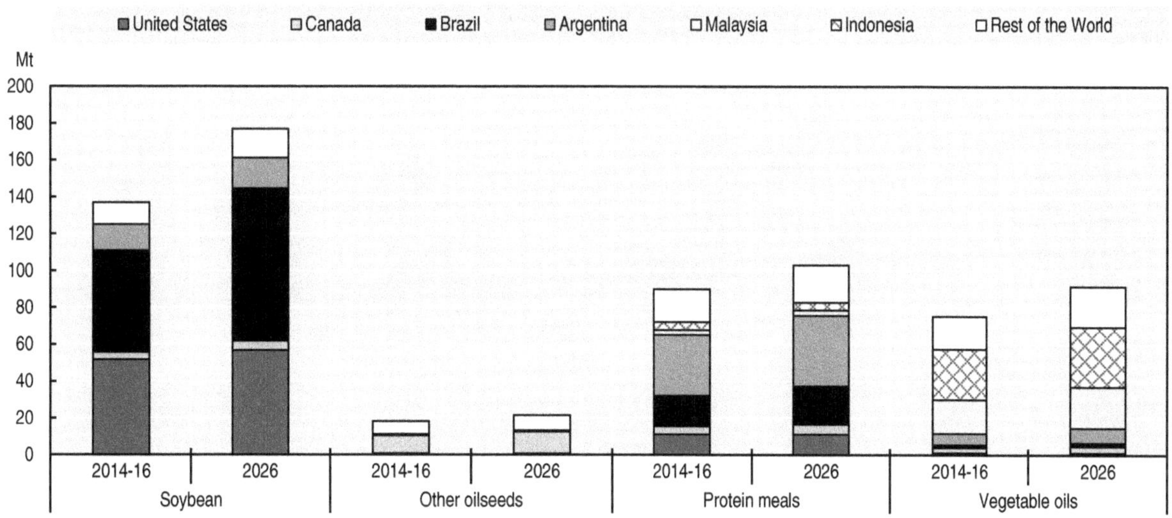

Source: OECD/FAO (2017), "OECD-FAO Agricultural Outlook", OECD Agriculture statistics (database), *http://dx.doi.org/10.1787/agr-data-en.*

StatLink *http://dx.doi.org/10.1787/888933522035*

The expected expansion of soybean and palm oil production will depend on the availability of additional new land, which could be constrained by new legislation seeking to protect the environment. This concerns notably oil palm plantations. Biofuel policies in the United States, the European Union and Indonesia are also major sources of uncertainty because they account for a considerable share of the vegetable oil demand in these countries. In addition, the issues and uncertainties common to most commodities (e.g. the macroeconomic environment, crude oil prices, and weather conditions) have considerable influence on the oilseed complex.

The expanded oilseeds and oilseed products chapter is available at
http://dx.doi.org/10.1787/agr_outlook-2017-8-en

SUGAR

Market situation

After five consecutive seasons of a global production surplus in the international sugar market, the 2015 marketing year marked the start of a production deficit period. Preliminary data suggest that a production deficit will also prevail in the 2016/17 season, as the anticipated production increases are considered insufficient to cover world sugar demand. This global supply shortage can be partially attributed to production setbacks in some key exporting countries, namely Brazil and Thailand, but also to shortfalls in India, the world's second largest sugar producer. It is not expected, however, that the global sugar stock-to-use ratio will return to the low levels observed in 2009 and 2010, despite stock releases on the domestic market undertaken by China.

In contrast to other basic agricultural commodities, current international sugar prices are relatively high. They started to rise sharply in mid-2015 due to tighter market conditions, ending four seasons of relatively weak world prices. High fructose corn syrup, the main competitive alternative representing 10% of the market for sweeteners, also experienced a price increase in 2016 with a realignment of supply-to-demand in the United States, the main exporting country. These elevated international sugar quotations augur well for production prospects in the coming years.

Projection highlights

The start of this outlook period is marked by relatively high sugar market prices, which conditions the market balance for the coming years. Assuming normal weather conditions and low input prices, increased crushing is expected throughout the projection period, thus increasing sugar availability. Sugar prices are expected to come down for some years before increasing slightly in nominal terms, but to decline further in real terms. Slowing population growth and changes in consumer attitudes will most likely moderate future sugar demand growth. The market will continue to be influenced by production shocks, macroeconomic factors, and domestic policies which shape the performance of the sugar sub-sector. Efforts to liberalise this market have taken place in key producing regions, including the European Union (abolition of sugar quota by 2017) and India, and Thailand is expected to reform its sugar programme in reaction to a complaint lodged by Brazil at the WTO.

Sugar crop production is projected to expand in many parts of the world, driven by remunerative returns in comparison to other crops. Sugarcane, cultivated largely in developing countries (Africa, Asia and South America), will continue to be the main crop used to produce sugar. The share of sugar from sugar beet is expected to decline slightly from 14% during the base period to 12.9% in 2026. Brazil is the world's largest sugar producer and exporter, and its sector is expected to recover from the severe financial problems of the last several years. As a sign of recovery, investments for the renewal of sugarcane plantations have strengthened and are anticipated to expand. In addition, on the basis of lower international oil prices, sugar is set to be relatively more profitable in comparison to ethanol at the start of the outlook period but a higher growth is expected in ethanol production throughout the outlook period.

In Asia, robust growth in sugar demand will continue to support expansion of the sugar sector over the outlook period. Efforts to deregulate the sector are not likely to lead to a complete removal of domestic support policies and associated border measures, but will have an impact on the market. Expansion is also foreseen in Africa as the number of operational factories increases (notably in Ethiopia). Globally, the production of sugar crops and sugar should increase by respectively 17% and 24% over the next ten years, and the growth in the share of sugarcane production devoted to producing ethanol should be slightly reduced from about +0.6% p.a. during the last decade to 0.4% this decade.

Figure 3.3. **World nominal and real sugar prices**

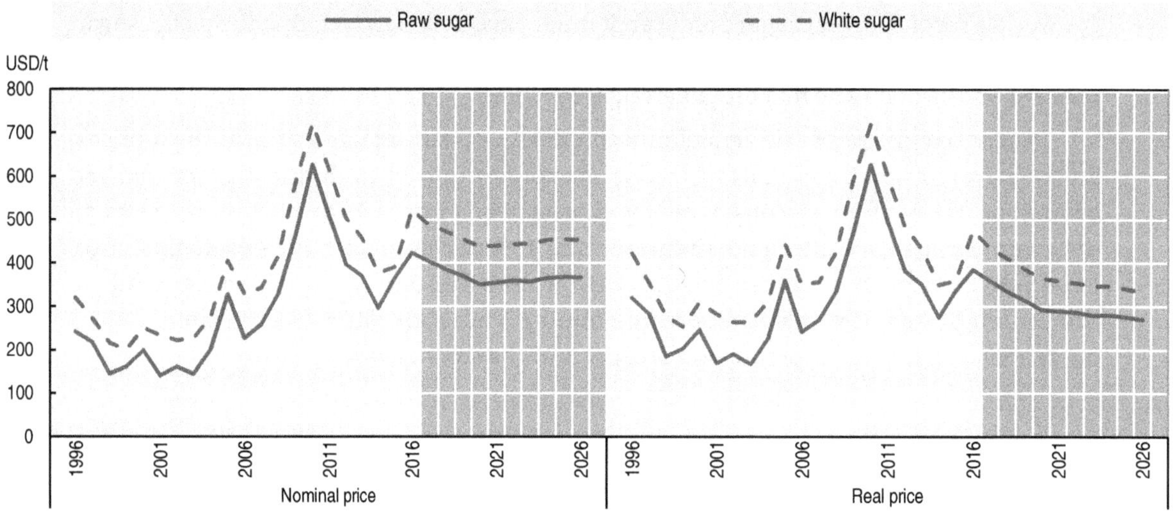

Note: Raw sugar world price, Intercontinental Exchange contract No.11 nearby futures price; Refined sugar price, Euronext Liffe, Futures Contract No. 407, London. Real sugar prices are nominal world prices deflated by the US GDP deflator (2010=1).
Source: OECD/FAO (2017), "OECD-FAO Agricultural Outlook", OECD Agriculture statistics (database), *http://dx.doi.org/10.1787/agr-outl-data-en.*
StatLink *http://dx.doi.org/10.1787/888933522054*

Per capita global demand growth for sweeteners is not foreseen to change much over the outlook period compared to the last decade (0.7% p.a. versus 0.6%). Slower population growth will put a brake on demand growth, as will changing attitudes towards sweetened products, which are increasingly linked to obesity and other associated health issues. Some companies have recently taken measures to reduce sugar content in their products. Although no growth is foreseen in sugar consumption in developed countries over the next decade, the reverse is true for developing countries due to population growth and increasing urbanisation, where a higher share of the consumers' budgets is allocated to beverages and food. Globally, the consumption of sweeteners is foreseen to increase by 20.3% over the next ten years.

Sugar will continue to be highly traded, with about 33% of total production expected to be exported over the outlook period. Exports are projected to remain concentrated, with 48% originating from Brazil where sugar cane production is shared between supply of sugar of which 72% are exported and ethanol for domestic use. Sugar exports are likely to expand in countries that have modernised or reformed their sugar sectors (notably Australia, European Union and Thailand). Imports will remain diversified, mostly driven by demand from Africa and Asia.

Following four seasons of steady decline, international sugar prices are at a relatively high level since 2015, although about 28% below the previous peak recorded in 2010. Nominal prices are projected to decline over the next few years and then remain at a relatively high plateau when compared to the long-term average, prior to the 2009 price hike. Prices are projected to reach USD 367/t in 2026, with a premium for white sugar estimated at USD 86/t. In real terms, sugar quotations are expected to decline consistently and average lower than the previous ten years.

The outlook for sugar production is dependent on a number of factors, such as weather events, macroeconomic conditions and national policies. Any changes to these factors will condition the results of the projections and alter the outcome of the sugar balance and prices. For example, any changes to the value of the Brazilian currency (real) against the United States dollar, or changes in the assumed level of world crude oil prices will alter the producer sugar margin and affect the sugar trade. The projections could also be affected by market movements of other competing crops, the feed sector, biofuels, or price fluctuations of other caloric sweeteners.

The expanded sugar chapter is available at
http://dx.doi.org/10.1787/agr_outlook-2017-9-en

MEAT

Market situation

Overall world meat production increased by only 1% to 317 million tonnes in 2016, with growth in the Americas and Europe offset by a down-turn in output in China in particular, but also in Australia. This was the second lowest annual increase in the last decade. Among the various sectors, poultry and bovine meat production expanded, while a decline was evident in pigmeat and sheepmeat production.

Measured by the FAO Meat Price Index, prices began 2016 at low levels, equivalent to those last seen at the end of 2009, and despite some recovery during the course of the year, annual average prices compare to levels attained in 2010, well below recent peaks. Prices rose for all categories of meat, in particular ovine, pig and poultry meat, with bovine meat recording more modest growth. Limited supplies of pigmeat in the European Union and of sheepmeat from Oceania lent support to prices for these products, while firm international demand, in particular from Asia, underpinned poultry meat prices. Meanwhile, recovery in bovine meat production in the United States reduced import requirements, contributing to a smaller lower increase in international prices for this product than for other categories of meat.

Global meat trade recovered in 2016, rising by 5% to 30 Mt. This represents a return to trend levels following the decline in 2015. Trade increased for pigmeat by 9%, poultry meat by 5%, and bovine meat by 3%, while sheepmeat decreased by 3%. At the country level, China in particular increased its imports of meat, along with Chile, Korea, Mexico, the European Union, the Philippines, South Africa, and the United Arab Emirates. By contrast, growth in domestic production reduced imports by the United States and Canada. Australia, the Russian Federation and Angola also imported less. The expansion in world meat exports was led by Brazil and the European Union, followed by the United States, with sales also rising for Argentina, Canada, Mexico, New Zealand, Paraguay and Thailand. Meanwhile, exports by Australia, China, India, South Africa and Turkey fell.

Projection highlights

The outlook for the meat market remains relatively favourable for producers. Feed grain prices have declined and assuming stable weather are set to remain low for the projection period. This lends stability to a sector that had been operating in an environment of particularly high and volatile feed costs over extended periods through the past decade. This is particularly relevant for regions such as the Americas, Australia and Europe, where feed grains are being used more intensively in the production of meat.

Global meat production is projected to be 13% higher in 2026 relative to the base period (2014-16). This compares with an increase of almost 20% in the previous decade. Developing countries are projected to account for the vast majority of the total increase, with a more intensive use of feed in the production process. Poultry meat is the primary driver of the growth in total meat production in response to expanding global demand for this more affordable animal protein compared to red meats. Low production costs and lower product prices have contributed to making poultry the meat of choice both for producers and consumers in developing countries. In the bovine meat sector, cow herds are being rebuilt in several major producing regions, but the decline in cattle slaughter in these regions is projected to be offset by higher carcass weights. Production is further increased by rising slaughter numbers in countries that are further along in the rebuilding cycle. This resulted in slightly higher beef production starting in 2016. Production growth is expected to accelerate from 2017 onwards, as slaughter volumes continue to increase. Pigmeat production will also increase after 2017, driven by slow herd expansion in China. The increase in herd size is, however, slowed by increased environmental regulations and animal welfare concerns affecting the pork sector. Production is also expected to increase in the sheepmeat sector with an expected global growth of 2.0% p.a., a higher rate than last decade. Production increases will be led by China, with expansion also in Algeria, Australia, Bangladesh, Islamic Republic of Iran, Nigeria, Pakistan and Sudan.

Globally, the traded share of meat output is expected to remain fairly constant, at around 10%, over the projection period, with most of the increase in volume coming from poultry meat. Import demand growth will be weak during the first years of the outlook period, mainly due to lower imports from China and the Russian Federation. Import demand will strengthen in the second half of the projection period, due to import growth in the developing world. The most significant growth in import demand originates from the Philippines and Viet Nam as well as Sub-Saharan Africa, which captures a large share of additional imports for all meat types. Although developed countries are still expected to account for slightly more than half of global meat exports by 2026, their share decreases steadily relative to the base period. On the other hand, the share of the two largest meat exporting countries, Brazil and the United States, in global meat exports is expected to increase to around 44%, contributing to almost 70% of the expected increase in global meat exports over the projection period.

At the start of the outlook, nominal meat prices are expected to be at levels similar or lower to those registered in 2016. Meat prices are projected to trend only marginally upwards as the market expands and exerts downward pressure on prices. Despite normal cycles for meats with longer production cycles, e.g. beef and sheepmeat, nominal prices for all meats are projected to be higher in 2026 relative to current levels. By 2026, the price for beef is projected to increase to USD 3984/t carcass weight equivalent (c.w.e.) and to increase to USD 3938/t c.w.e. for sheepmeat, while world pigmeat and poultry prices are expected to rise to around USD 1500/t c.w.e. and USD 1 709/t product weight (p.w.) respectively. Poultry meat demand is expected to increase more rapidly than the demand for pigmeat. In real terms, prices are expected to trend downwards for all meat types (Figure 3.4), although meat-to-feed price margins will generally remain within historical trends.

Global meat consumption per capita is expected to stagnate at 34.6 kg retail weight equivalent (r.w.e.) by 2026, an increase of less than half a kg r.w.e. compared to the base period. Nonetheless given high population growth rates in much of the developing world, total consumption is still expected to increase by nearly 1.5% per annum. Additional per capita consumption will consist mainly of poultry while pigmeat will decline globally on a per capita basis. In absolute terms, total consumption growth in developed countries over the projection period is expected to be approximately a fifth of that in developing regions, where rapid population growth and urbanisation remain the core drivers. These drivers are particularly important in Sub-Saharan Africa, where the rate of total consumption growth over the outlook period is faster than any other region. The composition growth is also different, with beef accounting for most of the total growth. Import demand is also expected to continue increasing in South East Asia.

Figure 3.4. **World meat prices**

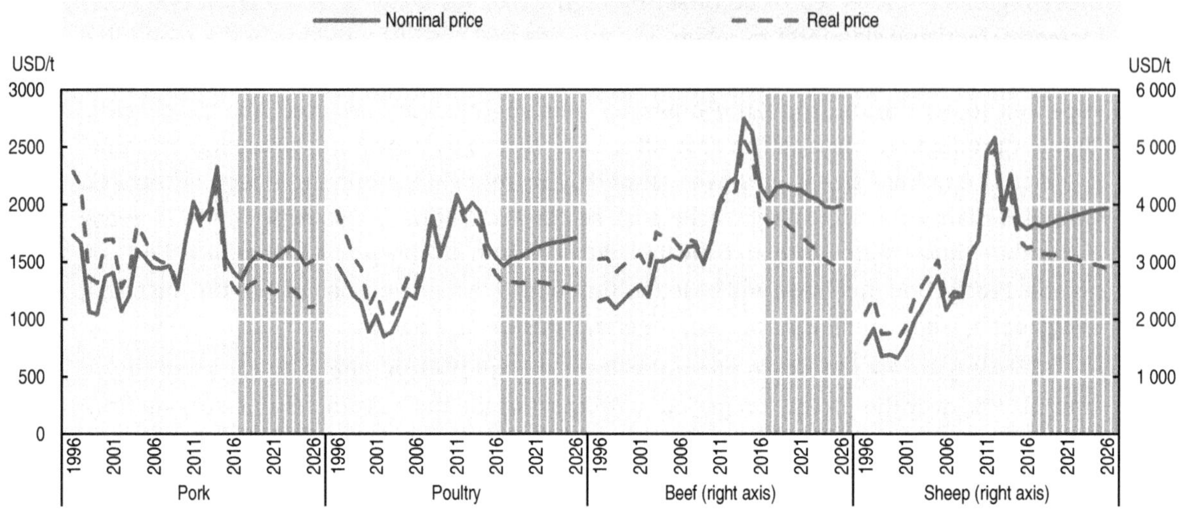

Note: US Choice steers, 1 100-1 300 lb dressed weight, Nebraska. New Zealand lamb schedule price dressed weight, all grade average. US Barrows and gilts, No. 1-3, 230-250 lb dressed weight, Iowa/South Minnesota. Brazil: Export unit value for chicken (f.o.b.) product weight.
Source: OECD/FAO (2017), "OECD-FAO Agricultural Outlook", OECD Agriculture statistics (database), *http://dx.doi.org/10.1787/agr-outl-data-en*.
StatLink *http://dx.doi.org/10.1787/888933522073*

Globally, animal disease outbreaks and trade policies remain among the main factors driving the evolution and dynamics in world meat markets. The implementation of various trade agreements, such as the ratified China-Australia Free Trade Agreement (ChAFTA), or the signed Canada-Ukraine Free Trade Agreement (CUFTA) and the Comprehensive Economic and Trade Agreement (CETA) over the outlook period could increase and diversify meat trade. Domestic policies will also impact the meat sector such as the review in 2018 of the US Farm Bill. Further factors that could impact the meat outlook include consumer preferences and attitudes towards meat consumption. Consumers are showing a preference for free-range meat and antibiotic-free meat products, but the extent to which they are willing and able to pay a premium for them remains unclear.

The expanded meat chapter is available at

http://dx.doi.org/10.1787/agr_outlook-2017-10-en

DAIRY AND DAIRY PRODUCTS

Market situation

International dairy prices started to increase in the last half of 2016, with butter and whole milk powder (WMP) accounting for most of this increase. This reversed a decline in dairy prices that started in 2014 following a decrease in Chinese demand, the Russian Federation's ban on imports from several countries, and an increase in production from some key exporters. From January to December 2016, butter and WMP prices increased by around 40% and 56% respectively.

Butter prices have recovered significantly and future increases will be limited compared to other dairy products. The prices of other milk-based products, such as cheese and skim milk powder (SMP), have increased more slowly but are expected to continue to increase through 2017. The increase in dairy prices in 2016 was due to a slump in milk production in Australia, New Zealand and Argentina and the European Union (only in the second half of 2016), as well as a strong demand for some dairy products, particularly cheese and butter.

In Oceania, milk production has been limited for several reasons, including low dairy prices in 2015-16, adverse weather conditions related to *El Niño,* poor pasture conditions, and higher prices of cull dairy cows which resulted in a contraction of the dairy herd by 1.6% in 2016. This has encouraged a renewal of dairy herds with younger, more productive cows, although the monthly culling rate is slowing down as international dairy prices improve. Considering the production cycle of dairy herds, this suggests a slow recovery in inventories but an increase in yields. Although China, the largest importer of milk products, has decreased its imports, mainly WMP, from the highs of 2013-14, Oceania's dairy exports are slowly recovering, through higher exports to countries such as Algeria, Indonesia, Mexico, the Russian Federation, Yemen, Bangladesh, and Egypt. New Zealand has reduced its production of WMP, but increased its production of cheese in response to world demand.

Several factors (in particular the import ban imposed by the Russian Federation, production increases in New Zealand, Australia and the United States, the elimination of the quota restrictions; decreases in WMP and SMP exports to China) created a challenging environment for the EU dairy sector in 2015. This changed in mid-2016. On the supply side, 351 029 tonnes of skim milk powder (SMP) were removed from the market via public purchases through the EU intervention policy. The stock is projected to be released over the next two years. Both domestic and international cheese and butter consumption increased, and some key producers reduced their production. The European Union, however, increased its production, and its exports of cheese and butter grew by 9.5% and 23% respectively, while exports of SMP and WMP decreased by 18% and 5% respectively.

Projection highlights

There is renewed consumer enthusiasm in developed countries for butter and dairy fat over substitutes based on vegetable oil. This trend can be attributed to such factors as more positive health assessments on dairy fat, a change in consumer perceptions towards taste and towards less processed food, with the result that these products are increasingly used in bakery products and recipes. As incomes and population increase, and diets become more globalised, more dairy products are expected to be consumed in developing countries. In developed countries, per-capita consumption is projected to grow from 20.2 kg in 2014-16 to 21.4 kg in 2026 in milk solids, compared with an increase from 10.9 kg to 13.2 kg in developing countries. There are, however, significant regional disparities amongst developing countries, where fresh dairy products will remain by far the most consumed; this contrasts with developed countries, where consumer preferences tend towards processed products (Figure 3.5).

Figure 3.5. **Per capita consumption of processed and fresh dairy products**
Milk solids

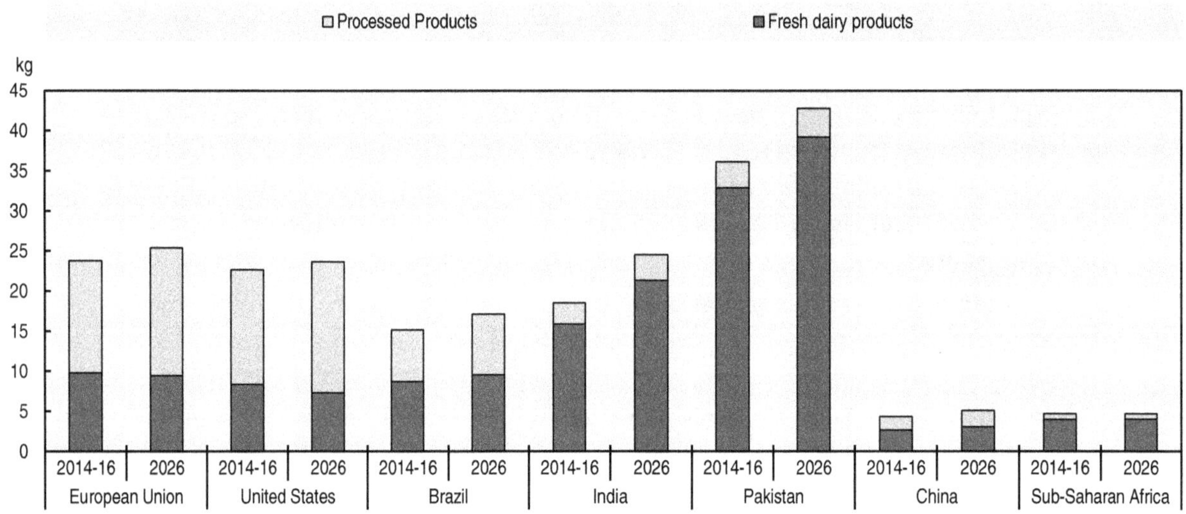

Note: Milk solids are calculated by adding the amount of fat and non-fat solids for each product; Processed products include butter cheese, skim milk powder and whole milk powder

Source: OECD/FAO (2017), "OECD-FAO Agricultural Outlook", OECD Agriculture statistics (database), *http://dx.doi.org/10.1787/agr-data-en.*

StatLink *http://dx.doi.org/10.1787/888933522092*

Although in some countries world milk production has been limited in recent years, it is projected to increase by 178 Mt (22%) in 2026, compared to the 2014-16 base period. The share of production from developed countries decreases over time, from 49% in 2016 to 44% in 2026. The majority of the increase in milk production (77%) is anticipated to come from developing countries, in particular Pakistan and India, which are expected to account for 29% of total milk production by 2026, compared to 24% in the base year. The expansion of milk production in developing countries at a rate of 2.7% p.a., is expected to be largely consumed domestically as fresh dairy products. At the world level, production of WMP is increasing at 1.9% p.a.; production of butter and SMP is expected to grow faster at 2% p.a. and 2.5% p.a. respectively, while cheese production should grow at 1.4% p.a.

Starting from a relatively low base in 2016, demand growth will support increases in dairy prices over the medium term. By 2026, cheese prices, currently lower than butter prices, will surpass the latter and be 38% higher than in the base period. The prices of milk powders increase slowly in the short term, due to the slow recovery of powder demand from China. Even though they are not expected to return to the highs of 2013-14, prices of SMP and WMP will increase by 76% and 60% respectively, between the base period and 2026, implying modest increases in real terms.

The projected depreciation over the medium term of the Argentinian and Brazilian currencies with respect to the United States dollar will encourage growth in exports from these countries as they become more competitive. On the import side, the currencies of most large importers – namely Philippines, Egypt, Islamic Republic of Iran, and Indonesia – are expected to depreciate, which will reduce their import demands. In the case of Japan, import demand is constrained by an ageing population, while in Canada the response is limited by the country's domestic dairy policies. Between the base period and 2026, the export share of dairy commodities increases for European Union from 24% to 28%. India – as the world's largest milk producing country – has a large expanding domestic market, and is not projected to become an important player on the export market.

The expanded dairy and dairy products chapter is available at
http://dx.doi.org/10.1787/agr_outlook-2017-11-en

FISH AND SEAFOOD

Market situation

The global fishery and aquaculture sector continued to expand in 2016, albeit at a modest rate. This reflects a number of factors, including diseases in aquaculture production, *El Niño*, regulatory constraints, and the ongoing inability of capture production to continue growing under current exploitation conditions. Aquaculture was responsible for the overall growth in production as capture fisheries experienced lower catches of selected major species including anchoveta (mainly used to produce fishmeal and fish oil).

Although several exporting countries faced supply constraints, the value of international fish trade increased in 2016, recouping part of the losses registered in 2015. This growth in value terms was mainly due to improved prices for a number of highly traded seafood commodities, in particular salmon. According to the FAO Fish Price Index, international fish prices were 7% higher on average in the second half of 2016 compared to the same period in the previous year. Despite higher prices, consumer demand for fish was sustained, with an overall slight increase in per capita fish intake. Due to a revision of historical capture fisheries data new statistics indicate that since 2013 aquaculture has become the main global source of fish for human consumption, rather than 2014 as previously believed.

Projection highlights

Average nominal traded fish prices are projected to continue increasing at a rate of 0.8% p.a. over the outlook period and are expected to grow by a total of 7.3% by 2026 when compared to the 2014-16 base period. Average nominal prices for both aquaculture and capture species are expected to remain relatively flat or decrease slightly up to 2020 but then begin growing up to 2026. Nominal prices for fishmeal and fish oil continue trending upwards over the outlook period with respective growth rates of 3.4% p.a. and 2.0% p.a.

Total fish production at the global level is anticipated to grow by just over 1% p.a. over the outlook period, a substantial reduction when compared to the 2.4% p.a. growth rate witnessed over the previous decade. In absolute terms total production is expected to reach 193.9 Mt by 2026, growing by a total of 15.2% (25.6 Mt) from the base period, partly affected by the assumed *El Niño* event in 2026. This slowdown is driven by the combined effect of growth rates falling in both capture fisheries and aquaculture. The annual rate of growth in world capture production is anticipated to be negative over the projected time period, at -0.1% p.a., compared with a positive 0.3% p.a. rate of growth observed over the previous decade (2007-16).

The observed slowdown in aquaculture growth is expected to continue, falling from 5.3% p.a. over the period 2007-16 to 2.3% p.a. for 2017-26. Aquaculture production is expected to surpass total capture fisheries production (including that utilised for non-food uses) in 2021, a year when capture production is assumed to be lower as a consequence of *El Niño*, and then continue to increase in absolute terms until the end of the outlook period. Global aquaculture production is anticipated to exceed the 100 Mt mark for the first time in 2025 and to reach 102 Mt in 2026. Continuing profitability as a consequence of relatively low feed prices is behind the ongoing growth of aquaculture, and profitability in the sector is expected to remain high in the short term, especially for species that require small amounts of fishmeal and fish oil. Production of selected freshwater species, including catfish/pangas, tilapia, and carp are expected to grow fastest over the next decade, all by more than 35%, while salmon/trout and shrimp will grow by around 27% and 28%, respectively, and molluscs by around 24%.

Figure 3.6. **Regional contributions to world fish and seafood production**

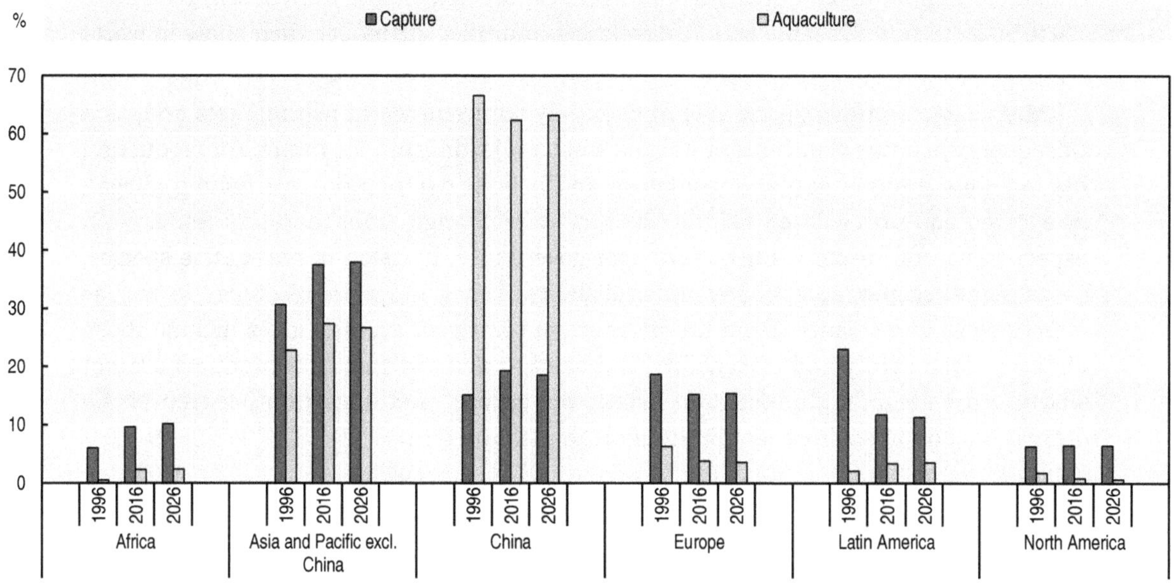

Source: OECD/FAO (2017), "OECD-FAO Agricultural Outlook", OECD Agriculture statistics (database), *http://dx.doi.org/10.1787/agr-data-en.*

StatLink *http://dx.doi.org/10.1787/888933522111*

The share of capture fisheries production that is reduced into fishmeal and fish oil will continue to fall over the next decade, with 3.4% less fish being crushed in 2026 than the base period. Efficiency increases, that are enabling greater quantities of oil and fishmeal to be recovered from fish waste, mean that the reduced share going to crushing is not expected to affect total world fishmeal and fish oil production, which will be relatively stable (except in *El Niño* years). Production of fishmeal and fish oil from fish residue will continue to increase, both at rates of 1.6% and 1.5% p.a., respectively, over 2017-26. Between the base period and 2026 the proportion of total fish oil obtained from waste fish will grow from 35.7% to 40.1%; for fishmeal this proportion increases from 26.9% to 29.2% over the same period. With growing demand from aquaculture and a stable supply, the price of fishmeal will continue to increase relative to oilseed meals.

Fish consumed as food is expected to increase at the global level from 148.8 Mt in the base period to 177.4 Mt by 2026 but, mirroring changes in production, the rate of increase is slowing and expected to be 1.4% p.a. over the period 2017-26, down from 2.9% p.a. in 2007-16. Growth in per capita consumption is also anticipated to slow, from 1.7% p.a. in 2007-16 to 0.4% p.a. over the projection and to reach 21.6 kg in 2026. At the world level, proportionally more of the fish being produced will be consumed as food by 2026 (91.5%) than in the base period (88.4%). At the regional level, per capita consumption is expected to continue an increasing trend in the Americas and in Europe, whilst rates of growth will decline in Asia (from 2.5% p.a. over 2007-16 to 0.7% p.a. in 2017-26) and become negative in Africa (-0.3% p.a. over 2017-26). This prospective decline for Africa raises an alarm in terms of food security.

About 35% of total fish production (30% excluding intra-EU trade) is expected to be exported in different product forms for human consumption, fishmeal and fish oil. After falling in 2015-16 world trade of fish for human consumption will once again increase, at a rate of 1.5% p.a. over the outlook period and by a total of 12.9% by 2026 (5.0 Mt lw), but this rate of increase is flatter than that observed in the previous decade. Being the major producers, Asian countries are expected to continue to be the main exporters of fish for human consumption, with their share in world exports to increase from 50% in 2014-16 to 53% in 2026. During the same period, developed countries will reduce their share in world imports from 53% to 52%.

Many factors influence the evolution and dynamics of world fish markets and, as a consequence, a range of uncertainties exist when projecting into the future. For production this includes: environmental degradation and habitat destruction, overfishing, illegal, unreported and unregulated fishing (IUU), climate change, transboundary issues with respect to natural resource utilisation, poor governance, invasion of non-native species, diseases and escapes, accessibility and availability of sites and water resources, as well as to technology and finance. From the perspective of market access, issues include those related to food safety and traceability, the need to demonstrate that products are not derived from illegal and proscribed fishing operations, and uncertainties around the international trade environment in the short to medium term.

The expanded fish and seafood chapter is available at
http://dx.doi.org/10.1787/agr_outlook-2017-12-en

BIOFUELS

Market situation

International prices of biodiesel and ethanol stabilised in 2016. Demand for biofuels was sustained by bioenergy obligatory blending and by the surge in demand for transportation fuels due to continued weak energy prices. Unfavourable price ratios of biofuels to conventional fuels resulted in a limited demand for non-mandated use of biofuels, with the notable exception of Brazil where recent policy reforms in several states favour hydrous ethanol which can be used directly by their flex-fuel vehicle fleet. Despite low crude oil prices, policy decisions were favourable to biofuels in 2016 with developments such as mandate increases and differential taxation systems or subsidies enacted in several countries.

In the United States, the Environmental Protection Agency's (EPA) final rulemaking for 2017 increased the maximum potential access for corn ethanol under the program to the statutory limit of 15 billion gallons and specified an "advanced" mandate that is higher than it would have been if it fully reflected the reduction of the cellulosic mandate. This translates into a strong demand for ethanol and biodiesel, despite the blend wall[1] constraint. The European Commission provided a nuanced message in a July 2016 communication on the limited role that food-based biofuels would play in decarbonising the transport sector post-2020. A revision to the European legislation – the RED2 legislation[2]– was proposed in February 2017 but is not considered in these projections. It sets a limit of 3.8% for the portion of renewable energy in the transport sector coming from food and feed crops below the current 7% cap.

Projection highlights

International crude oil prices are expected to double in nominal terms over the baseline period. This should lower demand for gasoline and diesel fuels, especially in developed countries. Biofuel prices, similar to biofuel feedstock prices, should trend upward but at a slower pace than energy prices. The evolution of ethanol and biodiesel markets over the baseline period is expected to continue to be driven by policies. Biofuel policies are subject to uncertainty and projections; they are based in this *Outlook* on a specific set of assumptions concerning the continuation of the same policies over the next ten years.

For the United States, all mandates are assumed to remain at their announced levels for 2017 except the cellulosic mandate, which should continue to increase moderately. The ethanol blend wall is set to increase to 11.3% by 2026. This *Outlook* thus assumes a limited development of mid-blends of ethanol. In addition, biodiesel use is assumed to increase in the early years of the outlook period, above the biodiesel mandate, to meet part of the advanced mandate (Figure 3.7). The Canadian Federal program called ecoENERGY for biofuels that started in 2008 with incentives of CAD 0.10 per litre for ethanol and CAD 0.26 per litre for biodiesel is gradually phased out with payments reduced to CAD 0.03 and CAD 0.04 respectively for ethanol and biodiesel.

1. The term blend wall refers to short-term technical constraints that act as an impediment to increased ethanol use.
2. *http://eur-lex.europa.eu/legal-content/EN/TXT/?uri=CELEX:52016PC0767R%2801%29*

Figure 3.7. **Evolution of ethanol blending in gasoline fuels and of biodiesel blending in diesel fuels**

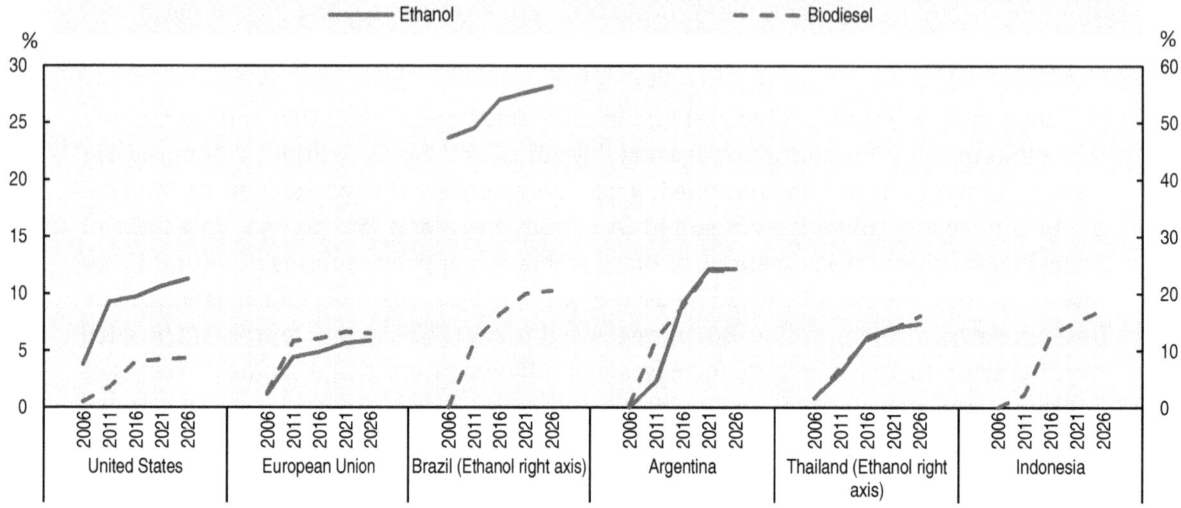

Note: Shares are expressed in volume.

Source: OECD/FAO (2017), "OECD-FAO Agricultural Outlook", OECD Agriculture statistics (database), *http://dx.doi.org/10.1787/agr-data-en*.

StatLink *http://dx.doi.org/10.1787/888933522130*

The use of biofuels in the European Union is assumed to be governed by the 2009 Renewable Energy (RED) and Fuel Quality Directives and the 2015 ILUC Directive, as well as by national legislations. The proportion of total transportation energy accounted for biofuels, including double counting for waste- and residue-based biofuels, is expected to reach 6.4% by 2020 and to remain stable thereafter. The remainder of the 10% RED target should be met from other renewable energy sources.

It is assumed that the Brazilian taxation system will remain favourable to hydrous ethanol rather than gasohol, which corresponds to the mandatory mix of 27% ethanol with gasoline. Brazilian ethanol demand is expected to expand by 6 blnL over the outlook period. The Brazilian biodiesel mandate should reach 10% by 2019, leading to an increase in production of more than 40% over the next ten years. In Argentina, it is assumed that the 12% blending mandate for biodiesel and ethanol will be fulfilled by 2020. Argentinean biodiesel production should be also driven by US import demand to meet the latter's advanced mandate.

Thailand is expected to be a significant player on biofuel markets, with most of its biofuel use met by domestic production. The Thai government plan to increase use of biofuels entails a differential taxation and subsidy system that is favourable to higher blends of ethanol in gasoline. The Indian government should continue to support the production of ethanol from molasses. It is assumed, however, that the observed blending share of ethanol in gasoline remains lower than the 5% mandate. The Indonesian government has a 20% biodiesel blending mandate, but this *Outlook* assumes that this mandate will not be fulfilled. The development of biodiesel production in Indonesia is related to the potential attribution of subsidies to biodiesel producers. Chinese use of ethanol should expand by about 1 blnL with mandates in place in some cities. Chinese ethanol is expected to be produced domestically from maize – thus helping to lower domestic stocks – and from cassava.

Given these expected developments, global ethanol production should expand from 120 blnL in 2016 to 137 blnL by 2026, while global biodiesel production should increase from 37 blnL in 2016 to 40.5 blnL by 2026. By 2026, 55% of global ethanol production should be based on maize and 35% on sugar crops. In 2026, about 30% of global biodiesel production should be based on waste vegetable oils. Advanced biofuels based on residues are not expected to take off over the projection period due to lack of investment in research and development.

Biofuel trade will remain limited. Potential ethanol exporters are the United States where the blend wall limits further increases in domestic demand and Brazil where ethanol could fulfil part of the US advanced ethanol mandate. Brazilian ethanol exports are not expected to expand as US ethanol is likely to remain cheaper over the outlook period. Argentina is expected to be a major biodiesel exporter with most exports directed towards the United States. The future of European biodiesel anti-dumping duties is an important uncertainty in the evolution of biodiesel trade.

The expanded biofuels chapter is available at
http://dx.doi.org/10.1787/agr_outlook-2017-13-en

COTTON

Market situation

There was a light recovery in the world cotton market during the 2016 marketing year following a strong drop in production in 2015, from 26.2 Mt in 2014 to 21.2 Mt. Global cotton production recovered by about 7% in 2016 due to improved yields. In addition, on-going stock releases sustained world consumption, although total world stocks remain at a very high level (18 Mt, 7.5% less than 2015, but still the equivalent of about eight months of world consumption). Production increased in almost all major cotton producing countries, with the exception of China. Pakistan, the United States, Brazil and India increased production by 17%, 24%, 7% and 1%, respectively due to improved yields that over-compensated a contraction in the area planted.

Global cotton demand stagnated at around 23.9 Mt during the 2016 marketing year. Mill consumption estimates in India remained stable at 5.3 Mt, but in China, decreased by 2.0% to 7.2 Mt. Mill consumption increased in Viet Nam by 12% and in Bangladesh by 11%. The increase in Pakistan was 1%. Global cotton trade recovered slightly, increasing by 3.8% in 2016 to 7.7 Mt. Increases in imports by Bangladesh, Pakistan and Viet Nam were insufficient to offset the decline in many countries' import demand since 2015. China's new cotton support policy, which narrowed the price gap between domestic and imported cotton, is behind this sluggish consumption; its domestic cotton price was below the imported price for a limited time in 2016. Moreover, US exports continued to increase, to 2.7 Mt or 27%, over the previous year, and Australia's exports increased by 17% as production recovered.

Projection highlights

Although the world cotton price remains under pressure due to high stock levels and fierce competition from synthetic fibres, cotton prices are expected to be relatively stable in nominal terms. This makes cotton less competitive because prices for polyester are significantly lower than international and domestic cotton prices and likely to decrease further. During 2017-26, relative stability is expected as government support policies continue to stabilise markets in major cotton-producing countries. However, world cotton prices are expected to be lower in real terms than the average during the base period (2014-16).

World production is expected to grow at a slower pace than consumption during the first few years of the outlook period, reflecting anticipated lower price levels and projected releases of global stocks accumulated between 2010 and 2014. More cotton may be auctioned if sales are strong and market prices increase. Last year, around 2.6 Mt were sold through to the end of September 2016. The stock-to-use ratio is expected to fall to 39% in 2026 from 83% in the base period. The global land use devoted to cotton is projected to decrease slightly below the average in the base period. Global cotton yields will grow slowly as production gradually shifts from relatively high yielding countries, notably China, to relatively low-yielding ones in South Asia.

World cotton use is expected to grow at 0.9% p.a. as a result of slower economic and population growth in comparison with 2000s, reaching 26.0 Mt in 2026. Consumption in China is expected to fall by 15% from the base period to 6.2 Mt following the downward

Figure 3.8. **Cotton consumption by region**

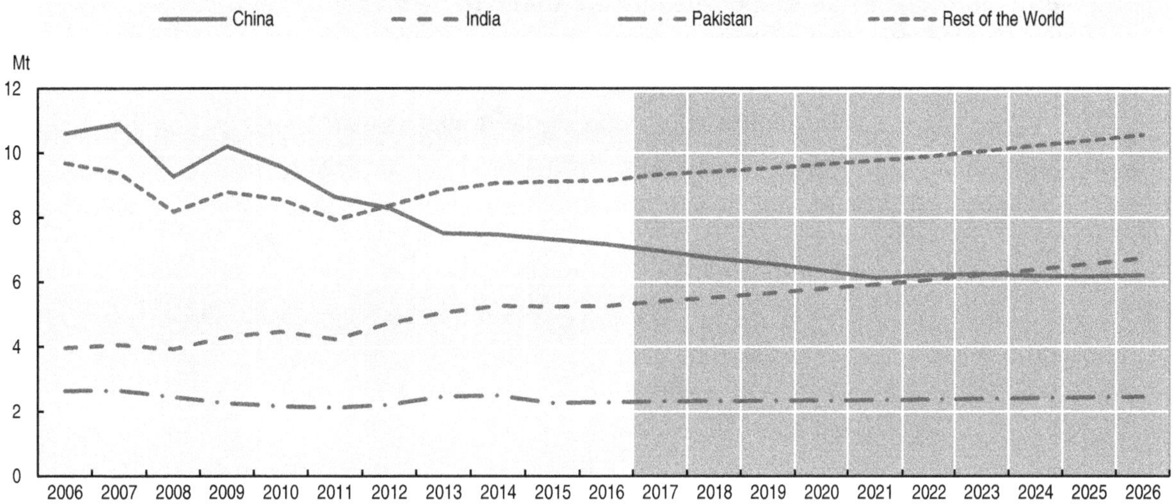

Source: OECD/FAO (2017), "OECD-FAO Agricultural Outlook", OECD Agriculture statistics (database), *http://dx.doi.org/10.1787/agr-data-en.*

StatLink *http://dx.doi.org/10.1787/888933522149*

trend since 2010, while India will become the world's most important country for cotton mill consumption with 6.7 Mt in 2026. Higher cotton mill consumption by 2026 is also foreseen for Viet Nam, Bangladesh, Indonesia and Turkey, with consumption increasing by 45%, 47%, 10% and 8% respectively.

It is expected that global cotton trade will grow more slowly compared to previous years, especially 2011-13 when growth was driven by surging Chinese imports. Trade in 2026 is expected, however, to exceed the average of the 2000s. To obtain value-added from mills, there has been a shift in the past several years from trading raw cotton to cotton yarn and man-made fibres, and which is expected to continue. Global raw cotton trade will nevertheless reach 8.5 Mt by 2026, 12% higher than the average of the 2014-16 base period, despite cotton being less competitive as prices for polyester are expected to be significantly lower. The United States retains its position as the world's largest exporter, accounting for 33% of world trade, a percentage that will remain stable. Brazil is ranked second with exports expected to reach 1.1 Mt, from 0.9 Mt. Cotton producing countries in Sub-Saharan Africa, as a whole, are expected to increase their exports to 1.5 Mt by 2026. After a strong decrease of cotton imports by China 2012 and 2016 it is expected that import increase over the outlook period to about 1.3 Mt in 2026. Its dominant role in the world cotton market will be significantly challenged as other importing countries emerge and India is assumed to be the largest cotton importer in 2026. It is projected that imports in Bangladesh and Viet Nam will increase to 1.5 Mt, each.

While increases in farm labour costs and competition for resources with other agricultural crops place significant constraints on growth, higher productivity driven by technological progress, including greater adoption of bio-tech cotton, creates significant potential for cotton production to expand in the next decade. Although the medium-term prospects are for sustained growth, there may be potential short-term uncertainties in the current outlook period which may result in short-term volatility in demand, supply and prices. A sudden slow-down in the global economy, a sharp drop in global textiles and clothing trade, competitive prices and quality from synthetic fibres, and changes in government policies are important factors that can affect the cotton market. The unprecedented high level of stocks is currently a key driver of the world cotton price.

The expanded cotton chapter is available at
http://dx.doi.org/10.1787/agr_outlook-2017-14-en

OECD-FAO Agricultural Outlook 2017-2026

ANNEX

Commodity snapshot tables

Table 3.A1.1. **World cereal projections**

Marketing year

		Average 2014-16est	2017	2018	2019	2020	2021	2022	2023	2024	2025	2026
WHEAT												
World												
Production	Mt	742.1	744.2	755.5	763.3	771.4	780.0	788.1	796.3	804.4	812.4	820.8
Area	Mha	222.7	222.8	223.5	224.0	224.4	224.9	225.3	225.6	226.0	226.4	226.7
Yield	t/ha	3.33	3.34	3.38	3.41	3.44	3.47	3.50	3.53	3.56	3.59	3.62
Consumption	Mt	722.4	754.2	753.2	760.6	767.9	775.9	783.2	791.1	798.9	806.9	815.3
Feed use	Mt	138.5	148.5	146.4	148.0	149.8	152.0	153.9	155.9	157.8	159.9	162.3
Food use	Mt	491.5	507.1	512.8	517.7	522.4	527.3	532.3	537.1	542.1	547.0	551.9
Biofuel use	Mt	13.1	13.2	13.6	13.7	13.6	13.3	13.6	13.4	13.4	13.5	13.3
Other use	Mt	79.2	85.5	80.4	81.3	82.2	83.2	83.5	84.7	85.6	86.5	87.8
Exports	Mt	165.8	168.8	173.9	176.5	178.5	180.4	182.7	184.8	186.9	189.1	191.1
Closing stocks	Mt	226.3	226.1	226.0	226.3	227.3	229.0	231.6	234.4	237.4	240.4	243.5
Price[1]	USD/t	207.3	200.5	202.5	208.2	215.9	225.3	232.7	238.5	243.6	246.2	248.9
Developed countries												
Production	Mt	397.5	396.7	403.7	407.0	410.8	414.6	418.0	421.2	424.4	427.6	430.9
Consumption	Mt	275.2	279.9	277.9	279.5	281.0	282.9	284.4	286.1	287.7	289.4	291.1
Net trade	Mt	115.4	121.4	126.8	129.0	130.6	132.0	133.6	135.0	136.5	138.1	139.5
Closing stocks	Mt	78.4	81.1	80.1	78.7	77.8	77.5	77.5	77.5	77.7	77.9	78.3
Developing countries												
Production	Mt	344.6	347.4	351.8	356.3	360.6	365.4	370.2	375.1	380.1	384.8	389.9
Consumption	Mt	447.2	474.3	475.3	481.1	486.9	492.9	498.8	504.9	511.3	517.6	524.2
Net trade	Mt	-112.9	-119.0	-124.3	-126.6	-128.2	-129.5	-131.2	-132.6	-134.1	-135.6	-137.0
Closing stocks	Mt	147.9	145.0	145.8	147.6	149.5	151.5	154.1	156.8	159.7	162.6	165.3
OECD[2]												
Production	Mt	298.0	294.0	298.2	300.8	303.4	306.1	308.4	310.7	312.8	315.0	317.1
Consumption	Mt	224.5	230.0	227.4	228.6	229.7	231.1	232.1	233.3	234.4	235.6	236.7
Net trade	Mt	68.5	69.2	71.8	73.7	74.6	75.4	76.5	77.4	78.4	79.4	80.1
Closing stocks	Mt	58.7	58.6	57.5	56.0	55.2	54.8	54.6	54.6	54.6	54.5	54.7
MAIZE												
World												
Production	Mt	1 024.7	1 042.4	1 050.8	1 066.2	1 078.9	1 096.0	1 109.7	1 123.0	1 136.0	1 149.4	1 163.7
Area	Mha	177.9	178.0	178.0	178.7	179.0	179.9	180.4	180.8	181.0	181.4	181.8
Yield	t/ha	5.76	5.85	5.90	5.96	6.03	6.09	6.15	6.21	6.28	6.34	6.40
Consumption	Mt	1 015.1	1 041.3	1 058.3	1 072.2	1 083.2	1 096.0	1 106.6	1 119.6	1 132.1	1 147.0	1 161.2
Feed use	Mt	574.1	600.9	609.3	621.7	629.9	642.1	650.8	662.2	672.8	683.8	695.4
Food use	Mt	131.5	135.7	137.9	140.0	142.1	144.4	146.8	149.2	151.5	153.9	156.3
Biofuel use	Mt	167.5	176.6	181.0	181.4	183.4	182.8	182.7	182.3	181.9	181.5	180.8
Other use	Mt	99.0	84.0	85.4	83.6	81.5	79.8	78.7	77.8	77.3	78.6	78.9
Exports	Mt	135.3	137.9	138.4	139.3	140.6	143.0	145.6	148.1	150.2	152.4	154.5
Closing stocks	Mt	228.8	222.1	213.3	206.1	200.6	199.4	201.3	203.5	206.2	207.5	208.8
Price[3]	USD/t	164.4	156.5	161.1	164.9	173.5	179.4	183.8	185.5	190.2	193.6	196.7
Developed countries												
Production	Mt	504.7	513.1	515.0	521.7	526.6	533.4	538.4	543.6	548.4	553.3	558.6
Consumption	Mt	447.5	465.6	472.4	478.4	482.3	486.7	488.8	493.1	496.8	500.8	505.1
Net trade	Mt	46.9	47.9	46.4	46.9	47.1	47.4	48.2	49.8	51.2	52.2	53.2
Closing stocks	Mt	80.3	86.3	82.5	78.8	76.0	75.3	76.6	77.3	77.8	78.1	78.3
Developing countries												
Production	Mt	520.0	529.4	535.8	544.5	552.3	562.7	571.3	579.5	587.6	596.1	605.1
Consumption	Mt	567.6	575.7	586.0	593.8	600.9	609.3	617.8	626.6	635.4	646.2	656.0
Net trade	Mt	-45.4	-46.7	-45.2	-45.7	-45.9	-46.2	-47.0	-48.6	-50.0	-51.0	-52.0
Closing stocks	Mt	148.5	135.8	130.8	127.3	124.6	124.1	124.7	126.2	128.4	129.4	130.5
OECD[2]												
Production	Mt	474.8	478.5	479.6	485.7	489.9	496.2	500.7	505.3	509.6	513.9	518.7
Consumption	Mt	466.3	485.8	492.6	498.5	502.3	506.8	509.0	513.2	516.9	521.0	525.3
Net trade	Mt	-1.9	-5.8	-7.8	-8.5	-9.6	-9.8	-9.6	-8.4	-7.7	-7.2	-6.8
Closing stocks	Mt	78.3	84.6	79.4	75.1	72.3	71.6	72.9	73.4	73.8	74.0	74.2

Table 3.A1.1. **World cereal projections** *(cont.)*

Marketing year

		Average 2014-16est	2017	2018	2019	2020	2021	2022	2023	2024	2025	2026
OTHER COARSE GRAINS												
World												
Production	Mt	301.4	302.1	305.4	308.5	311.8	315.2	318.6	321.9	325.1	328.5	331.8
Area	Mha	156.2	153.9	154.0	154.2	154.3	154.4	154.6	154.8	154.9	155.1	155.3
Yield	t/ha	1.93	1.96	1.98	2.00	2.02	2.04	2.06	2.08	2.10	2.12	2.14
Consumption	Mt	292.5	298.1	300.3	304.1	307.2	310.4	313.2	316.5	319.7	323.1	326.5
Feed use	Mt	165.1	166.5	166.7	169.1	172.2	174.3	175.7	177.6	179.2	180.7	182.0
Food use	Mt	75.5	77.9	79.6	81.0	82.4	83.8	85.3	86.8	88.4	89.9	91.5
Biofuel use	Mt	7.8	9.8	10.1	10.1	10.2	10.2	10.1	9.9	9.9	9.9	9.9
Other use	Mt	44.2	43.9	43.9	43.9	42.4	42.1	42.2	42.1	42.1	42.6	43.0
Exports	Mt	49.2	43.4	43.9	44.9	45.9	46.7	47.7	48.7	49.5	50.3	51.2
Closing stocks	Mt	58.1	61.4	61.5	60.8	60.4	60.1	60.5	60.9	61.3	61.5	61.8
Price[4]	USD/t	179.4	154.6	155.6	162.3	170.2	181.1	186.8	187.8	191.9	195.3	198.3
Developed countries												
Production	Mt	188.9	185.4	186.8	188.1	189.3	190.4	191.5	192.5	193.5	194.5	195.5
Consumption	Mt	150.1	156.1	156.1	156.9	157.2	157.5	157.5	157.7	157.9	158.4	158.6
Net trade	Mt	36.2	30.4	30.7	31.6	32.4	33.1	34.0	34.8	35.5	36.1	36.9
Closing stocks	Mt	37.1	41.2	41.2	40.8	40.4	40.3	40.4	40.4	40.5	40.5	40.4
Developing countries												
Production	Mt	112.5	116.7	118.6	120.4	122.6	124.8	127.1	129.4	131.6	134.0	136.4
Consumption	Mt	142.4	142.0	144.2	147.2	150.0	152.8	155.7	158.7	161.7	164.8	167.8
Net trade	Mt	-30.1	-25.3	-25.6	-26.5	-27.4	-28.0	-28.9	-29.8	-30.4	-31.1	-31.9
Closing stocks	Mt	21.0	20.2	20.2	20.0	19.9	19.9	20.1	20.5	20.8	21.1	21.5
OECD[2]												
Production	Mt	155.0	150.2	151.4	152.4	153.3	154.3	155.3	156.2	157.1	158.0	159.0
Consumption	Mt	129.3	133.2	132.7	133.3	133.4	133.6	133.5	133.9	134.3	134.9	135.4
Net trade	Mt	24.9	18.8	19.0	19.6	20.3	20.7	21.4	22.1	22.6	23.0	23.6
Closing stocks	Mt	30.9	31.7	31.4	30.9	30.6	30.5	30.8	31.0	31.2	31.4	31.4
RICE												
World												
Production	Mt	494.9	506.5	512.5	518.2	524.2	530.0	536.1	542.1	548.3	554.6	560.9
Area	Mha	162.3	163.8	163.8	163.9	164.0	164.0	164.0	164.1	164.1	164.2	164.2
Yield	t/ha	3.05	3.09	3.13	3.16	3.20	3.23	3.27	3.30	3.34	3.38	3.42
Consumption	Mt	494.7	507.6	513.5	518.1	524.3	530.1	535.8	541.8	547.8	553.9	560.1
Feed use	Mt	20.6	21.9	22.6	23.0	23.3	23.7	23.9	24.2	24.5	24.8	25.2
Food use	Mt	399.9	409.6	414.4	418.9	423.8	428.2	432.6	437.0	441.4	445.8	450.3
Exports	Mt	44.0	42.7	43.7	44.7	45.6	46.6	47.4	48.3	49.3	50.2	51.2
Closing stocks	Mt	171.7	169.4	167.9	167.5	166.9	166.4	166.2	166.1	166.2	166.5	166.8
Price[5]	USD/t	375.1	389.0	393.5	398.4	400.3	405.0	407.6	409.5	411.1	412.9	415.5
Developed countries												
Production	Mt	18.1	17.3	18.2	18.2	18.3	18.4	18.4	18.5	18.5	18.6	18.6
Consumption	Mt	19.1	19.3	19.3	19.3	19.3	19.3	19.3	19.3	19.3	19.3	19.3
Net trade	Mt	-1.1	-1.4	-0.9	-1.0	-1.0	-1.0	-1.0	-1.0	-1.0	-0.9	-0.9
Closing stocks	Mt	5.1	4.4	4.2	4.1	4.1	4.1	4.2	4.3	4.5	4.7	4.9
Developing countries												
Production	Mt	476.8	489.2	494.3	499.9	505.9	511.6	517.6	523.7	529.8	536.0	542.3
Consumption	Mt	475.6	488.3	494.3	498.8	505.0	510.8	516.5	522.5	528.4	534.6	540.8
Net trade	Mt	1.5	1.8	1.4	1.4	1.5	1.4	1.4	1.4	1.4	1.4	1.3
Closing stocks	Mt	166.5	165.0	163.7	163.4	162.9	162.3	162.0	161.7	161.7	161.8	161.9
OECD[2]												
Production	Mt	21.8	20.8	21.7	21.6	21.7	21.7	21.7	21.7	21.7	21.7	21.7
Consumption	Mt	22.9	23.3	23.2	23.1	23.0	23.0	22.9	22.9	22.8	22.8	22.7
Net trade	Mt	-1.4	-1.6	-1.2	-1.3	-1.3	-1.3	-1.3	-1.3	-1.3	-1.3	-1.3
Closing stocks	Mt	6.6	5.8	5.4	5.2	5.1	5.1	5.2	5.3	5.4	5.6	5.8

Note: Marketing year: See Glossary of Terms for definitions.
Average 2014-16est: Data for 2016 are estimated.

1. No.2 hard red winter wheat, ordinary protein, United States FOB Gulf Ports (June/May).
2. Excludes Iceland but includes all EU28 member countries.
3. No.2 yellow corn, United States FOB Gulf Ports (September/August).
4. Feed barley, Europe, FOB Rouen.
5. Milled 100%, grade b, nominal price quote, FOB Bangkok (January/December).

Source: OECD/FAO (2017), "OECD-FAO Agricultural Outlook", *OECD Agriculture statistics* (database). doi: dx.doi.org/10.1787/agr-outl-data-en

Table 3.A1.2. **World oilseed projections**

Marketing year

		Average 2014-16est	2017	2018	2019	2020	2021	2022	2023	2024	2025	2026
SOYBEAN												
World												
Production	Mt	325.6	338.6	344.6	350.7	358.2	364.7	372.9	378.7	386.7	393.1	401.3
Consumption	Mt	322.2	341.9	347.0	352.0	358.6	365.3	372.5	379.0	386.2	393.3	401.1
Crush	Mt	288.1	306.3	310.8	315.5	321.6	327.9	334.6	340.6	347.5	354.1	361.4
Closing stocks	Mt	36.3	33.5	31.1	29.8	29.4	28.8	29.1	28.8	29.3	29.0	29.2
Price[1]	USD/t	402.2	389.7	398.2	408.6	412.0	430.6	434.0	439.6	439.5	442.2	446.1
Developed countries												
Production	Mt	127.3	128.0	128.9	129.7	131.6	133.3	135.2	136.4	138.2	139.6	141.1
Consumption	Mt	86.7	88.2	89.0	89.2	90.4	91.5	92.8	93.5	94.7	95.6	97.1
Crush	Mt	77.7	79.6	80.3	80.6	81.7	82.8	84.0	84.8	86.0	86.9	88.2
Closing stocks	Mt	11.3	13.2	11.4	10.6	10.3	10.3	10.6	10.7	11.2	11.2	11.7
Developing countries												
Production	Mt	198.3	210.7	215.7	220.9	226.6	231.4	237.7	242.3	248.4	253.4	260.2
Consumption	Mt	235.5	253.7	258.0	262.8	268.2	273.8	279.8	285.5	291.5	297.7	304.0
Crush	Mt	210.4	226.7	230.5	234.9	239.9	245.1	250.5	255.8	261.4	267.2	273.2
Closing stocks	Mt	25.0	20.3	19.7	19.2	19.0	18.5	18.5	18.2	18.1	17.8	17.6
OECD[2]												
Production	Mt	119.6	119.4	120.1	120.7	122.3	123.7	125.3	126.3	127.9	129.0	130.2
Consumption	Mt	87.5	89.1	89.8	89.9	91.1	92.0	93.1	93.8	94.9	95.8	97.2
Crush	Mt	78.4	80.3	81.0	81.1	82.2	83.2	84.3	84.9	86.1	86.9	88.2
Closing stocks	Mt	11.2	12.9	11.1	10.3	10.0	10.0	10.3	10.4	10.9	10.9	11.3
OTHER OILSEEDS												
World												
Production	Mt	139.9	146.0	147.7	149.4	151.1	152.7	154.3	156.3	158.0	159.3	161.2
Consumption	Mt	141.1	145.2	147.5	149.6	151.4	152.9	154.4	156.2	158.0	159.5	161.0
Crush	Mt	119.5	123.2	125.4	127.4	129.1	130.6	131.9	133.6	135.2	136.6	138.0
Closing stocks	Mt	8.1	8.2	8.4	8.2	7.9	7.8	7.7	7.8	7.8	7.6	7.8
Price[3]	USD/t	420.0	431.3	425.0	428.3	441.7	451.4	454.4	459.0	465.8	477.3	483.2
Developed countries												
Production	Mt	84.3	88.1	89.1	90.3	91.4	92.5	93.4	94.9	96.0	96.7	98.0
Consumption	Mt	76.6	79.7	81.1	82.2	82.9	83.6	84.3	85.2	86.0	86.7	87.4
Crush	Mt	69.5	72.5	73.8	74.7	75.3	76.0	76.5	77.3	78.0	78.7	79.2
Closing stocks	Mt	6.2	6.5	6.7	6.5	6.2	6.0	5.9	6.0	6.0	5.8	6.0
Developing countries												
Production	Mt	55.6	57.9	58.6	59.1	59.7	60.2	60.9	61.4	62.0	62.6	63.3
Consumption	Mt	64.6	65.4	66.4	67.4	68.5	69.2	70.1	71.1	72.0	72.8	73.7
Crush	Mt	50.0	50.7	51.7	52.7	53.8	54.6	55.4	56.3	57.2	58.0	58.8
Closing stocks	Mt	1.9	1.7	1.7	1.7	1.7	1.8	1.8	1.8	1.8	1.9	1.9
OECD[2]												
Production	Mt	57.9	58.6	59.0	59.5	59.9	60.3	60.5	61.2	61.6	61.5	62.0
Consumption	Mt	54.4	54.6	55.5	56.0	56.2	56.4	56.5	56.8	57.0	57.1	57.1
Crush	Mt	49.3	49.6	50.4	50.8	50.9	51.1	51.2	51.4	51.6	51.7	51.6
Closing stocks	Mt	5.4	5.6	5.7	5.5	5.3	5.1	5.0	5.0	5.0	4.8	5.0
PROTEIN MEALS												
World												
Production	Mt	314.5	331.2	335.8	340.3	346.1	352.2	358.6	364.6	371.2	377.5	384.3
Consumption	Mt	308.8	330.1	335.0	340.5	346.4	352.5	358.7	364.8	371.3	377.5	384.2
Closing stocks	Mt	16.0	16.4	17.1	16.9	16.6	16.3	16.2	16.0	15.8	15.8	15.9
Price[4]	USD/t	340.2	296.4	294.9	297.9	302.6	313.1	313.0	318.7	321.0	327.2	335.3
Developed countries												
Production	Mt	101.2	104.3	105.2	105.7	106.9	108.1	109.4	110.4	111.7	112.8	114.0
Consumption	Mt	116.8	122.0	123.0	123.7	124.8	125.7	126.8	127.8	128.9	129.9	130.8
Closing stocks	Mt	1.8	1.7	1.7	1.7	1.7	1.7	1.7	1.7	1.7	1.7	1.7
Developing countries												
Production	Mt	213.3	226.8	230.5	234.6	239.3	244.1	249.2	254.2	259.5	264.8	270.2
Consumption	Mt	192.0	208.1	212.0	216.8	221.6	226.8	231.9	237.1	242.4	247.7	253.4
Closing stocks	Mt	14.2	14.7	15.4	15.2	14.9	14.6	14.5	14.3	14.1	14.1	14.2
OECD[2]												
Production	Mt	94.0	95.9	96.6	96.7	97.7	98.6	99.6	100.3	101.4	102.2	103.2
Consumption	Mt	122.2	128.1	129.2	129.9	131.2	132.1	133.2	134.1	135.3	136.3	137.3
Closing stocks	Mt	1.7	1.6	1.6	1.6	1.6	1.6	1.6	1.6	1.6	1.6	1.6

Table 3.A1.2. **World oilseed projections** *(cont.)*

Marketing year

		Average 2014-16est	2017	2018	2019	2020	2021	2022	2023	2024	2025	2026
VEGETABLE OILS												
World												
Production	Mt	179.0	189.9	193.2	196.4	199.6	202.8	206.0	209.3	212.9	216.4	219.8
of which palm oil	Mt	61.8	66.9	68.4	69.9	71.2	72.5	73.7	75.1	76.5	77.9	79.3
Consumption	Mt	180.0	189.5	192.6	196.1	199.5	202.6	205.8	209.1	212.7	216.0	219.5
Food	Mt	141.4	147.8	150.1	153.0	156.2	159.3	162.4	165.5	168.8	171.9	175.2
Biofuel	Mt	23.9	26.2	26.8	27.1	27.0	26.7	26.6	26.5	26.5	26.4	26.4
Exports	Mt	75.3	79.1	80.2	81.6	82.7	84.1	85.5	87.0	88.6	90.0	91.5
Closing stocks	Mt	22.7	21.7	22.2	22.5	22.5	22.7	22.8	23.1	23.3	23.7	24.0
Price[5]	USD/t	768.3	827.7	829.2	838.2	849.9	862.2	871.8	884.2	896.6	897.4	902.0
Developed countries												
Production	Mt	46.0	47.7	48.2	48.5	49.0	49.5	50.0	50.4	51.0	51.4	51.9
Consumption	Mt	51.2	52.0	51.9	52.1	52.2	52.5	52.6	52.7	52.8	52.7	52.6
Closing stocks	Mt	4.4	4.2	4.2	4.1	4.0	4.0	4.0	3.9	3.9	3.9	3.9
Developing countries												
Production	Mt	132.9	142.2	145.0	147.8	150.6	153.3	156.0	158.9	162.0	164.9	167.9
Consumption	Mt	128.7	137.5	140.7	144.0	147.3	150.2	153.3	156.4	159.8	163.3	166.9
Closing stocks	Mt	18.3	17.5	18.0	18.4	18.6	18.7	18.9	19.1	19.4	19.7	20.0
OECD[2]												
Production	Mt	37.9	38.3	38.7	38.8	39.0	39.3	39.6	39.8	40.1	40.4	40.6
Consumption	Mt	50.8	51.7	51.8	52.0	52.2	52.5	52.7	52.9	53.1	53.1	53.1
Closing stocks	Mt	3.8	3.5	3.5	3.4	3.3	3.3	3.3	3.3	3.2	3.2	3.2

Note: Average 2014-16est: Data for 2016 are estimated.

1. Soybean, U.S., CIF Rotterdam.
2. Excludes Iceland but includes all EU28 member countries.
3. Rapeseed, Europe, CIF Hamburg.
4. Weighted average protein meal, European port.
5. Weighted average price of oilseed oils and palm oil, European port.

Source: OECD/FAO (2017), "OECD-FAO Agricultural Outlook", *OECD Agriculture statistics* (database). doi: dx.doi.org/10.1787/agr-outl-data-en

Table 3.A1.3. **World sugar projections**

Marketing year

		Average 2014-16est	2017	2018	2019	2020	2021	2022	2023	2024	2025	2026
WORLD												
SUGARBEET												
Production	Mt	261.9	276.3	276.2	270.8	269.5	268.8	268.9	268.7	269.1	270.4	271.4
Area	Mha	4.5	4.6	4.6	4.5	4.4	4.4	4.4	4.3	4.3	4.3	4.3
Yield	t/ha	58.72	59.99	60.12	60.84	61.11	61.41	61.69	61.95	62.24	62.59	62.91
Biofuel use	Mt	13.2	11.4	10.3	10.0	9.9	10.0	9.4	9.4	9.4	9.4	9.3
SUGARCANE												
Production	Mt	1 844.0	1 918.8	1 947.2	1 977.9	1 998.0	2 018.0	2 044.3	2 078.0	2 116.6	2 157.6	2 197.9
Area	Mha	27.0	27.7	27.9	28.2	28.4	28.5	28.7	29.0	29.4	29.8	30.3
Yield	t/ha	68.39	69.34	69.69	70.11	70.45	70.78	71.17	71.54	71.91	72.28	72.65
Biofuel use	Mt	343.5	362.6	371.3	381.4	391.9	399.0	407.4	412.7	418.9	426.0	432.9
SUGAR												
Production	Mt tq	168.6	179.2	184.1	187.2	190.0	192.4	195.3	198.8	202.2	205.9	209.5
Consumption	Mt tq	168.3	174.3	176.7	179.8	183.0	186.5	189.7	192.9	196.3	199.7	203.3
Closing stocks	Mt tq	72.8	67.1	69.8	72.5	74.8	76.1	77.0	78.1	79.3	80.7	82.3
Price, raw sugar[1]	USD/t	361.6	403.2	383.9	369.2	350.8	354.5	359.2	357.4	365.7	367.3	367.1
Price, white sugar[2]	USD/t	429.9	487.7	471.4	453.4	437.6	439.3	442.9	443.6	452.2	454.1	452.6
Price, HFCS[3]	USD/t	651.5	609.5	538.3	524.3	511.3	516.5	523.8	523.0	535.1	542.9	543.6
DEVELOPED COUNTRIES												
SUGARBEET												
Production	Mt	217.4	218.8	217.3	211.2	209.4	208.2	207.9	207.1	206.5	207.0	206.9
SUGARCANE												
Production	Mt	81.1	83.4	85.0	86.6	87.3	87.1	87.2	87.3	87.6	88.2	88.4
SUGAR												
Production	Mt tq	40.3	43.9	44.3	43.6	43.5	43.4	43.6	43.7	43.8	44.1	44.3
Consumption	Mt tq	47.6	47.8	47.8	47.7	47.8	48.0	48.2	48.4	48.6	48.8	49.1
Closing stocks	Mt tq	14.8	14.6	15.5	16.0	16.5	16.8	16.9	17.0	17.0	17.1	17.2
HFCS												
Production	Mt	9.4	9.7	9.8	10.0	10.3	10.4	10.5	10.5	10.6	10.6	10.7
Consumption	Mt	8.3	8.6	8.6	8.8	9.0	9.2	9.2	9.2	9.2	9.3	9.3
DEVELOPING COUNTRIES												
SUGARBEET												
Production	Mt	44.5	57.5	59.0	59.6	60.1	60.6	61.0	61.7	62.5	63.4	64.5
SUGARCANE												
Production	Mt	1 763.0	1 835.4	1 862.2	1 891.3	1 910.7	1 930.8	1 957.1	1 990.6	2 029.0	2 069.4	2 109.6
SUGAR												
Production	Mt tq	128.3	135.3	139.9	143.6	146.5	149.0	151.7	155.1	158.3	161.8	165.2
Consumption	Mt tq	120.6	126.6	128.9	132.1	135.1	138.4	141.5	144.5	147.7	150.9	154.2
Closing stocks	Mt tq	58.0	52.5	54.3	56.5	58.3	59.3	60.1	61.1	62.2	63.6	65.1
HFCS												
Production	Mt	3.5	3.7	3.7	3.8	3.8	3.9	3.9	4.0	4.0	4.1	4.2
Consumption	Mt	4.5	4.7	4.8	4.8	4.9	5.0	5.0	5.1	5.2	5.3	5.3
OECD[4]												
SUGARBEET												
Production	Mt	170.1	183.6	182.7	176.8	175.1	173.9	173.3	172.0	171.2	171.6	171.5
SUGARCANE												
Production	Mt	120.3	123.1	125.1	127.2	128.3	128.3	129.3	130.3	131.3	132.4	133.3
SUGAR												
Production	Mt tq	39.5	43.4	43.9	43.2	43.2	43.1	43.2	43.3	43.5	43.7	43.9
Consumption	Mt tq	44.9	45.3	45.3	45.1	45.3	45.4	45.5	45.8	46.0	46.3	46.5
Closing stocks	Mt tq	13.1	12.7	13.5	13.8	14.2	14.3	14.4	14.5	14.7	14.8	14.9
HFCS												
Production	Mt	10.6	10.9	11.0	11.3	11.5	11.7	11.7	11.8	11.8	11.9	11.9
Consumption	Mt	10.3	10.6	10.7	11.0	11.2	11.4	11.4	11.5	11.5	11.6	11.6

Note: Marketing year: See Glossary of Terms for definitions.
Average 2014-16est: Data for 2016 are estimated.
tq : tel quel.
HFCS: High fructose corn syrup.

1. Raw sugar world price, ICE contract No11 nearby, October/September.
2. Refined sugar price, White Sugar Futures Contract No. 407, Euronext market, Liffe, London, Europe, October/September.
3. United States wholesale list price HFCS-55, October/September.
4. Excludes Iceland but includes all EU28 member countries.

Source: OECD/FAO (2017), "OECD-FAO Agricultural Outlook", *OECD Agriculture statistics* (database). doi: dx.doi.org/10.1787/agr-outl-data-en

Table 3.A1.4. **World meat projections**

Calendar year

		Average 2014-16est	2017	2018	2019	2020	2021	2022	2023	2024	2025	2026
WORLD												
BEEF AND VEAL												
Production	kt cwe	68 471	69 942	70 652	71 187	71 854	72 621	73 400	74 146	74 766	75 496	76 341
Consumption	kt cwe	67 538	69 723	70 371	70 898	71 557	72 312	73 090	73 843	74 464	75 196	76 041
PIGMEAT												
Production	kt cwe	116 907	117 975	118 639	120 090	121 441	122 515	123 299	124 531	125 683	126 685	127 526
Consumption	kt cwe	116 912	117 931	118 653	120 092	121 437	122 513	123 298	124 525	125 677	126 679	127 521
POULTRY MEAT												
Production	kt rtc	113 875	118 080	119 205	120 885	122 461	124 036	125 608	127 196	128 737	130 256	131 609
Consumption	kt rtc	113 228	118 081	119 208	120 887	122 463	124 036	125 605	127 192	128 734	130 254	131 607
SHEEP MEAT												
Production	kt cwe	14 318	14 711	15 045	15 343	15 760	16 103	16 405	16 719	16 978	17 237	17 515
Consumption	kt cwe	14 288	14 712	15 052	15 354	15 770	16 114	16 410	16 715	16 976	17 238	17 515
TOTAL MEAT												
Per capita consumption[1]	kg rwt	34.1	34.3	34.2	34.3	34.4	34.4	34.4	34.5	34.5	34.6	34.6
DEVELOPED COUNTRIES												
BEEF AND VEAL												
Production	kt cwe	29 428	30 024	30 240	30 223	30 259	30 337	30 458	30 636	30 739	30 880	31 045
Consumption	kt cwe	28 347	29 025	29 137	29 181	29 276	29 331	29 458	29 650	29 781	29 930	30 096
PIGMEAT												
Production	kt cwe	43 006	44 562	44 036	44 182	44 538	44 760	44 746	45 036	45 347	45 540	45 596
Consumption	kt cwe	39 989	41 151	40 854	41 058	41 455	41 634	41 553	41 776	42 041	42 170	42 140
POULTRY MEAT												
Production	kt rtc	47 328	49 261	49 364	49 939	50 466	50 932	51 361	51 810	52 173	52 520	52 756
Consumption	kt rtc	44 873	46 983	47 004	47 438	47 828	48 127	48 440	48 735	48 997	49 215	49 343
SHEEP MEAT												
Production	kt cwe	3 393	3 348	3 385	3 429	3 462	3 496	3 534	3 572	3 600	3 628	3 662
Consumption	kt cwe	2 699	2 732	2 771	2 795	2 816	2 840	2 857	2 875	2 893	2 912	2 934
TOTAL MEAT												
Per capita consumption[1]	kg rwt	66.4	68.3	68.0	68.2	68.5	68.7	68.7	68.9	69.2	69.3	69.3
DEVELOPING COUNTRIES												
BEEF AND VEAL												
Production	kt cwe	39 043	39 917	40 411	40 964	41 595	42 284	42 943	43 510	44 027	44 616	45 297
Consumption	kt cwe	39 191	40 698	41 234	41 718	42 281	42 981	43 632	44 192	44 683	45 266	45 945
PIGMEAT												
Production	kt cwe	73 901	73 412	74 603	75 908	76 903	77 755	78 554	79 496	80 336	81 145	81 930
Consumption	kt cwe	76 923	76 780	77 799	79 034	79 982	80 879	81 745	82 750	83 635	84 509	85 381
POULTRY MEAT												
Production	kt rtc	66 546	68 819	69 842	70 945	71 995	73 104	74 247	75 386	76 564	77 737	78 852
Consumption	kt rtc	68 355	71 098	72 205	73 449	74 635	75 909	77 166	78 457	79 737	81 039	82 265
SHEEP MEAT												
Production	kt cwe	10 926	11 362	11 660	11 915	12 298	12 607	12 871	13 147	13 378	13 610	13 853
Consumption	kt cwe	11 590	11 979	12 281	12 559	12 954	13 275	13 553	13 841	14 083	14 326	14 581
TOTAL MEAT												
Per capita consumption[1]	kg rwt	26.5	26.5	26.5	26.6	26.7	26.8	26.9	27.0	27.0	27.1	27.2
OECD[2]												
BEEF AND VEAL												
Production	kt cwe	27 605	28 317	28 570	28 597	28 636	28 704	28 811	28 968	29 052	29 192	29 350
Consumption	kt cwe	26 448	27 261	27 425	27 518	27 598	27 623	27 717	27 876	27 970	28 091	28 240
PIGMEAT												
Production	kt cwe	41 120	42 546	41 987	42 091	42 459	42 719	42 717	43 004	43 327	43 548	43 620
Consumption	kt cwe	38 548	39 663	39 384	39 573	39 993	40 205	40 149	40 387	40 663	40 818	40 802
POULTRY MEAT												
Production	kt rtc	45 585	47 402	47 497	48 078	48 612	49 096	49 537	49 994	50 391	50 764	51 018
Consumption	kt rtc	42 865	45 034	45 079	45 521	45 939	46 280	46 612	46 935	47 249	47 514	47 695
SHEEP MEAT												
Production	kt cwe	2 736	2 693	2 729	2 767	2 797	2 825	2 856	2 889	2 911	2 934	2 964
Consumption	kt cwe	2 062	2 096	2 133	2 151	2 168	2 186	2 198	2 210	2 223	2 238	2 256
TOTAL MEAT												
Per capita consumption[1]	kg rwt	67.1	69.0	68.6	68.8	69.1	69.1	69.1	69.3	69.4	69.5	69.5

Note: Calendar Year: Year ending 30 September for New Zealand.
Average 2014-16est: Data for 2016 are estimated.

1. Per capita consumption expressed in retail weight. Carcass weight to retail weight conversion factors of 0.7 for beef and veal, 0.78 for pigmeat and 0.88 for both sheep meat and poultry meat.
2. Excludes Iceland but includes all EU28 member countries.

Source: OECD/FAO (2017), "OECD-FAO Agricultural Outlook", *OECD Agriculture statistics* (database). doi: dx.doi.org/10.1787/agr-outl-data-en

Table 3.A1.5. **World dairy projections: Butter and cheese**

Calendar year

		Average 2014-16est	2017	2018	2019	2020	2021	2022	2023	2024	2025	2026
BUTTER												
World												
Production	kt pw	10 905	11 379	11 644	11 902	12 161	12 412	12 662	12 888	13 108	13 348	13 593
Consumption	kt pw	10 831	11 379	11 609	11 869	12 131	12 380	12 631	12 857	13 077	13 317	13 561
Stock changes	kt pw	13	-3	3	1	-3	0	-1	-2	-1	-2	-1
Price[1]	USD/t	3 396	3 925	3 736	3 788	3 852	3 935	3 982	4 063	4 130	4 214	4 248
Developed countries												
Production	kt pw	4 725	4 877	4 966	5 068	5 155	5 221	5 296	5 350	5 403	5 464	5 526
Consumption	kt pw	4 131	4 316	4 356	4 434	4 501	4 547	4 597	4 631	4 659	4 702	4 745
Developing countries												
Production	kt pw	6 180	6 503	6 678	6 835	7 006	7 191	7 367	7 538	7 705	7 884	8 067
Consumption	kt pw	6 700	7 064	7 252	7 435	7 630	7 833	8 033	8 227	8 419	8 615	8 815
OECD[2]												
Production	kt pw	4 528	4 691	4 780	4 881	4 968	5 034	5 107	5 159	5 210	5 270	5 330
Consumption	kt pw	3 930	4 156	4 193	4 268	4 332	4 378	4 425	4 456	4 480	4 522	4 564
Stock changes	kt pw	13	-3	3	1	-3	0	-1	-2	-1	-2	-1
CHEESE												
World												
Production	kt pw	22 471	23 139	23 526	23 888	24 240	24 520	24 856	25 197	25 520	25 849	26 193
Consumption	kt pw	22 273	23 064	23 401	23 760	24 101	24 381	24 714	25 054	25 376	25 711	26 049
Stock changes	kt pw	37	-51	0	2	14	14	17	17	18	13	19
Price[3]	USD/t	3 633	3 644	3 604	3 700	3 775	3 863	3 946	4 038	4 121	4 210	4 276
Developed countries												
Production	kt pw	17 843	18 410	18 673	18 930	19 184	19 365	19 602	19 854	20 090	20 338	20 600
Consumption	kt pw	16 964	17 609	17 805	18 051	18 283	18 451	18 672	18 900	19 109	19 330	19 555
Developing countries												
Production	kt pw	4 628	4 729	4 853	4 958	5 057	5 156	5 254	5 343	5 430	5 512	5 594
Consumption	kt pw	5 309	5 455	5 596	5 709	5 818	5 929	6 041	6 155	6 267	6 380	6 494
OECD[2]												
Production	kt pw	17 334	17 896	18 174	18 435	18 691	18 873	19 108	19 354	19 586	19 831	20 092
Consumption	kt pw	16 593	17 280	17 471	17 714	17 942	18 107	18 324	18 547	18 753	18 970	19 192
Stock changes	kt pw	37	-51	0	2	14	14	17	17	18	13	19

Note: Calendar year: Year ending 30 June for Australia and 31 May for New Zealand in OECD aggregate.
Average 2014-16est: Data for 2016 are estimated.

1. FOB export price, butter, 82% butterfat, Oceania.
2. Excludes Iceland but includes all EU28 member countries.
3. FOB export price, cheddar cheese, 39% moisture, Oceania.

Source: OECD/FAO (2017), "OECD-FAO Agricultural Outlook", *OECD Agriculture statistics* (database). doi: dx.doi.org/10.1787/agr-outl-data-en

Table 3.A1.6. **World dairy projections: Powders and casein**

Calendar year

		Average 2014-16est	2017	2018	2019	2020	2021	2022	2023	2024	2025	2026
SKIM MILK POWDER												
World												
Production	kt pw	4 474	4 445	4 396	4 586	4 796	4 917	5 016	5 134	5 240	5 343	5 452
Consumption	kt pw	4 316	4 431	4 596	4 711	4 804	4 911	5 009	5 130	5 239	5 344	5 456
Stock changes	kt pw	16	2	0	2	2	-3	-1	-3	-3	-4	-6
Price[1]	USD/t	2 637	2 522	2 554	2 739	2 859	2 977	3 100	3 217	3 307	3 424	3 530
Developed countries												
Production	kt pw	3 878	3 840	3 787	3 959	4 152	4 258	4 341	4 443	4 536	4 625	4 718
Consumption	kt pw	2 019	2 066	2 158	2 222	2 258	2 305	2 345	2 398	2 443	2 486	2 532
Developing countries												
Production	kt pw	595	604	608	627	644	659	674	691	704	718	734
Consumption	kt pw	2 297	2 365	2 438	2 490	2 546	2 606	2 664	2 732	2 795	2 858	2 924
OECD[2]												
Production	kt pw	3 646	3 621	3 575	3 745	3 937	4 043	4 125	4 227	4 320	4 408	4 500
Consumption	kt pw	2 047	2 127	2 222	2 290	2 330	2 381	2 425	2 482	2 531	2 578	2 632
Stock changes	kt pw	16	2	0	2	2	-3	-1	-3	-3	-4	-6
WHOLE MILK POWDER												
World												
Production	kt pw	5 166	5 404	5 497	5 596	5 695	5 816	5 939	6 050	6 162	6 265	6 372
Consumption	kt pw	5 238	5 394	5 495	5 595	5 694	5 816	5 939	6 050	6 163	6 266	6 372
Stock changes	kt pw	1	8	0	0	0	0	0	0	0	0	0
Price[3]	USD/t	2 889	3 120	3 066	3 207	3 302	3 417	3 513	3 613	3 696	3 803	3 883
Developed countries												
Production	kt pw	2 387	2 371	2 398	2 431	2 469	2 522	2 568	2 615	2 665	2 716	2 759
Consumption	kt pw	615	608	591	604	618	632	646	660	674	686	694
Developing countries												
Production	kt pw	2 779	3 033	3 099	3 165	3 226	3 295	3 371	3 434	3 497	3 549	3 612
Consumption	kt pw	4 623	4 786	4 904	4 990	5 076	5 184	5 293	5 390	5 489	5 579	5 677
OECD[2]												
Production	kt pw	2 566	2 554	2 585	2 620	2 660	2 714	2 762	2 811	2 863	2 918	2 964
Consumption	kt pw	784	783	771	789	808	827	847	866	885	904	919
Stock changes	kt pw	1	8	0	0	0	0	0	0	0	0	0
WHEY POWDER												
Wholesale price, United States[4]	USD/t	981	948	978	1 031	1 075	1 127	1 157	1 205	1 234	1 279	1 319
CASEIN												
Price[5]	USD/t	7 404	7 138	7 268	7 669	7 990	8 283	8 588	8 873	9 096	9 390	9 649

Note: Calendar year: Year ending 30 June for Australia and 31 May for New Zealand in OECD aggregate.
Average 2014-16est: Data for 2016 are estimated.

1. FOB export price, non-fat dry milk, 1.25% butterfat, Oceania.
2. Excludes Iceland but includes all EU28 member countries.
3. FOB export price, WMP 26% butterfat, Oceania.
4. FOB export price, sweet whey non-hygroscopic, Western Europe.
5. Export price, New Zealand.

Source: OECD/FAO (2017), "OECD-FAO Agricultural Outlook", *OECD Agriculture statistics* (database). doi: dx.doi.org/10.1787/agr-outl-data-en

Table 3.A1.7. World fish and seafood projections

Calendar year

		Average 2014-16est	2017	2018	2019	2020	2021	2022	2023	2024	2025	2026
FISH[1]												
World												
Production	kt	168 293	175 969	178 702	182 271	184 953	185 154	187 894	189 614	191 752	193 936	193 875
of which aquaculture	kt	76 369	82 291	85 171	88 805	91 535	93 864	94 695	96 220	98 332	100 426	102 128
Consumption	kt	168 212	176 761	179 393	182 863	185 444	185 546	188 186	189 805	191 843	193 927	193 866
of which for food	kt	148 756	155 821	159 020	162 928	165 910	167 681	169 522	171 436	173 757	176 112	177 367
of which for reduction	kt	14 187	15 929	15 664	15 517	15 399	13 998	15 050	14 991	14 892	14 817	13 698
Price												
Aquaculture[2]	USD/t	2 095.5	2 109.0	2 119.1	2 119.5	2 100.0	2 139.4	2 172.2	2 204.4	2 230.2	2 286.2	2 312.7
Capture[3]	USD/t	1 568.3	1 564.7	1 580.6	1 577.3	1 577.8	1 610.6	1 631.0	1 655.1	1 677.2	1 699.3	1 724.8
Product traded[4]	USD/t	2 837.2	2 850.0	2 867.5	2 826.0	2 800.0	2 852.5	2 896.3	2 939.2	2 973.6	3 008.2	3 043.0
Developed countries												
Production	kt	29 154	29 378	29 464	29 614	29 684	29 704	29 682	29 624	29 597	29 616	29 684
of which aquaculture	kt	4 546	4 748	4 876	5 059	5 228	5 314	5 318	5 317	5 345	5 391	5 471
Consumption	kt	37 148	37 372	37 369	37 286	37 341	37 197	37 497	37 260	37 759	37 721	38 231
of which for food	kt	31 718	32 200	32 306	32 307	32 442	32 326	32 752	32 577	33 132	33 149	33 651
of which for reduction	kt	4 494	4 330	4 263	4 218	4 178	4 188	4 099	4 066	4 031	3 999	4 032
Developing countries												
Production	kt	139 139	146 592	149 238	152 657	155 268	155 450	158 213	159 990	162 156	164 320	164 190
of which aquaculture	kt	71 823	77 544	80 295	83 746	86 307	88 550	89 377	90 903	92 986	95 035	96 657
Consumption	kt	131 064	139 389	142 024	145 577	148 103	148 349	150 689	152 545	154 084	156 206	155 634
of which for food	kt	117 038	123 621	126 714	130 621	133 469	135 355	136 770	138 859	140 625	142 963	143 716
of which for reduction	kt	9 692	11 598	11 401	11 299	11 221	9 811	10 950	10 925	10 861	10 818	9 667
OECD												
Production	kt	31 211	31 536	31 696	31 853	31 968	31 699	31 832	31 939	31 981	32 068	31 694
of which aquaculture	kt	6 299	6 454	6 611	6 837	7 049	7 174	7 188	7 200	7 256	7 325	7 432
Consumption	kt	39 372	39 993	40 099	40 029	40 125	39 822	40 267	40 145	40 717	40 728	41 024
of which for food	kt	32 736	33 330	33 584	33 640	33 833	33 740	34 214	34 110	34 715	34 756	35 307
of which for reduction	kt	5 542	5 656	5 561	5 485	5 438	5 275	5 286	5 300	5 288	5 281	5 053
FISHMEAL[5]												
World												
Production	kt	4 385.2	4 942.2	4 921.4	4 932.4	4 944.6	4 635.5	4 933.1	4 948.1	4 957.0	4 973.2	4 721.4
from whole fish	kt	3 205.6	3 752.9	3 709.9	3 694.9	3 686.0	3 362.0	3 634.4	3 630.7	3 617.8	3 610.0	3 343.3
Consumption	kt	4 457.5	4 856.0	4 929.2	4 944.0	4 957.2	4 811.1	4 771.5	4 958.4	4 967.3	4 985.2	4 877.5
Variation in stocks	kt	-72.4	85.8	-8.2	-12.1	-13.0	-176.0	161.2	-10.7	-10.7	-12.4	-156.5
Price[6]	USD/t	1 592.3	1 280.9	1 200.3	1 252.9	1 291.0	1 558.6	1 372.1	1 412.0	1 442.0	1 487.8	1 834.9
Developed countries												
Production	kt	1 414.8	1 423.2	1 427.5	1 439.8	1 448.8	1 469.3	1 460.7	1 463.7	1 467.3	1 472.8	1 493.4
from whole fish	kt	1 025.1	1 024.3	1 018.6	1 018.4	1 019.0	1 032.0	1 013.6	1 008.7	1 003.3	998.6	1 010.1
Consumption	kt	1 618.9	1 677.8	1 675.6	1 619.2	1 581.4	1 444.4	1 437.4	1 463.5	1 429.7	1 402.6	1 299.1
Variation in stocks	kt	3.6	28.8	2.8	-1.1	-2.0	-47.0	44.2	0.3	0.3	-1.4	-47.5
Developing countries												
Production	kt	2 970.4	3 518.9	3 493.9	3 492.6	3 495.9	3 166.2	3 472.3	3 484.4	3 489.7	3 500.4	3 228.0
from whole fish	kt	2 180.5	2 728.6	2 691.4	2 676.5	2 667.0	2 330.0	2 620.7	2 622.1	2 614.5	2 611.4	2 333.2
Consumption	kt	2 838.7	3 178.3	3 253.6	3 324.8	3 375.8	3 366.7	3 334.1	3 495.0	3 537.5	3 582.6	3 578.4
Variation in stocks	kt	-76.0	57.0	-11.0	-11.0	-11.0	-129.0	117.0	-11.0	-11.0	-11.0	-109.0
OECD												
Production	kt	1 604.4	1 687.2	1 685.6	1 691.5	1 699.4	1 681.2	1 695.6	1 709.7	1 718.8	1 730.6	1 692.0
from whole fish	kt	1 210.6	1 282.0	1 270.4	1 263.6	1 263.0	1 237.1	1 241.5	1 247.4	1 247.5	1 248.9	1 201.0
Consumption	kt	1 810.5	1 864.0	1 862.9	1 815.1	1 780.2	1 635.0	1 633.7	1 669.6	1 638.7	1 615.6	1 501.5
Variation in stocks	kt	-9.0	62.8	1.8	-2.1	-3.0	-68.0	63.2	-0.7	-0.7	-2.4	-53.5

Table 3.A1.7. **World fish and seafood projections** (*cont.*)

Calendar year

		Average 2014-16est	2017	2018	2019	2020	2021	2022	2023	2024	2025	2026
FISH OIL[5]												
World												
Production	kt	881.2	968.1	962.2	962.3	962.8	909.0	959.2	962.3	964.0	966.9	925.6
from whole fish	kt	566.8	645.0	634.0	628.5	623.8	565.0	609.9	607.7	603.9	601.1	554.0
Consumption	kt	905.1	894.4	963.9	964.0	964.4	961.6	912.7	961.8	963.5	966.4	976.1
Variation in stocks	kt	-23.9	73.7	-1.7	-1.6	-1.6	-52.6	46.4	0.5	0.5	0.5	-50.5
Price[7]	USD/t	1 808.3	1 607.9	1 622.9	1 641.3	1 667.2	1 907.2	1 720.2	1 747.0	1 774.4	1 794.8	2 055.8
Developed countries												
Production	kt	394.2	354.3	354.2	356.0	357.1	360.0	359.3	360.6	362.0	363.7	367.8
from whole fish	kt	206.1	171.9	169.4	168.3	167.1	167.9	164.8	163.9	163.0	162.1	163.8
Consumption	kt	534.6	502.0	529.8	526.6	524.8	540.1	482.2	515.2	511.8	510.2	536.9
Variation in stocks	kt	-4.7	28.7	0.3	0.4	0.4	-25.6	21.4	0.5	0.5	0.5	-25.5
Developing countries												
Production	kt	487.0	613.9	608.0	606.3	605.7	549.0	599.9	601.7	602.0	603.2	557.8
from whole fish	kt	360.7	473.1	464.6	460.2	456.7	397.1	445.0	443.8	440.9	438.9	390.2
Consumption	kt	370.5	392.4	434.1	437.4	439.6	421.5	430.5	446.7	451.7	456.3	439.2
Variation in stocks	kt	-19.2	45.0	-2.0	-2.0	-2.0	-27.0	25.0	0.0	0.0	0.0	-25.0
OECD												
Production	kt	513.6	469.2	468.4	469.1	470.5	466.8	470.6	474.4	477.3	480.7	474.7
from whole fish	kt	274.4	238.0	234.0	230.8	228.8	221.9	222.4	222.9	222.4	222.1	212.6
Consumption	kt	682.9	640.8	673.2	670.5	669.2	671.7	621.1	660.9	658.4	657.2	669.7
Variation in stocks	kt	-8.0	43.7	0.3	0.4	0.4	-35.6	31.4	0.5	0.5	0.5	-35.5

Note: The term "fish" indicates fish, crustaceans, molluscs and other aquatic animals, but excludes aquatic mammals, crocodiles, caimans, alligators and aquatic plants.

Average 2014-16est: Data for 2016 are estimated.

1. Data are in live weight equivalent.
2. World unit value of aquaculture fisheries production (live weight basis).
3. FAO estimated value of world ex vessel value of capture fisheries production excluding for reduction.
4. World unit value of trade (sum of exports and imports).
5. Data are in product weight.
6. Fishmeal, 64-65% protein, Hamburg, Germany.
7. Fish oil, any origin, N.W. Europe.

Source: OECD/FAO (2017), "OECD-FAO Agricultural Outlook", *OECD Agriculture statistics* (database). doi: dx.doi.org/10.1787/agr-outl-data-en

Table 3.A1.8. **World biofuel projections**

		Average 2014-16est	2017	2018	2019	2020	2021	2022	2023	2024	2025	2026
ETHANOL												
World												
Production	mln L	117.4	123.7	126.8	128.4	130.7	131.5	132.8	133.7	134.7	135.8	136.7
of which maize based	mln L	68.2	71.9	73.7	73.9	74.7	74.5	74.5	74.3	74.2	74.0	73.7
of which sugar cane based	mln L	27.9	29.5	30.2	31.1	31.9	32.5	33.3	33.7	34.3	34.9	35.5
of which advanced[1]	mln L	0.8	0.8	0.9	0.9	0.9	1.0	1.0	1.1	1.1	1.2	1.2
Consumption	mln L	117.2	124.6	127.0	128.8	130.8	131.8	133.0	134.0	134.9	136.0	136.9
of which fuel use	mln L	96.2	103.1	105.4	107.0	108.9	109.6	110.7	111.4	112.1	113.0	113.6
Exports	mln L	8.2	8.9	9.0	8.9	8.9	8.8	8.7	8.5	8.2	8.1	7.9
Price[2]	USD/hl	51.0	44.5	46.0	47.3	48.4	49.7	50.9	51.9	53.2	54.5	55.3
Developed countries												
Production	mln L	68.1	71.7	73.2	73.2	74.0	73.6	73.6	73.3	73.2	73.0	72.7
Consumption	mln L	67.7	72.7	74.0	74.4	74.9	74.7	74.8	74.5	74.3	74.1	73.8
of which fuel use	mln L	62.0	66.7	67.9	68.3	68.8	68.7	68.7	68.4	68.1	68.0	67.6
Net trade	mln L	0.2	-0.5	-0.8	-0.9	-0.9	-1.0	-1.1	-1.0	-1.0	-1.0	-1.0
Developing countries												
Production	mln L	49.4	51.9	53.6	55.2	56.7	57.9	59.3	60.4	61.5	62.8	64.0
Consumption	mln L	49.5	51.9	53.1	54.4	56.0	57.1	58.3	59.5	60.7	61.9	63.1
of which fuel use	mln L	34.2	36.4	37.5	38.7	40.0	41.0	42.0	43.0	44.0	45.0	46.0
Net trade	mln L	-0.2	0.5	0.8	0.8	0.9	0.9	1.1	1.0	1.0	1.0	0.9
OECD[3]												
Production	mln L	67.2	70.8	72.3	72.3	73.0	72.6	72.6	72.4	72.2	72.0	71.7
Consumption	mln L	67.9	72.8	74.1	74.5	75.0	74.8	74.9	74.6	74.4	74.2	73.9
of which fuel use	mln L	62.0	66.7	68.0	68.4	68.8	68.7	68.7	68.4	68.1	68.0	67.6
Net trade	mln L	-0.8	-1.5	-1.8	-1.9	-1.9	-2.0	-2.1	-2.1	-2.0	-2.0	-2.0
BIODIESEL												
World												
Production	mln L	33.8	37.3	38.6	39.6	40.3	40.2	40.1	40.2	40.4	40.4	40.5
of which vegetable oil based	mln L	24.3	27.6	28.4	29.0	29.2	29.0	28.8	28.8	28.8	28.8	28.8
of which waste based	mln L	8.2	9.0	9.4	9.8	10.2	10.2	10.3	10.4	10.4	10.5	10.5
of which advanced[1]	mln L	0.3	0.4	0.4	0.4	0.4	0.5	0.5	0.5	0.5	0.6	0.6
Consumption	mln L	33.8	37.5	38.8	39.7	40.4	40.3	40.2	40.4	40.5	40.6	40.6
Exports	mln L	3.5	3.8	4.3	4.2	3.8	3.6	3.3	3.2	3.1	3.1	3.1
Price[4]	USD/hl	86.9	86.1	88.0	89.4	90.4	90.9	91.3	92.1	92.7	93.2	93.6
Developed countries												
Production	mln L	20.4	21.7	22.2	22.4	22.3	22.1	21.9	21.8	21.7	21.2	20.9
Consumption	mln L	22.4	24.3	25.3	25.4	24.8	24.4	24.0	23.7	23.5	23.0	22.6
Net trade	mln L	-2.2	-2.6	-3.0	-2.9	-2.5	-2.3	-2.0	-1.9	-1.8	-1.8	-1.8
Developing countries												
Production	mln L	13.4	15.6	16.4	17.2	18.0	18.1	18.2	18.4	18.7	19.2	19.6
Consumption	mln L	11.3	13.2	13.5	14.3	15.6	15.9	16.3	16.6	17.0	17.5	18.0
Net trade	mln L	2.1	2.5	2.9	2.8	2.4	2.2	1.9	1.8	1.7	1.7	1.6
OECD[3]												
Production	mln L	21.0	22.4	23.0	23.2	23.0	22.8	22.7	22.6	22.4	21.9	21.6
Consumption	mln L	22.9	24.9	25.9	26.0	25.5	25.1	24.7	24.4	24.1	23.7	23.3
Net trade	mln L	-2.1	-2.5	-3.0	-2.9	-2.5	-2.3	-2.0	-1.8	-1.8	-1.7	-1.7

Note: Average 2014-16est: Data for 2016 are estimated.

1. Advanced biofuels corresponding to biofuels produced out of agricultural residues, forest residues and dedicated energy crops.
2. Wholesale price, United states, Omaha.
3. Excludes Iceland but includes all EU28 member countries.
4. Producer price Germany net of biodiesel tariff and energy tax.

Source: OECD/FAO (2017), "OECD-FAO Agricultural Outlook", *OECD Agriculture statistics* (database). doi: dx.doi.org/10.1787/agr-outl-data-en

Table 3.A1.9. **World cotton projections**

Marketing year

		Average 2014-16est	2017	2018	2019	2020	2021	2022	2023	2024	2025	2026
WORLD												
Production	Mt	23.4	22.7	22.6	22.7	23.2	23.7	24.2	24.7	25.2	25.6	26.1
Area	Mha	31.7	30.2	29.7	29.5	29.5	29.6	29.7	29.8	29.9	29.9	30.0
Yield	t/ha	0.74	0.75	0.76	0.77	0.79	0.80	0.81	0.83	0.84	0.86	0.87
Consumption[1]	Mt	24.0	24.0	24.0	24.1	24.1	24.2	24.6	24.9	25.2	25.6	26.0
Exports	Mt	7.6	7.8	7.8	7.9	7.9	8.0	8.0	8.1	8.2	8.4	8.5
Closing stocks	Mt	19.8	16.5	14.9	13.3	12.1	11.4	10.9	10.4	10.2	10.1	10.0
Price[2]	USD/t	1 582.8	1 480.7	1 467.2	1 442.1	1 460.5	1 546.7	1 568.2	1 572.3	1 572.5	1 573.3	1 576.0
DEVELOPED COUNTRIES												
Production	Mt	5.6	6.0	5.9	5.9	6.0	6.0	6.1	6.2	6.3	6.4	6.5
Consumption	Mt	1.7	1.8	1.8	1.8	1.8	1.8	1.9	1.9	2.0	2.0	2.0
Exports	Mt	4.1	4.6	4.6	4.6	4.6	4.6	4.6	4.7	4.7	4.7	4.8
Imports	Mt	0.4	0.4	0.4	0.4	0.4	0.4	0.4	0.4	0.4	0.4	0.4
Closing stocks	Mt	1.8	2.1	2.0	1.8	1.7	1.7	1.7	1.7	1.7	1.7	1.7
DEVELOPING COUNTRIES												
Production	Mt	17.7	16.7	16.7	16.8	17.2	17.6	18.1	18.5	18.9	19.3	19.7
Consumption	Mt	22.3	22.2	22.2	22.3	22.3	22.3	22.7	23.0	23.3	23.6	23.9
Exports	Mt	3.5	3.2	3.2	3.2	3.3	3.4	3.4	3.5	3.5	3.6	3.7
Imports	Mt	7.0	7.3	7.3	7.3	7.4	7.4	7.5	7.6	7.7	7.8	7.9
Closing stocks	Mt	18.0	14.4	12.9	11.5	10.4	9.8	9.2	8.7	8.5	8.3	8.3
OECD[3]												
Production	Mt	5.2	5.5	5.4	5.4	5.5	5.6	5.6	5.7	5.8	5.9	5.9
Consumption	Mt	3.3	3.3	3.3	3.3	3.3	3.3	3.3	3.3	3.4	3.4	3.4
Exports	Mt	3.3	3.9	4.0	4.0	4.0	4.0	3.9	4.0	4.0	4.1	4.1
Imports	Mt	1.7	1.7	1.7	1.7	1.7	1.7	1.6	1.6	1.6	1.6	1.6
Closing stocks	Mt	2.5	2.8	2.6	2.5	2.4	2.3	2.3	2.3	2.4	2.4	2.4

Note: Marketing year: See Glossary of Terms for definitions.
Average 2014-16est: Data for 2016 are estimated.
1. Consumption for cotton means mill consumption and not final consumer demand.
2. Cotlook A index, Middling 1 3/32", c.f.r. far Eastern ports (August/July).
3. Excludes Iceland but includes all EU28 member countries.

Source: OECD/FAO (2017), "OECD-FAO Agricultural Outlook", *OECD Agriculture statistics* (database). doi: dx.doi.org/10.1787/agr-outl-data-en

OECD PUBLISHING, 2, rue André-Pascal, 75775 PARIS CEDEX 16
(51 2017 05 1 P) ISBN 978-92-64-27547-8 – 2017

www.ingramcontent.com/pod-product-compliance
Lightning Source LLC
Chambersburg PA
CBHW061219240926
51846CB00006B/1275
* 9 7 8 9 2 6 4 2 7 5 4 7 8 *